Sounds of the Sea

By

Anne Sogorka Cook

1stBooks - rev. 04/18/02

DEDICATION

To my father, who first took my hand and led me to the sea.
To my mother, who encourages me every step of the way.
To my husband, who is my editor and advisor, and still takes my
hand and leads me to the sea
To my children, who ride the waves, build the castles and teach me
what life and love are all about.

CHAPTER ONE

I woke to the sounds of the sea. Each breath I took echoed the restless haunting symphony of tumbling waves whether the ocean was outside my window or a hundred miles away. For the past sixty years the sea surged and crested in its endless cycle fifty yards beyond the front porch of the sandcastle that was my home on the island that encircled my life.

A soft breeze blew the racket of the gull's sunrise feeding through the window. I imagined the scene; sky competing with sea for the deepest shade of Autumn blue, white birds squawking furiously, darting high and low, flapping wings to hover, then take aim and swoop down to snatch a mullet breaking water. If the tide had brought in clams the hungry gulls would feast on them as well; pluck one from the sand and drop it again and again, until the shell broke open and revealed the raw treat inside.

I lay still and listened closer. A strange squeal I could not identify disturbed the usually harmonious morning melody. I dressed and went downstairs to investigate, holding on tight to the smooth, worn banister, checking familiar bumps and grooves, concentrating on my feet and legs, a necessary habit of old age. They moved well enough for eighty, but not as fast as the rest of me would like them to.

I walked through the empty, quiet rooms, not a book out of place, not a cushion disturbed, opened the back door and went outside, breathed in the sweet salty air and paused, listening. A flock of honking geese took sudden flight over the sparkling bay waters to the west. Again, the strange squeal intruded.

I started around the side of the house, following the sound. A walk once led around the north corner to the beach but dunes had claimed the path years ago. Mountains of sand roamed aimlessly, covered with beach grass as tall as the second story windows. I took a step back, looked up, and discovered the source of the noise. The old weathervane on the peak of the roof had come loose. The post was swaying back and forth precariously as the points spun steadily in the persistent rhythm of a stiffening southeast wind.

Stepping back for a better view I lost my balance and fell into the tremendous dune, sprawled among the reeds. At that moment, a voice shouted from the driveway. "Hello! Is that you Sara?"

I scrambled clumsily to get up. "Yes, Elizabeth. It's me. Who else would it be?"

Elizabeth Morgan, my neighbor, appeared around the corner of the garage with her daughter Jane. They stared at me as I awkwardly attempted to straighten my hair and adjust my skirt.

"Are you all right Sara? What on earth were you doing over there?"

I tried to catch my breath. "I heard a noise, and I was looking around to see what it was," I said, hearing how foolish it sounded. I wanted to tell her it was

1

my yard and if I wanted to run around naked I would, but I didn't dare say that. Virginia Bennett had been my dear friend and neighbor and her grandaughter, Elizabeth was forever trying to be the same. She was eager to help; to walk, to bake, to shop, to listen, whatever I needed, whatever I wanted.

The truth was, all I wanted was for Elizabeth to leave me alone, and I hated myself for feeling that way. Elizabeth embodied everything missing from my life. My house was empty while Virginia's house was filled to the rafters with the constant hum of life.

Virginia's children had come, and then their children with them, every season of every year; cars, trucks, toys, swings, babies, boyfriends, girlfriends, an endless parade. But the irony was that Virginia was not at the head of the line receiving all the love. She had not been allowed that luxury any more than I had, for Virginia was long dead.

Dead but not forgotten as opposed to alive and abandoned. My hand trembled slightly as the word stung; abandoned. Is that what people see in me? Is that what I am?

Elizabeth held out her hand. "What's wrong Sara?"

I reached for it and steadied myself. I looked into her face and saw Virginia's beautiful hazel eyes blasting me to my senses. There was no pity there, only genuine concern and compassion.

I pulled her close to me, savoring the unfamiliar closeness of another body. Elizabeth was startled, but she held my embrace. Then she pulled back. "Sara. Say something. Are you OK?"

"Of course I am." I smiled my brightest smile. "Don't be silly. Please excuse my moment of weakness."

"Well, we just stopped over to say good-bye. We're all packed up." Elizabeth eyed me like a physician would a strange new patient.

"Oh. I thought you'd stay 'til Labor Day," I said.

"Well we had planned to but Ted's worried about the storm. We don't want to get stuck and have the kids miss the first day of school," Elizabeth said.

"Better safe than sorry I always say. Ted thinks it's coming then?" I asked.

"Well, he thinks something's coming, not the end of the world like they're predicting, of course. Is Charley coming to do your shutters? Why don't I send Ted and the boys over to put them up before we go…"

"Oh, don't worry about me. If they need to go up they'll get up."

Jane tugged impatiently on her mother's jeans. "Oh I almost forgot, Sara… Happy Birthday!!" Elizabeth said as the little girl pulled a bunch of Black-eyed Susans from behind her back and handed them to me. I bent down and took the flowers, gazed into the little girl's face until tears stung my eyes. I stood up and looked away.

"Thank you ladies, aren't you sweet to remember an eighty year old fart like me." We laughed together. "Yes. You never forget, Elizabeth. You are your grandmother's image. I know I always tell you that but it's true. Inside and out. Virginia would have treasured the both of you..." my voice quivered.

"I know, Sara. And thank you. But now you've really got me worried. All this sentiment. It's not like you, and good-byes are hard enough. I hate leaving you here all...winter." Elizabeth changed her thought in mid sentence. That image flashed once more.

I laughed it off. "Well, I am eighty, senility cannot be far away. Perhaps it's the new me. You may return in the spring and find me drooling and incontinent, holed up in the garage with a shopping cart full of dirty rags. Or maybe I'll go the other extreme and get engaged or married!"

Elizabeth lightened up a bit. "Seriously Sara, why don't you come stay with us up home for awhile? If not now, how about for the holidays? We'd all love to have you."

I smiled mischievously. "I'll give it some thought dear, really I will."

Elizabeth was satisfied. "Well at least that sounds more like you. You have no intention of coming but you'll say so to make me feel better and leave you alone!"

I waved them on their way. "You better run along now. I hear Ted slamming doors over there. Tell the boys I said so long."

Halfway down the driveway Elizabeth turned. "You have the number Sara. If you need anything, anything at all, you just call."

I waved at them, wondering what Elizabeth really thought about me. She was safe in the cocoon of her family's love, as I once was. Most likely she could not imagine ending up alone, as I once would never have imagined it for myself.

They turned and waved then disappeared around the corner. I hated to see them go, actually. It did get quiet when the summer residents packed up and headed to their winter homes. But every Labor Day I remembered when I was the one saying good-bye and said a prayer of thanks that I would never have to leave again.

Eastwind is a barrier island five miles long, surrounded by the Atlantic Ocean, Fish Hawk Bay, and the Squan River. At its narrowest point the island is a mere half mile wide. Some say years ago every northeaster carved a healthy inlet out of the center of the island, forming two separate parcels. But never in my lifetime. As long as I knew it Eastwind was one continuous stretch, though it was divided in another way.

The island was home to two distinct communities. From the mainland bridge in the center to the rocky jetty on the northern point was Sandy Point, a seasonal hamlet of small bungalows centered around a mile long boardwalk, where I spent my childhood summers in an old gray bungalow a stone's throw from the sea.

From the bridge to the lighthouse on the southernmost edge is Eastwind, where my husband, Mike grew up. When he was young, this end of the island was home to only a handful of wealthy families that owned the huge, rambling beach and bay front homes. Some were summer homes, but many of the families lived there all year, crossing Fish Hawk Bay by boat or walking the wooden footbridge into town for shopping and school. In town, two dozen more venerable families lived in equally grand homes on the tidy tree-lined streets branching off from the quaint main street.

The primitive foot crossing was eventually replaced with an automobile drawbridge, named after the family who donated the land to the state to build it. Some applauded the family for the gesture, others cursed them, for if one factor led to the subsequent development of the island, it was that bridge.

An ancient argument; some say change is always good and others say it's always bad. I say it's neither, but a span connecting the past to the future, and life is merely the perpetual motion of the journey back and forth across it.

If I had been given a vote in the matter of that bridge many years ago my choice would have been clear; fix the old wooden footpath, or better yet knock it down and widen the channel, so only a few true souls would make the island their home, and I know that somehow Mike and I would still have found each other and wound up here together.

I sighed, wondering at my romantic notions, bent down and picked up the newspaper and went inside. I brewed a pot of tea, toasted a muffin and sat at the table. The headline blared: IRIS IS COMING! RUN FOR YOUR LIVES!!!!. I abruptly flipped it over to the back page, read the comics, then tossed the whole thing into the fireplace.

I poured myself another cup of tea and went out to the front porch, surveying the canvas laid out before me. The white sand sparkled like a new carpet, windswept clean each night, every grain in place and glistening in the fresh rays of the sun.

I placed my mug on the wicker table and shaded my eyes to look beyond the sand to the sea. Blues and greens floated lazily together; sun light suspended in the spray of the waves as they arched and crested. The gulls were far out, white dots against a blue sky, riding the swells in silence.

The rocking chair creaked as I settled into it. My cat Henry stirred from his favorite sunny spot at the far end of the porch. He stretched and arched his back, scratching his claws on the wooden floor. He jumped onto the railing running the length of the porch and gingerly traveled end to end like a tight-rope walker. Then he jumped off, brushed hard against my bare legs, and rubbed his face on my sneakers seeking attention. He got none and moved away.

My gaze never left the sea while Henry made his morning rounds of the empty porch. It was once furnished with white wicker plant stands and tables; and chairs with plump flowery cushions, a shady welcome haven on hot afternoons. An old-fashioned porch for an old-fashioned girl. That's what Mike used to say. Now there were two rocking chairs and a table. I wondered what Mike would have said about that.

Henry had a brief encounter with an enormous dragonfly. He knocked it to the ground and batted it around, watched it buzz furiously on its back for awhile then lost interest and moved to the top of the steps and plopped there. Henry never set paw on the sand. His domain was the house, the yard, the driveway and the porch, never the sand.

Henry was a seventieth birthday present from John; my oldest son. I didn't think cats lived that long, but Henry was too stubborn to get old and die. We were a lot alike.

I rocked back and forth sipping my tea, dozing in the warm sun, serenaded by the sounds of my constant companion, the sea. I witnessed the magic of many sunrises, slept, woke, worked and played beside it and that was an awesome fortune I never took for granted. An infinite cast of characters entertained me; graceful terns and mighty whales, moonlight, sunlight, clouds and wind, snows of winter, rains of spring.

That morning the ocean was uneasy, troubled by some unsettled matter, a nagging worry that refused to recede. A storm was coming; its scent simmered in the damp salty air and I welcomed it, for nothing reconciles turmoil like a good blow. Perhaps this would be the big one, 'the storm of the century', and if so maybe it was time. Perhaps mother nature was tired of the perpetual abuse and ready to unleash her fury, wipe the slate clean and reclaim what she had lost. Her warnings and threats had gone unheeded, leaving her this last recourse; a terrible, beautiful storm. A storm powerful enough to teach a lesson none could ignore and leave long awaited peace in its wake.

I listened closer, for my heart was as plagued as the sea. Was the answer there, rolling in and out with the tide? If mother nature could calm her troubled waters with a storm, could I? And then I wondered if these were the musings of a woman with a romantic bent or a demented mind.

I thought about the storm, enveloped already in the analysis and intrigue accompanying all blips on the ever present weather maps, debated and discussed by those who think they know and fueled by those who think they want to know, and together they all ignore the only truth, that no one knows. They know it's a hurricane; they've determined the speed of its winds and taken its temperature, they've assigned it a name and countless projected paths. With each storm the number of projections multiply as if by predicting every possible scenario, eventually the weathermen will be vindicated.

I listened for the wind. It had not yet spoken. Or maybe it had, so many miles out and under that no one heard it but the whales and the squid. Maybe the wind and the sea did know and issued their own silent warning to the creatures of the deep, and it's only a matter of time, but all we mortals can do, is wait and watch and wonder.

The gulls were quiet, yet one persistent hunter cried his mournful wail. There was always one; ever hungry, diving for another fish, searching for one more clam. I pictured him circling his unsuspecting prey, gaining speed, diving with his beak open, plucking the squirming fish up, bending his neck for a better grip, then throwing his head back and swallowing it whole.

I opened my eyes quickly. I didn't want to think about that fish, gasping its last breath dangling from a gull's mouth yearning for release. Mike always said I was too sensitive, that fish and gulls don't act on emotion or feelings, only instinct. The mullet's purpose is to feed the gulls and the bluefish who chase them to the surface, all part of nature's plan. And the wind and sea don't think or decide anything, they simply follow a course driven by forces of tide and temperature.

Mike was a naturalist. He understood the elements of the island and how and why they harmonized or didn't. He knew the unwritten laws; the reason for a heron's erratic dance, the implications of a subtly shifting breeze, why the shoreline is littered with whole white clam shells one morning, snail shells the next and tiny black mussels the day after that. He could identify a double crested cormorant hidden in the cattails, a common loon diving in black water, and the entire contents of a seining net filled with such odd creatures as stony coral and staghorn coral, spider crabs and fairy shrimp.

He could tell an egg belonging to an American Golden Plover from one laid by a common gull. To Mike seagulls were Ringed Plovers and Common Terns, Black-Legged Kittiwakes and Herring Gulls. He could tell time by the sun and describe the next day's sunrise by staring at the night sky. He was as much a creature of the island as the wildlife that scampered swam and soared there; constantly aware of and in tune with the nuances of their existence in a way I never would be. It wasn't something you could learn because it was wisdom that couldn't be taught. Mike did his best and he was a patient teacher, but he didn't have to teach me to love it. I fell in love with the sea long before I fell in love with Michael Franklin Hankins.

I respected the sea and feared its power. Mike shared the respect but if he ever felt the fear it didn't show. Nature inspired him, compelled him to experience it without hesitation, whether it was a daring rescue in raging surf or a challenging sail on a storm tossed bay.

"But age never got the chance to slow you down my dear," I whispered to him as if he were rocking in the chair next to me.

I stretched my hands up over my head.

Inventory. I took inventory every morning to make sure everything was still there and working. According to the annoying little charts on everything from panty hose to doctor's pamphlets I was boringly average; medium height, medium weight, normal blood pressure and cholesterol, type O blood, all very solid, very middle of the road. Wrinkles covered my entire body, and those wrinkles were covered with freckles that had darkened into age spots long ago.

I suffered no serious illnesses, had never been hospitalized except to give birth. No medical condition threatened to be my end; unless I was struck by lightning or a speeding car I would probably live to be a hundred and eighty. My cranky peers were anxious for me to develop something and join in their complaining jags. What none of them realized and I couldn't begin to explain was that my ailment didn't cause me to limp, or catch my breath, or put my car keys in the toaster, but it slowed me down just the same.

My self diagnosed affliction was not rare. The classic lonely old lady is everywhere; she's your neighbor, your aunt, your mother's best friend, but when she's in your mirror every morning she's not as easily dismissed.

Every aspect of my appearance was quite ordinary for a woman of eighty years. No reason for a second glance. The only outward indication of the inner mass of confusion that I considered myself to be were my eyes. They changed from blue to green as often as I changed my mind. My mother said they were 'blue as the sea' but my father said they were as green as Ireland's meadows. Mike called them 'hazy', which I thought romantic until I looked it up in the dictionary and read the definition; 'somewhat vague'. I asked him if he meant my eyes or my mind, and he laughed the question away without ever really answering it.

'Somewhat vague' was an apt description. I lived my whole life in a state of indecision, never quite sure if I was saying or doing the right thing; forever hesitant and insecure. I held back my true feelings so well that other people's perceptions of me became who I was.

For awhile I grew up and was capable of making confident decisions, but somehow the older I got the more I regressed to my anxious and uncertain self. Had I only imagined that temporary sureness or did Mike's strength empower me and losing him diminished it? It was a question I could dwell on for hours and never make up my mind which answer I liked best.

Lately my mind drifted more and more; over and around thoughts and memories like waves over glass, softening the edges, clouding them like treasured bits of blue sea glass washed in with the tide. I kept the most precious recollections within easy reach, where I could retrieve and savor them whenever I wanted to.

Other memories I purposely kept out of reach; the rough and jagged-edged shards of glass picked up on shore and quickly tossed back to the sea. I rarely looked past the precious ones, but every so often, in a peaceful moment my guard slipped, my thoughts veered, and Mary crept in. Memories of Mary were always sharp and painful. There were not enough waves in the sea to soften the piercing grief she conjured up in my heart.

I gripped the arms of my chair to regain control, to turn away from the progression of events that followed Mary, the frustrating nightmare that had become my reality for the past ten years.

John gave me a cat on my seventieth birthday and took his daughter, my only grandchild home. It was so hard to say good-bye to them, but it would have been impossible if I had known that it was forever.

I heard the Morgan's car beep as they pulled away. I thought about Virginia, how I still missed running next door to talk over tea, her laughter scaring away my worries and fears. When Mike died Virginia was my anchor and losing her set me adrift again. Then Mary came along and filled the empty spaces in my heart like red glitter glue in a child's valentine until I lost her too, in the slow motion surge that scattered my family like wind dissipates sea spray. But the wave never broke, the storm never landed; it swirled around us, pulling us under but never drowning us, a constant threat of downpour but then only dark clouds.

I walked to the top of the steps, stared at the horizon trying to back track my thoughts. It was no use. The memories were more powerful than any resolve I had left. A lump rose in my throat and strangled me. Tears welled in my eyes.

Mary; sitting in the sand filling a bucket with shells as her golden hair danced in the morning sun, racing to the water's edge to toss them into the sea and running back, climbing clumsily up the stairs, arms outstretched calling, "Nana, Nana! Come see what I found!"

I backed away from the steps and reached for the front door. The quiet of the hallway calmed me. I had made peace with the quiet long ago. When you live alone it is necessary to make silence your friend for it can quickly become your enemy. Rooms that had once been filled with noise were still.

I paused to turn off the lamp on a small table at the bottom of the stairs. I lit it every night, for I had not yet made friends with darkness. The lamp was a wine jug filled with shells. I remembered a little boy proudly handing it to me on another birthday that seemed, suddenly, to belong in some other woman's past.

I walked into the front room where a wall of windows looked out at the sea night and day. The room was comfortable with a faded blue couch and easy chair under the windows, and a large oak rolltop desk on the north wall. Mike used to say that if I had my way every room would have only two pieces of furniture; a rocking chair and a desk.

I wasn't much of a decorator, but the house didn't require much; the contrasting hues of sea and sky framed in every window, the scents drifting through the screens, the murmur of the sea and sea birds grabbed your senses at every turn. Shelves and bookcases were filled with the bounty of my front yard; sea glass and sea shells in boxes and baskets, old buoys and decoys, driftwood creations and hand carved ships.

The wall facing the windows was a mural of a whimsical pelican, Petey, painted by my grandfather many years before and almost destroyed once, but rescued at the last second and placed there to age gracefully, staring out to sea. For a long time after Mike died I stayed out of this room altogether because for twenty-five years it was the nucleus of our lives; the gathering place for quiet evenings of homework and reading newspapers, discussions and debates, board games and card games.

We sat here on damp and rainy days, passing time with hot chocolate and stories, watching clouds layer over the ocean like neatly folded cotton blankets. The boys peered intently out the windows keeping watch for the stormy petrel, mysterious dark sea bird who legend said flew before storms to warn sailors. When the clouds burst we scrambled to the couch as the drops splattered on the window and lightning assaulted the sea with sparking swords of power, whipping the water into a frenzy and sending angry waves tumbling to shore. When the skies cleared and the ocean calmed in retreat, we grabbed our beach combing pails and ran barefoot out the front door to reap the harvest the sea had left us.

I sat down in the chair where I had rocked my babies to sleep, calming our fears by gentle moonlight over the dark sea, listening, always, to the rhythm of the tides. I walked across the braided rug and listened for a second to my little boy's laughter, sat on the couch and smoothed out the wrinkles in the coarse fabric.

I remembered the feel of Mike's rough, weathered skin. I could smell his cologne, see the smile spread across his face and into the laugh wrinkles around his sea green eyes. After all these years, I could still recall his presence in an instant.

I believed in ghosts, but I didn't believe you had to die to become one. Or maybe you had to die to become a good one, a ghost who could whisper in a song, or a phrase in just the right tone, the glint in a baby's eye, the tilt of an old man's head, and bring back a memory that comforts you when you're lonely, makes you smile when you're sad, takes you someplace better…

I stared ahead into the dining room at the gallery of pictures on the breakfront. I walked over, reached out and touched the framed memories. Those were the living ghosts that haunted me, visiting not in a whisper but a thundering roar. They stared at me blankly, the frame as cold in my hand as the sentiments they should have inspired were frozen in my heart. My own flesh and blood. I couldn't face them, so I placed the picture down gently and walked away.

Soft southern sunlight streamed through the kitchen windows. I filled my watering can at the sink and went out to the screened sun porch. Red geraniums in clay pots were lined up patiently on a low white dresser in the southeast corner where they bloomed brightly in winter, spring, summer and fall. I could never get them to bloom outside, some pesky bug was forever feasting on their precious buds. I watered them, carefully pulling off dead leaves and spent blooms, then took the straw broom from its hook and swept the green wooden floor.

The floorboards were old friends. I knew every splinter and stain in every crack and crevice of every corner of the house. A childish notion I had never outgrown, assigning human qualities to inanimate objects. I cried when we sold our first car, and the second one too. I only lived in three houses my entire life and had loved them all, felt guilty packing up and moving away.

This house was built by men who faced the wrath of the sea every day and believed a home should be a garrison to protect loved ones from the harsh elements not by defying them but by harmonizing with them. The Hankins' homestead had braved wind and wave for so long it had become one with them, a part of the scape without which the others would lose some of their brilliance and much of their meaning.

It was two stories, shingled in weathered brown cedar shakes and trimmed in dark green. Silent, strong and stoic, with an air of history, of stories and secrets never revealed. I had lived there so long the house had become a mental fortress as much as physical shelter.

I put down the broom, braced my arms on the window sill on the far side of the porch and gazed at the flat lawn reaching the dunes beyond it. Terns flit busily about, making breakfast of the tiny crabs and grubs beneath the sand. A low picket fence enclosed the yard. My garden meandered along the street side on the west, a rustic tool shed stood in the far corner and still plenty of open space for a rowdy game of touch football, or endless sunny hours of steal the flag and hide and seek.

As fast as the memories surfaced I pushed them back, determined to keep the past at bay. I was alarmed and annoyed by the sudden struggle, since I had become quite good at avoiding it. Was it Elizabeth leaving? Labor Day blues? The approaching storm? Or was it Jane, just about Mary's age last time she reached out to me with a birthday bouquet? I pushed away thoughts of garden tours and picnics, intimate evening strolls, slow swings and soft sighs on the hammock while children slept soundly in their rooms. How things change. The hammock disappeared into the past as quickly as the footsteps of the children and the sound of their laughter.

I looked out over the lawn. Mike had been proud of it. The dunes periodically threatened to overtake the grass, and that was a serious dilemma because the dunes surrounding the house were held in high esteem. The sand was built up now after a summer of dry weather and normal tides. Mike would call that mother nature's flood insurance.

The Hankins' believed in the power of dunes as protectors long before it became a popular belief. While neighbors flattened their dunes to make way for additions, pools and decks, they just shook their heads. The green picket fence prevented the dunes from taking over the lawn entirely. The sand still came in whenever and wherever it pleased, but the grass adapted, staying low and coarse and the color of moss. I had been frustrated by the sandy soil but over the years I too adapted, learning how to enhance the soil with compost, and to make the most of what did thrive; mums, day lilies, daisies, and shore rose.

I gave up my vegetable garden when the tomatoes rotted on the window sills and the zucchini quiches took over the freezer. I hired a landscaper to arrange an assortment of flowering shrubs to anchor the garden. Forsythia, lilac, viburnum, and rose of sharon, provided a succession of blooms yet demanded only an occasional invigorating pruning. I also had him put a purple martin house high on a white post to ensure music on spring mornings.

I went out the side door, down the steps and followed the flagstone path to the garden. I had faithfully cut back the mums all summer and they were ready to burst. The lilies needed taming, a few weeds taunted me, the shasta daisies were dying fast and the Montauk daisies were about to pop, but I resisted the urge to fetch my tools and dig in.

I maintained a daily schedule from which I rarely strayed. It started innocently enough from chores to pass the time, but gradually became a ritual to nurture normalcy and foster sanity.

On Saturday I gardened. My intentions were always light; a bit of weeding and watering, but I would find myself involved in some ambitious project or simply lose track of time snipping away, raking a little pile here, another one there, and before I knew it fall into bed filthy and exhausted without any supper. As a result I would spend Sunday recovering from gardening; sleep late and attend noon mass, then visit old friends at the cemetery. Monday was reserved for laundry and Tuesday I cleaned the house. Wednesday was bridge day, Thursday I shopped in town, visited the library, and lunched with friends.

Friday was an easy day, an unconscious left-over from working years, when the week was full of obligations and finally waned and dropped lazily off into the weekend. I was to tend my houseplants, and tackle miscellaneous chores like sweeping the porches, walkways and driveway, tidying the tool shed. I retrieved the broom and worked at a slow steady pace, hypnotized by the motion of the broom whisking the sand high into the morning sky.

Sweeping, weeding, mopping, all mundane chores inviting quiet contemplation. I solved many a puzzle that way and knew twice the feeling of accomplishment; to sort out the weeds from the flowers, and the answers to a current quandary. These days there was less work, perhaps that was why although the puzzles were fewer, the few seemed enormous, and the hours were easy to find but difficult to fill.

Suddenly I was exhausted. I hung the broom, walked stiffly to my chair on the porch and collapsed in it. Henry brushed my leg. I reached down to scratch his smooth backside. Henry was a Manx cat; he had no tail. John never explained how he found a Manx. He had been rather mysterious about it actually, which probably meant it was just a cat with no tail he happened to find.

John and his younger brother David, had always been fascinated with tales of the island long ago. Mike told them the stories his grandfather had told him, of the strange ways of people who lived by the sea; who fished not for a living but to live, who traveled miles to shop in a dusty general store for a luxury like soap.

They loved to hear Mike tell his stories, but nothing compared to listening to Charley Duncan, master storyteller and unofficial historian of Eastwind Island. Charley and Mike grew up together on the island, sharing their love for every inch of it. My boys loved the shipwreck stories best. They were filled with heroes; ordinary men who left their warm dry homes on cold and rainy nights, crossed harsh land to the beach and rescued the poor souls clinging to huge ships tossed about like tiny bits of driftwood in stormy seas. The men formed human chains in the icy water, or launched small fishing boats to save men, women, and sometimes children, from a watery death.

The story of the Manx cats was John's favorite. The Isle of Man is one of the British Islands. A wealthy New York merchant learned of a breed of tailless cats native to the Isle of Man, and ordered three hundred of the strange creatures. The ship was caught in a spring storm off the coast of Eastwind and went down. Captain and crew never made it to shore, but the cats drifted in on the towering waves like drowned rats and took cover in the jetties and pilings along the beach, rebuffing any attempts to be 'saved'. Over the years they disappeared although each new generation of Eastwind boys claim to spot one or two living in secret caves under the huge jetty rocks.

Henry rested on my foot. I picked him up and held him. I gazed out at the beach. Something caught my eye on the sand. I put Henry down and went to look closer, my sneakers sinking into the warm sand. I bent over and picked up a perfect Quahog, Indian name for a cherry stone clam shell, the underside just deepening into a dark shade of purple.

I climbed the stairs and as I reached the top the phone rang. It startled me. I didn't get many phone calls. I stopped, listened, it rang again.

I went inside and picked up the phone.

"Hello," I said.

"Sara, is that you?" a voice demanded.

I recognized Clare's shrill voice immediately.

"Clare," I said slowly. "Why hello dear. What on earth are you doing up at this hour of the morning?"

"Now don't you dear me Sara. I can't believe you're still there. I want you to pack a bag and drive over here this instant!"

I carried the phone to the door, smiling as I listened to her tirade. "Why Clare, whatever do you mean? The sun is shining, it is a glorious September morning. As a matter of fact I was putting on my suit when you called, I thought I'd take a little dip. Do you remember how we loved swimming in September? A summer bonus we called it, when Labor Day came late and we could enjoy these warm days before we…"

She interrupted me. "Sara. 'Iris' is coming whether you believe it or not. They're already planning an evacuation, you know. Are you going to be stubborn and get dragged out in your underwear at midnight by the National Guard? Is that what you want? That would be a fine sight on the morning news!"

I leaned against the door frame, laughing. It was a funny picture. I could imagine the scandal, they'd lock me up for sure. I let her continue talking, no use trying to stop her. She had to get it out of her system.

"......and you are too old for toughing out these storms any more, Sara. Why if I had a car I'd......" I tuned her out. I didn't mind Clare calling me old because she had a couple years on me.

Clare Jordan had been my friend as long as I could remember. Her family had a bungalow near mine in Sandy Point. She endured three financially successful but emotionally disastrous marriages, that took her from Texas to Vermont, and back again. Now she wintered each year in Florida and summered inland in an exclusive retirement village where she played bridge every afternoon, and went to dances every Friday night with all the other silly old fools who lived there. She was forever inviting me to come along but I would have no part of it.

She was still lecturing, "and selfish too I might add. Why when John called me this morning to find out what was going on, I......"

"John!" She had my attention then. I straightened up and gripped the reciever tightly, my body bristling. "Why in heaven's name, did John call you?" I shouted. "If he wants to know what's going on, why doesn't he call me? I am so tired of this nonsense. You listen to me Clare Jordan Busybody Monroe Jackson Anderson, because I'll tell you exactly what is going on and then you can tell my son. I am staying right here in my home where I belong. Where I have been one hundred percent OK for the past ten years and where I intend to be one hundred percent OK for the next ten, God willing. And no hurricane, or flood watch, or interfering friend or relative is going to stop me!"

I slammed the receiver in her ear, then slammed the phone down on the table so hard the receiver bounced off and fell on the floor with a thud. I left it where it landed. My whole body was shaking, but I was proud of myself. I had told Clare all right, my voice was clear and steady. But I knew Clare wouldn't be telling John that. I could hear the conversation: Clare would say, "I just don't know what she could be thinking John." And he would sigh and say, "Well, we've seen it coming, Clare. She's alienated herself a little more each year."

Yes. That was just the word he would use. Alienated. I would say ignored, cast off, left to die, and he would call it voluntary alienation.

The phone buzzed obnoxiously on the floor where I left it. I replaced the receiver and the minute I did, it rang.

I picked it up and held my nose, saying, "Good morning. I'm sorry but this number, 555-1357 has been permanently disconnected at the request of the demented old lady who lives here. Thank you for calling, please don't try again." And I slammed it down again with all my might. I groped behind the table for the plug and yanked it out of the wall grinning like a naughty child. I went out to the porch and Henry looked up, startled by my quick movements. I dragged my chair to the top of the steps and threw myself into it rocking so fiercely my feet lifted right off the floor with each angry push.

I felt like I might explode, burst into the sky in a million fragments and float over the ocean like fireworks on the fourth of July. I had to do something. I stood up so fast I nearly tumbled headfirst down the steps. My chair continued rocking wildly behind me. I walked onto the beach and stopped halfway between the house and the water, looked down at my fisted hand and opened it slowly. I was still holding the shell, it's form imprinted like a fossil in the palm of my hand. I stared at it for a second. Then I held out my left arm to brace myself and with the other arm hurled the shell with all my strength and watched it sail across the clear blue sky to the sea.

CHAPTER TWO

The shell landed beyond the breakers with a splash. I chased the foamy wash along the shoreline dancing with delight as my father tossed another clam shell into the sea. It was the first day of my seventh summer at Sandy Point and I was eager to reach for every promise the new season held for me.

Shell throwing was a Boyle family tradition. "Wow, Daddy! That must be a record," I shouted as he tossed another one. I raced from the water's edge back to him.

"You say that every time Sara," he called out, laughing, as he caught me in his arms. John Boyle was a tall, slender Irishman, packed with strength and a mischievous sense of humor I adored.

"Can we throw some more? Please," I begged.

"No, we've been gone too long already," he said.

I wrapped my arms around his neck and peeked out at the colorful sailboats gliding over the ocean's swells. It was a different planet from the place I had left the night before. Like a princess in a fairy tale, I fell asleep in a dreary city and woke up in a faraway magical kingdom filled with sea gulls soaring and waves breaking under the brightest sun in the bluest sky.

My father shifted me on his hip. "We might get in your first swim lesson today. Are you ready to give up that bubble?"

"Oh I'm ready, Daddy. But promise you won't let go until I say, Okay?"

He laughed. "Something tells me you'll be ready to let go long before I am, my little fish. Look, there's Dave setting up. I'll race you to him."

The boardwalk that lined Marksion's Beach had five entrance gates. We used the inlet gate and Dave was the badge checker. As far as I knew he existed only in summer at his appointed position in my fantasy. I never knew his last name, where he went when the beach closed, if he had a family or lived alone; he simply appeared in June and disappeared into the sunset on Labor Day.

He was probably younger than he seemed to me then. He wore dark sunglasses and a faded gray hat, flannel slacks and a button down white shirt under a gray sweater vest. He sauntered out of the Markison Pavilion at 8:30 a.m. sharp; cigar in mouth, money box in hand, newspaper tucked under one arm, and set up his stand.

Then he'd swivel back on his chair and shout to one of the locker boys to bring him a cup of coffee from the food stand. If it was a rookie Dave would take him aside and speak very low, "Be a good boy and bring me a cup of coffee, then go and tell the lifeguards that Arnold wants them to bring him up fifty feet of shoreline, pronto."

If the boy hesitated Dave would grab him by the arm and say, louder, "You know who Arnold is don't you? He's the boss. Owns every speck of sand on this beach, owns every inch of this boardwalk. Yep. You can thank Arnold Markison come payday, my boy."

And off the boy would go. When the guards heard his urgent message they'd send him running to every lifeguard stand looking for fifty feet of shoreline with roars of laughter followed just out of his earshot.

When my brother Bobby was sent on his initiation mission he searched all morning and was frantic when he went home for lunch and told my grandmother about it. She looked him in the eye and said he had two seconds to set his mind straight and use the good brains God gave him or she'd box those brains out of his ears. Then they sat down and had a good laugh over a turkey club sandwich.

Dave smiled down at us. "Well look what the tide brought in, the biggest and the littlest Boyles," he said reaching out to shake my father's hand.

"Good to see you, Dave. How was your winter?"

"The only good winter is one that's over, I always say John. But tell me, how are you, the kids, Mary and her mom?"

My grandmother, we called her Nana, never went to the beach, so she never met Dave, but they knew each other well enough. Ever since Bobby's initiation Nana sent Dave samples of her delicious home baked goodies so he would play his practical jokes on somebody else's grandkids.

John answered, "Everybody's well. Nana is still going strong. The boys are anxious to start working, and Sara is anxious to start riding those waves. Right Sara?" He winked at me.

I didn't pay much attention to their conversation. They talked about Bobby working in the food stand at night and doing construction days to save money for college in the fall, and how my other brother Jimmy was desperate to get a job as locker boy even though he was too young.

I climbed up on the railing, lifted my face to the sun and took a deep breath of the cool salty air. I watched a sea gull poised on one foot high on top of the pavilion, turning his head from side to side. I wondered what he was thinking; did he hate summer? Hate us invading his territory?

I let the sensations of the new season wash over me. I could smell the suntan lotion, taste the sweet cotton candy, hear a train whistle at the other end of the boardwalk, see a beach crew pulling out lifeguard stands and line up red and white striped beach umbrellas, feel the smooth new boards beneath my bare feet and touch the fresh white paint on the walls of the pavilion.

The sea gull took flight suddenly and I watched him fly away, sure he was not as pleased by these signs as I was. But I didn't want to waste time worrying about him because I knew as quickly as he disappeared over the sea, that's how fast summer days fade into winter daydreams.

My Dad said, "Well, great to see you back Dave."

Dave called after us, "Great to be back, John. Great to be back!"

We walked along the south side of the pavilion, nodded greetings to a few familiar faces in the group of lifeguards bustling past us, shiny silver whistles swinging from their necks. Clean red shorts with GUARD emblazoned across them matched the hats they wore to protect skin that would be burnt to a crisp by the end of the day, then tanned deep brown by mid-July. The stiffness of the younger guards thick leather belts showed their rookie status while the veteran's belts hugged their waists like a second skin.

Two of them stopped and asked about Bobby, then casually inquired about my older sister, Joann.

We turned north at the corner of the pavilion where the boardwalk stretched for a quarter mile to the Inlet. Inside the pavilion was slowly coming to life. Behind one counter teen-aged boys in crisp white uniforms prepared the grill that would soon be smoking with burgers and dogs; baskets of french fries awaited the plunge into hot grease to spit and gurgle and turn crispy golden brown. White stools with red seats lined the counter and a dozen tables and chairs were scattered around an old jukebox in the center of the floor.

On the opposite wall a penny candy counter beckoned with a tempting assortment of treats neatly arranged in a glass display by teen-aged girls in red and white checked uniforms. They constantly flirted with the guys in the hamburger stand, encouraged by the dreamy songs humming out of the jukebox night and day as paddle fans whirled around overhead, chains slapping in time with the tunes.

We went into the paper store across from the pavilion and Dad bought the Daily News and a pack of Chicklets. Outside a man was setting up a display of beach toys and I watched him put the last plastic pinwheel in its hole. The wind caught the points and sent them spinning wildly in a kaliedescope of color.

"Let's take a quick walk to the inlet," Dad said.

The Sandy Point Inlet was a man-made channel. It had opened and closed for years at the whim of the tides hindering the ships docked along the Squan River. The state was eventually forced to fund the enormous undertaking of hauling huge granite stones from a subway excavation project in the city to form jetties on the north and south borders.

Mountains of sand were dredged out, allowing the salty Atlantic Ocean to flow freely in and mix with the fresh water of the Squan River. The brackish water harbored a plentiful supply of striped bass, fluke, and weakfish and attracted fishermen from sunup to sundown.

At high tide the jetties jutted out to sea 150 feet but at dead low a beach comber could walk to the point on a sandy carpet laid with shells, sea glass, star fish and clams. Light towers beamed at the end of both jetties; providing beacons for sailors of small pleasure boats as well as the commercial fishing ships that traveled in and out of the channel.

The boardwalk ended in a "T" at the inlet, where wooden benches welcomed walkers, runners or those who came just to gaze at the sailing ships, rugged fishermen, sea and shore birds and early morning surfers over on Squan Beach. West of the boardwalk untouched dunes rambled for two square miles covered with patches of primrose and wild daisies, pink and white marshmallows and beach rose; Bayberry bushes grew from pebbles scattered in sandy soil. Rabbits, raccoons, blue heron and snowy egrets thrived there, gulls and terns were infinite.

The hot wood of the bench burned the back of my legs. My father put his arm around me and we sat in silence. Then he leaned over and whispered what I was thinking "Sometimes I wish I could sit here forever."

He hoisted me onto his shoulders and we walked back past the dunes. I shaded my eyes to see the far end of the boardwalk; pastel cars dangled from the giant ferris wheel, the painted canopy of the carousel turned slowly on a test run, and the red roof of the south end Pavilion, identical to the north end only bigger, completed the picture.

The Pavilions were the hubs of Sandy Point. Summer bungalows of all shapes and sizes were scattered along the boardwalk between them in no particular order, as if they had been washed in with the tides and left where they landed. Narrow rows led down to Ocean Ave through the haphazard maze of stone paths and wooden walkways, clotheslines, sheds and sandy yards.

Up and down every row the same signs heralded the start of a new season; cars pulling in, possessions unloaded, windows thrown open, rugs airing out, and children flying out of doorways, set free upon the sand after the long winter's wait.

Residents of Sandy Point were without exception 'summer people'. It was the middle class of three on Eastwind Island; 'year rounders', 'summer people', and 'day people'. 'Day people', were the easiest to distinguish from the other two if you believed as the children did, that it all came down to which type of badge you pinned on your suit.

A day badge was an emblem of inferiority. The small square of brightly colored cloth pinking sheared around the edges allowed access to Markison Beach for that day only. A day visitor might also sport a black elastic band with a numbered disc around their wrist which meant they had rented a locker to change after the beach for a night on the boardwalk.

A day person could try to change in the public restroom, but the extra cost of a locker rental was less painful than the humiliation of being chased out onto the boardwalk by the diligent ladies who manned the restrooms.

'Summer people' and 'year rounders' purchased season badges; a shiny square of white plastic with Markison's printed in red and the bearer's name in black, allowing access to the beach from Memorial Day until Labor Day. These were badges of honor signifying that you belonged. There was only one step above a season badge; a Beach/Pool Badge.

The Markison Beach Complex included an olympic sized, salt water swimming pool. There was a section for sun bathing in red and white adirondak chairs and an employee lounge for changing.

There was a job for everyone at Markison's: lifeguards, badge checkers, locker boys, umbrella boys, waitresses and waiters, counter help for the grills, candy and ice cream stands, and maintenance crews. The beach had been in Arnold Markison's family for as long as anyone could remember. Arnold was over six feet tall; a thin, friendly fellow. He was personally involved in everything; from how long it took to grill a hot dog and get it on the customer's plate, to how long it took a guard from the south end stand to sprint down to the inlet and assist on a save. His children worked there, their cousins aunts and uncles, and everyone knew everyone.

Markison's was where the three classes met; kids from Sandy Point worked with kids from Eastwind and other towns on the mainland. The relationship between summer people and year round residents was symbiotic; they benefited from each other's existence even though they often denied it and in some cases, resented the other's presence. There were summer people who envied the locals their life by the sea all seasons of the year, and others who imagined it barren and isolated.

There were year round people who wished they could escape their every day lives for two months of vacation, and there were others who lived around the corner from the sea but never ventured near it. That attitude was one I could not comprehend, for even at the callow age of seven I clearly fit into the category of the envious. I had never been there before June or after September, but returning to Sandy Point each summer was marvelous, and leaving each fall was misery.

As we approached our row Dad said, "Looks like the Jordans are pulling in Sara. Let's go say hello."

Some rows had formal names, others were named from reference, like second row, or Jane's row, long after some forgotten child named Jane summered there. We lived on Pilgrim's Path and the Jordans lived two rows over on Lenape Lane. They pulled their shiny new station wagon into the garage at the bottom of the row. The Jordans owned all the bungalows on Lenape Lane and lived in the biggest one, at the top of the row facing the beach.

Walter Jordan was first out of the car. He was nineteen years old, tall and muscular with blonde hair and green eyes; star athlete, academic scholar, lifeguard captain, all around Mr. Popularity. He stretched his legs and arms as if preparing for a marathon, waved at us, then reached into the car and hoisted a footlocker onto his shoulders.

Chuck Jordan was next, feet barely touching the ground as he bounded up the row. He was eleven years old, a 'C' student in school, champion wrestler, and described by most as a 'handful'. His best buddy was my brother Jimmy.

He ran past us shouting in one breath, "Hi Mr. Boyle…Hey Sara!…Where's Jimmy?…Is the ocean calm or rough?…Is Bobby down?…Is anybody else here yet?" He raced past us to the top of the row and disappeared down the boardwalk.

Mrs. Jordan came up the walk holding Clare by the hand. I was immediately jealous of Clare's sunsuit; dainty yellow and white daisies on a pink background trimmed in white with ties at the shoulders. She carried a matching pink plastic bag with bright yellow sunglasses dangling from the strap.

Evelyn Jordan smiled warmly. She was a petite woman with dark hair and eyes. She held her hand out to my father.

"John. How good to see you. And look at Sara. You must have grown a foot since last summer."

She wrapped me in a hug and kissed my cheek lightly. Then she turned back to my father.

I stepped off the path and stared at my toes, wiggled them into the warm sand waiting for Clare to make the first move. Clare Jordan was my best friend, best summer friend anyway. She was two years older than I was and we really had no choice but to be friends. Our parents sat on the beach and played bridge together, my older brothers were friends with hers, and my older sisters would happily marry into the Jordan family any day.

My father and Mrs. Jordan were already planning a bridge game for that evening. Clare sat down, unbuckled her white sandals, wiggled her toes in the sand and smiled, handing me the bag. It was filled with tiny dolls, play make-up, hair combs and bright barrettes.

Walter Jordan Senior, loaded down with suitcases, huffed over to us. "Where did those boys run off to now Evelyn?" Excuse me not giving you a proper handshake," he gestured to my father.

"Here Walter, let me give you a hand with those," John said, reaching for a bag.

"Nonsense. I bet you just finished unloading your own car, you don't have to start on mine. I've got two strong boys I raised for this." His voice rose higher. "Although it's strange how they have a knack of disappearing when I need them!"

Mr. Jordan was loud and mean. The only good thing about him was he wasn't around much. He came down the first weekend and the last and two or three times in between. I never understood how he and my father got along. The only thing they had in common was bridge; my father said Mr. Jordan was a challenging player, but whether he meant his skill or his temperament I wasn't sure.

Clare didn't seem to mind her father's ranting. He never yelled at her, but just hearing his voice sent chills up my spine. He bellowed to his sons again as he continued up the row.

Dad called me and I was thankful for his gentle voice. I handed the bag back to Clare and whispered, "When you come to the beach later, bring the bag, OK?"

Mrs. Jordan said, "I don't know if we'll make it to the beach today, but come over later with your mom and we girls can get reacquainted."

We cut between the rows to Pilgrim's Path. The nicest bungalow on our row belonged to Catharine and Preston Folger. Preston Folger's great grandfather had been one of the first residents of Sandy Point.

Catharine and Preston were school teachers. My grandparents, Mary and James Molloy, taught with them in the city. They visited them in Sandy point and when a bungalow across the row went up for sale they bought it. My mother spent her childhood summers much the same way I did, and when she fell in love with John Boyle it was lucky for me that he fell in love with Sandy Point too.

We shared the bungalow with my grandparents until Grandpa Molloy passed away and the house, and Nana, got handed down to us. Nana woke at sun-up each morning and recited the rosary. I would find her kneeling beside the bed and inch closer, stealing into her early morning reverie. I listened to the faintly whispered prayers, watched her lips move as the silver beads flowed swiftly through her wrinkled hands and shared the peace she found there. After the rosary she began her chores; baking, washing; preparing breakfast and packing lunches. By 10 a.m. she was on the upper landing of the bungalow, pulling the first line of wash down and hanging the second load out to dry. Across the row Catharine Folger sat in the cool stillness of her porch reading the morning paper. She had fewer chores since her family was grown and gone.

Nana and Catharine gossiped back and forth across the pebbled path without so much as a glance exchanged, speaking in code and instantly knowing who the 'he' was who gambled away his paycheck, and the 'she' who should have known better, without names mentioned. I got pretty good at guessing who was who and learned intriguing secrets before they realized I was onto them.

Preston Folger was a fisherman. He left every morning before dawn, rain or shine, in hip boots and suspenders, pole under one arm, fish pail and lunch pail in the other, to fish from the inlet jetty. Sometimes he bought passage on a charter boat, full day or half, blues or fluke, and sailed out to the open sea to cast his line.

As we approached the Folgers' Preston was bent over his pail. I peered into it.

"Catch anything?" Dad asked.

Preston smiled. "Not much. A couple of sea robins." He reached out and held my hands. "And how is Miss Sara? You were sound asleep when Bobby carried you in last night. Let me see how much you've grown."

He backed me up against the 'measuring wall', a yard stick nailed to the corner of the house, covered with dated heights of Molloy, Boyle and Folger children, and noteworthy fish that had passed through over the years.

He sized me up, whipped a worn down pencil out of his breast pocket and marked it. "Jimmy was just here. Seems he and Chuck are anxious to get out fishing on the "Jane Marie" again as soon as possible." We stepped back to inspect the wall. "Well, Sara. You're almost as tall as Jimmy!"

Dad asked, "Which way did Jimmy go?"

"Right back inside. Mary called him in, something about a messy room..." Preston chuckled.

Dad threw up his hands. "A messy room? We just got here?!"

Our bungalow was shingled in light gray fish scales that squared off as they went down. The doors and windows were trimmed in white and scraped and painted every three years. The house was a simple structure, like a shoe box, but it held more magic for me than a trunk of pirate gold.

The screen door slammed behind us and the familiar scent of salty air mingled with musty cotton and old wood enveloped me. Another token of summer; the smell of the bungalow and everything in it from the sheets in the drawers to the towels in the shower, the plates in the cupboard and the curtains on the windows. I drew in a deep breath.

My eyes slowly adjusted to the darkness. Conch shells, chunks of driftwood and a huge dried out star fish dangled from a fishing net on one wall; a lumpy couch draped with a badly faded flowered slipcover slouched underneath it. On another wall a peg board was adorned with fishing poles and crabbing nets, beach hats, and fishing hats stuck with colorful lures. Tackle boxes and beach pails were stacked haphazardly next to fishing boots lined up on the floor.

The focal point of the room was 'Petey The Pelican'. Grandpa Molloy was an amateur painter and many of his works were properly framed and hung on the walls, but the summer before he died he painted the mural of an enormous brown pelican perched high on a grass covered dune; crabs and seashells scattered on the sand and seagulls and sand pipers flying across a vivid aqua sky. I whispered good morning to Petey. I didn't get a chance to know Grandpa Molloy but I figured if his spirit was around that's where it would be.

Chairs scraped upstairs and my mother called down angrily. "Is that you John? Where have you been? Bobby overslept and the girls won't stir!".

Dad went to the steps and called up, "It's beautiful out Mary. We couldn't resist poking around a bit. The Jordans just arrived, and Preston's already been out fishing."

He bent down and whispered in my ear. "Let's really rouse those lazy sisters of yours...Run in there and tell them Walter Jordan is here and I'm bringing him in to say hello."

I spent enough time listening in on my sister's conversations to know what kind of chaos that would cause. JoAnn was twenty, Eileen was nineteen. Nana called them Irish twins but they didn't seem one bit alike to me. JoAnn was bold and fearless, Eileen was timid. JoAnn was tall and curvy, Eileen was thin as a twig. JoAnn spent hours brushing her long brown hair and trying new styles and make up. Eileen wouldn't touch makeup, kept her curly hair short and barely combed. But they were alike in one way; they constantly talked about boys in general and Walter Jordan in particular.

I tiptoed quietly over to JoAnn's bed and whispered loud enough for Eileen to hear, "You guys better get up quick! Dad just let Walter in. He's out there talking and he'll be in here in a second!" And then I stepped aside.

There was a second's hesitation before they threw off their covers and jumped out of bed, stifling frantic screams, clawing past each other to get to the bathroom. Dad stood outside the door, arms folded across his chest grinning. "Well, well. What's the hurry ladies? You remind me of those wicked stepsisters. What were their names Sara?"

They pounced on him then, chased him up the stairs screaming, "How could you?!…That was so cruel!!" And then, "Is he down?…Did you see him?…Did he ask about me?!"

We met Jimmy half way up. Jimmy never walked, he ran. Dad caught him with both arms to keep us from colliding.

"Whoa boy. Slow down. Where do you think you're going?"

Jimmy looked at him and smiled, his clear blue eyes sparkling. "Mom said I could go Dad. You know. Up to see Arnold? About my job? Remember???"

"I remember. But you better remember it's Mr. Markison to you. And be polite. And don't be disappointed if the answer is no."

"Yes, sir," Jimmy backed down the stairs saluting.

"Good luck," Dad called after him as the screen door slammed again.

Upstairs, a sunroom wrapped around the northeast corner of the house with windows framing the view from the Squan River docks to the inlet and out as far as the light tower on the jetty point. The panorama continued out the dining room windows onto the boardwalk and beach beyond it.

JoAnn and Eileen dragged my father into the kitchen to complain about his cruel joke to my mother. I dallied in the sunroom, arranging my toys on a little pink bookcase in the corner. I had brought my favorite dolls, some coloring books and a brand new box of crayons from home. I opened the box and smelled them. It was a smell I usually liked, but it didn't belong here. It belonged at home, with pencils and books. I put them back and wandered into the dining room where Bobby sat at the table eating a bowl of cereal. He was staring out the window at the blinding vista ahead of him.

"Hey Sary Jane, Mary Jane. How ya doin'? How's things up at the boards? Any cute little seven year olds around?"

I climbed into the chair next to him and whispered, "I told you not to call me that. My name is Sara, just Sara!"

He pretended to be hurt. "You always let me call you Sary Jane Mary Jane. But if you insist I promise, from now on I'll call you 'Sara Just Sara'." He bent his head and continued eating.

I poked him in the ribs and we laughed together.

I liked Bobby best. He was never mean. JoAnn and Eileen and even Jimmy, weren't always mean, but they all were at one time or another. Bobby never seemed to get mad about anything.

He sat up straight suddenly and pointed out at the beach. "Look quick Sara!" he shouted.

I looked and saw nothing but the boardwalk and beach sparkling in the sun. "What?"

He said, "Aw, you missed it. It's gone. It was a pelican. You know, like Petey downstairs?"

I was doubtful. "Yeah. Sure."

"No, really. I'm not kidding. I think I just saw one. I read how they are spotting pelicans all along the coast. Dolphins too."

I turned to him cautiously. "Stop teasing Bobby."

He leaned all the way back in his chair. "I'm serious Sara. When I was your age we used to see pelicans and dolphins all the time. Then they disappeared because of all the junk in the water, but they're coming back. You'll see."

We stared out the window together in silence. "Wow," I whispered.

My mother entered the dining room quietly, kicked the legs of Bobby's chair out and sent him crashing to the floor. She stood over him with her hands on her hips trying not to laugh. "How many times do I have to tell you not to rock back on these chairs?"

My mother's hair was completely gray. Her eyes were exactly the same shade as mine, which was exactly no shade at all. She was dressed in her usual summer attire; navy blue shorts and a sleeveless flowered blouse, white sneakers, and a white kerchief holding her short hair off her freckled face. Her arms and legs were covered with freckles too, eventually the sun would connect them and turn her skin dark brown.

Bobby got to his feet and glared down at her from a good foot above. "Mom, suppose I really hurt myself?"

She smiled. "But you didn't get hurt now did you? Wish I could say the same for that chair. Now go and get your lunch pail or you'll miss your ride. I've packed it up as good as Nana."

"Ha! Doubt that Mom!" Bobby shouted as he took his plate into the kitchen quickly. "When is Nana coming down anyway, so a guy can get some decent food around here?...Just kidding Mom!" he yelled as he escaped out the kitchen door and down the rickety back staircase.

24

I poured a bowl of cereal, keeping a sharp eye on the horizon for pelican wings and dolphin fins. JoAnn and Eileen joined me, but I didn't tell them, they wouldn't understand.

Mom said, "Well girls, we'll be busy this morning." We all groaned.

Every member of the family had a part in opening the bungalow. Dad lit the pilot under the water heater; a mysterious ritual involving much burning newspaper and swearing and often resulting in a heated discussion with my mother before being successfully accomplished. Mom had to stock the refrigerator and cabinets and supervise everybody else.

The boys unloaded crates of kitchen staples and paper goods and took them upstairs and then lugged the footlockers to their appointed bedrooms. My things were packed with Nana's in a shiny black trunk lined with flowery, scented paper. JoAnn and Eileen shared a plain brown trunk with madras plaid lining, and the boys crammed Grandpa Molloy's beat up green Army trunk with new fishing hooks and lures, Jimmy's comic books and trading cards, baseballs, footballs, and a few articles of clothing.

"You know," said Eileen, "I don't see why we have to do all the dirty work. The boys carry in a few trunks and boxes and go along their merry way while we scrub nine months worth of grunge out of smelly toilet bowls!"

"That's right, Mom," added JoAnn, "I thought when we started working in the summer we weren't going to have to do that stuff anymore."

"That's funny. I don't seem to recall any deals like that, do you Mary?", asked Dad.

Mom ignored the whole conversation. She started clearing away the breakfast things. "Oh Eileen, don't forget to make up Nana's bed. She'll be down tomorrow with Mrs. Folger."

"Come on Sara. We can get started on the bathroom up here," said JoAnn.

"Oh, sure. Leave me all alone downstairs with the spiders and crickets," whined Eileen.

Later that afternoon I was bundled up in a soft warm terry cloth towel on my mother's lap in her beach chair, trying desperately to stay awake but the hum of my parent's voices blended with the distant harmony of children's laughter, gulls calling, life guard whistles, and the steady murmur of the sea into an irresistible lullaby.

The next thing I heard was Jimmy asking, "Hey, Dad, how many weeks 'til Labor Day? Cause I figure if I save 5 bucks a week I'll have enough for a new bike when we get home." I sat up. Did somebody say Labor Day? Had I missed the entire summer?

Jimmy and Dad were stretched out on a scratchy green army blanket in mirror poses; arms folded behind the neck, legs crossed at the ankles. Dad

25

answered, "I see a headline forming: "JAMES BOYLE...YOUNGEST LOCKER BOY ON EAST COAST......EARNS SMALL FORTUNE IN SINGLE SUMMER...""

JoAnn and Eileen wandered over from the lifeguard stand. Eileen was saying, "If you have to work until 9 why did you tell Walter you would meet him at the party at 8?"

JoAnn answered, "I've told you a million times Eileen, you have to keep them guessing!"

They plopped down on a towel and Eileen began complaining that none of the guards would be around for 'the game' because of a lifeguard meeting. 'The game' was a friendly match of touch football engaged in every evening by boys between the ages of eight and eighty.

"What about me and Bobby?" Jimmy asked, offended. "Those wimpy guards aren't the only ones who can play football you know!"

Eileen shot back, "Bobby has to be at work at 6 you idiot. He won't be around for many games this year either. I might as well get a night job too, there won't be anything going on around here."

"Stop whining Eileen," Mom said. "Since you don't have any plans you can babysit for Jimmy and Sara tonight, Clare and Chuck too. We're playing bridge with the Jordans." Eileen rolled her eyes.

I was happy to hear I would see Clare later. She had not come to the beach and I was anxious to brag about my swimming lesson. I knew I had done well, and I knew swimming was one area I could be better than Clare, because she didn't have anyone to teach her. Her father never came to the beach and her mother couldn't swim a stroke. She would be shipped up to Markison's Pool for lessons.

My father taught us all how to swim in the ocean. Goosebumps popped up and down my arms and legs as I thought about my lesson that morning; icy water swallowing me up from my toes to my chin while Dad held my hand and gently pulled me out past the breakers, my feet reluctantly leaving the safe sandy bottom to dangle in the cold depths.

"Kick and paddle, kick and paddle," he coaxed, and my free hand paddled like a puppy's paw while the other held fast to his arm. Kicking and paddling were easy, it was letting go of his arm that was terrifying. I wanted to. But I was sure I would slip under the shimmering sheet of water and drift swiftly and silently away, out of his reach. He kept encouraging, "You're doing great...That's it...You've got it......Let go just a bit now...A bit more...Look up Sara!......It's a pelican!"

I let go and looked up to see the enormous bird slowly approach, then pass above, his shadow falling over us as he ventured deliberately southward. I was ten yards south of my father before either of us realized I was swimming! Our eyes met and we laughed so hard I nearly swallowed a gallon of salt water but I kept on kicking and paddling and it worked.

I loved it, I never wanted to stop. I swam over to him and out again, swam around in circles, waved confidently to my mother on shore. I closed my eyes, held my breath and dove into the shadowy depths, did a somersault and opened my eyes to see the misty circle of sunshine from below, stayed under until I had just enough breath left to swim over to my father's legs, suspended like yellow flagpoles in the watery underworld.

He pulled me up. "Ready to get out blue lips?"

I wasn't, but he insisted. "Hold on a minute and I'll pick a good one for you to ride in."

I didn't have a chance to protest. He grabbed the back of my suit and said, "Now hold your arms out straight, keep your head up and your eye on shore. Don't stop kicking until you feel the sand under your feet. Then get up and run and don't look back." He gave me a push and off I went, kicking like crazy to keep up with the wave, then teetering on the crest waiting to crash, then racing through the foamy wash and into my mother's arms.

Dad was right behind me. "Did you see her? What a pro!"

Mom was less thrilled. "That was an awfully big one John!"

I broke away and ran down to the water, eager to do it again, but Dad called me back. We walked up to our blanket and he repeated the caution that always accompanied the lesson; "Swimming in the ocean is not like swimming in any other water Sara. The sea is unpredictable, but you'll discover a sixth sense for it, your instincts are good, trust them."

My seventh summer was the hottest on record. I perfected my swimming skills and learned to body surf. If the ocean was too rough or the tide washed thick with smelly green seaweed, Mrs. Jordan took Clare and I up to the pool where we taught each other how to dive off the high board, raced and played countless games of Marco Polo.

JoAnn and Eileen developed gorgeous tans. Eileen counted another Markison fortune at her job in the office and made a good sized fortune of her own to bank for college. JoAnn didn't save much of her earnings as a waitress in the luncheonette but she had a spectacular wardrobe ready for her senior year at state, had broken at least three hearts and considered herself practically engaged to Walter Jordan by late August. Jimmy managed to save a few bucks and Nana promised to match his fund for that new bike if he could make it to Labor Day without making her invoke the holy spirit in his name.

The week before Labor Day Bobby was ready to leave for college. Grandpa Molloy's old army trunk sat forlornly in the corner of the sunroom collecting his new khaki trousers and plaid button down shirts, underwear and socks with his name clearly printed on them in black laundry marker.

As his departure day neared Nana tucked in his rosary beads, extra spending money, and a two week supply of chocolate chip cookies and brownies. Mom and Dad gave him a subscription to National Geographic Magazine and advice to study hard, act sensibly, resist temptation, eat right, sleep well, and continue to make his family proud.

Bobby was going to UCLA. He wanted to be a Marine Biologist since he could pronounce the words, and the minute his eighth grade graduation was over he started investigating colleges to find the one with the best program. Unfortunately for us, that college turned out to be three thousand miles away.

Bobby's last day in Sandy Point dawned hot and humid, even the ocean was warm and sticky. When the sun went down heat lingered in heavy air as a rowdy crew assembled for 'the game'. I sat with Clare on the edge of the boardwalk and cheered as Jimmy, Bobby, Walter and Chuck and the others packed in the last precious flashes of summer fun. After the game a gang of kids headed to the water for a dip. I asked if I could go and Mom refused but Bobby convinced her to let me.

I played in the wash as the other kids horsed around. The ocean was dead calm. Swimming in the ocean after sundown made me feel creepy; dark, shadowy water gave me chills no matter how warm it was. I was glad when everyone left and Bobby called me to swim out to him. We floated on our backs holding hands, staring up at the sky, barely moving in the lazy swells.

"I'm going to miss you Bobby," I said.

"Yeah, I know. I'll miss everyone too. But Thanksgiving will be here before you know it," he answered.

I didn't detect any sorrow in his voice at all which amazed me. If I were about to leave home I was sure I would be upset, but he didn't seem to care. I wasn't sure how to ask him about it so I said, "I love you Bobby."

He squeezed my hand tighter and we drifted slowly and I felt better because at least he knew how I felt. A wave passed under us and our hands broke loose. I felt something brush against my side and thought it was Bobby's arm. I turned my head and panicked when I saw it wasn't him and I had the crawling sensation that something was passing underneath me.

I got my feet back under me just as Bobby did the same. The terrified look on his face sent me into a frenzy of fear as he grabbed my arms to pull me to shore. Our movements were awkward; my legs wouldn't work. The harder he pulled the more spastic I became. I wanted to tell him to let me swim, but he just kept yanking.

Then, suddenly, he let go. I slipped under the water and sank slowly to the bottom. I reached for the surface and stood and stared at Bobby swimming furiously away from me. I couldn't believe it.

He stopped then and yelled back to me, "They're dolphins Sara! They won't hurt us!"

28

Twenty dorsal fins sliced through the water and Bobby swam furiously to keep up with them. They took turns leaping from the sea into the air, diving, splashing, dancing in their own wakes. Bobby grabbed onto one and took a ride, felt its smooth slippery skin, looked into its unblinking eyes. Then as quick as they came they were gone, submerged as a single unit. They resurfaced thirty yards south to perform the act again. We stood on shore watching until they were out of sight, then raced home to tell everyone the unbelievable story.

When Bobby left the next morning it felt like the end of the world. We talked of nothing else but the dolphins all night, and now everything was all wrong. Dark clouds hovered ominously outside, and inside tears had been falling all morning. Bobby and Dad were at the airport, JoAnn and Eileen were back home getting ready for school, Nana and Mom were moping about, summer was almost over and I was miserable.

I sat at the dining room table watching the rain fall, streaks of lightning illuminating the dark sky, piercing the agitated sea. With the next crash of thunder the screen door slammed and Jimmy pounded up the stairs.

"Mom! Mr. Folger said he'd take me and Chuck out on the "Jane Marie" if it clears up tomorrow. Even if it doesn't, he says blues bite best in a storm. Can I go?"

"We'll see Jimmy. Certainly not if it stays like this." Mom sat down and sighed wearily.

"Can I go too?" I asked.

She turned her head slowly and stared at me. "Why on earth would you want to go out on that fishing boat, Sara?"

"She thinks she'll see her dolphin friends out there," teased Jimmy.

"That's enough Jimmy. We'll see. That's my answer to both of you for now."

"It could be for my birthday Mom. Please? Clare could come too, and Dad. He'll be back tonight right? It will be fun!"

She shook her head. "Well, I don't get it, but if that's what you really want...Maybe."

I stuck my tongue out at Jimmy and asked if I could go to Clare's. I put on my raincoat and skipped barefoot through the rows to the Jordan's.

Clare wasn't the least excited about a fishing trip. "Sara, I am not going anywhere on that smelly old boat!"

"But Clare, there's nothing else fun to do. It won't be nice enough to go swimming and besides, it's my birthday and I want to go. So if you're really my best friend you'll do it."

Mrs. Jordan didn't like the idea either but agreed to let Clare go.

Rain fell for three days straight and each time the fishing trip was postponed the anticipation mounted. Clare and I planned what to wear and what to pack for lunch. Jimmy and Chuck got bored and gave us fishing lessons in the Folger's basement. We learned how to tie a basic knot, bait a hook, cast a line, and tell the difference between a Blue and a Fluke, a Sea Bass and a Striped Bass.

The weather broke on Thursday of Labor Day weekend and Mr. Folger said we could give it a try. At 7am sharp the group assembled and headed to the dock. The "Jane Marie' was waiting; engine running, plank down, crew busily moving around buckets of disgusting slop. Clare and I walked over the plank just as a grungy guy in hip boots hauled it back onto the dock and gave a signal to the bridge. We grabbed the handrail as the boat lurched out of its berth and watched our mothers shrink to tiny waving dots.

The boys explored every corner of the boat. Dad and Mr. Folger picked a spot to set up the gear. Dad told us to get our bearings before we wandered too far off. Clare sat on the bench next to Mr. Folger looking sort of green.

I couldn't take my eyes off the scene rolling past me as the boat made its way steadily out of the channel into the inlet. We surged past the Coast Guard Station, cutters docked and ready. We passed the end of the boardwalk where I had stood and watched boats pass a thousand times and I was fascinated to see the other side of the scene.

The benches were empty. I was disappointed no one would watch me sail proudly past on my worthy vessel. We turned southeast at the mouth of the inlet; the light tower's green beacon flashed and the sun broke through the clouds and blinded me with glare off the endless water. Markison's Pavilions were tiny cottages, the bungalows were specks in the sand, and the bridge to the mainland was a cardboard span for toy cars as we headed away from the coast. The long stretch of beach on the southern end of the island appeared deserted, a few homes barely visible peeked out from behind overgrown dunes.

The most remarkable feature of the island stood in all its glory on the southern tip; red and white stripes spiraled up a hundred feet to the regal black crown. The Eastwind Lighthouse had overlooked these waters for centuries, guiding sea captains on endless voyages, a tangible link between land and sea, sailor and home. The actual light was no longer 'kept' as it was in the old days when it was a full time job to haul the oil up two hundred and thirty three steps, light the beacon, and tend it. Since it was electrified, the task was as simple as flicking on a light switch.

I had looked at it many times but never really seen it. From land it was just a tower, poking out of rooftops into the sky, a fixed and useless structure. But facing it from the sea, as it silently surveyed its infinite domain, the lighthouse was the commander-in-chief, the crowned king, and I was clearly the insignificant one. Houses and people disappeared but the lighthouse loomed larger than life.

With each swell we crested the ocean grew more menacing. The sun slipped back behind thick and threatening clouds, the boat pitched and rocked, and Clare, who hadn't moved from her spot on the bench turned a deeper shade of green.

I sat down next to her and she whispered, "I think I'm gonna be sick!"

I helped her up and we headed for the tiny closet they called a head. I opened the door and she stumbled in as the boat lurched.

Mr. Folger was packing up his tackle box. He shouted to me but his words got tossed in the wind so he pointed to the cabin. I got Clare and we staggered in the direction of the cabin when a wave crashed over the rail and soaked us through. We stood like two stunned rabbits until Chuck ran out and dragged us in.

We gathered around a long table with the other drenched sailors to regroup. Dad sat next to Clare and tried to comfort her but all she could do was rest her head on her arms and moan. Jimmy and Chuck were feeling okay, or too stubborn to admit it if they weren't. I was all right if I sat still and didn't move.

Mr. Folger calmly spread his newspaper out on the table like he was sitting in his dining room. He took his glasses from his breast pocket, slowly wiped each lens with his handkerchief and set them just so on the bridge of his nose. We were fixated on his every move. He looked over at us, sized us up, and commented dryly, "You kids ready for some lunch?"

We groaned in unison. The Captain's voice crackled over the loudspeaker: "Looks like we hit some rough weather folks. Not to worry. We've got an able crew on board to keep things together. You might want to stay inside though, seems "Elaine" is gonna pay us a little visit, so we'll head back to shore."

Jimmy asked the obvious question. "Who the heck is Elaine?"

Preston explained, "Elaine is a category one hurricane. She's been playing hide and seek with the weathermen all week. Last I heard she was supposed to be on her way to Nova Scotia, but these damn things do as they please."

We leaned farther across the table to hear him over the constant din of the wind wailing through the cabin windows. "Is this a hurricane?" asked Chuck.

"Oh no. This is no hurricane. If we were out here in a hurricane, well...It wouldn't be good. This is what you call the periphery of a hurricane. She'll wander here and there out at sea, gaining speed, stirring up wind and rain and tides for hundreds of miles from her eye until, and if, she's ready to land."

"She's got eyes?" I asked. We were enthralled. Clare shifted her head to hear.

Preston leisurely turned a page of his paper and smoothed out the crease; enjoying his captive audience. He took out his thermos, set two coffee cups on the table and carefully poured the steaming liquid, handing one to Dad.

Preston continued, "A hurricane has one eye Sara, but she can't see. The eye is the hollow core of the storm, where she gathers her strength and spins it into a mighty punch itching to land somewhere.

"So, how do you know it's not here?" asked Jimmy.

"Let me put it this way Jimmy. If "Elaine" was here we'd be fish bait by now."

31

"I wish she would come," said Chuck.

Preston smiled. "Careful what you wish for Chuck. A hurricane hitting this coast would be something you might not want to see."

"I think it would be neat," said Jimmy. "Huge waves, 50 mile an hour winds!"

"Actually, it isn't a hurricane until the winds are clocked at 75 miles an hour. Winds just below that make it a tropical storm and that's when it gets a name."

"Like a baby?" I asked.

The boys snickered. Preston said, "That's right Sara, a hurricane is one of Mother Nature's babies. When air that's too hot meets up with air that's too cold they get into a struggle and make a regular old storm. But when both sides gain force and neither one weakens, they slam into one another and create a phenomenon, a storm of storms."

"Did you ever see one?" asked Chuck.

Preston didn't answer right away. He gazed out a porthole dreamily. "I never did, but I know what hundred mile an hour winds and a forty foot storm surge can do and I'm not so sure I'd like to see one."

"Tell us, tell us. Please!", we begged.

He took off his glasses and set them down, leaned back and stretched, rubbing his eyes. He put his elbows on the table, scratched his chin and studied each one of us before he continued.

"When my great grandfather built our bungalow, it was fifty yards from the sea." He paused to let that image take shape. "That's right, up where the boardwalk is now. He came down every summer with his family just like we all do. Only they traveled in a horse and buggy over dusty clay roads and cut a path through the dunes to get to the house. Well one year my great granpappy decided to stay on a bit past Labor Day and enjoy the cool September breezes. And it was enjoyable for a few days, until the weather turned."

Preston paused to pour two more cups of coffee from his thermos. "Remember, there was no TV, no radio, no fancy storm tracking systems; no way to know a hurricane was roaring up the coast like a runaway freight train headed straight for Eastwind Island. Nope. The only thing that came knocking on their door was a ferocious wind. And then it was too late. All they could do was huddle together and pray that it would stop. My grandfather told me what scared him the most was the sound of it. Like no other sound he'd ever heard. A hurricane makes a noise like a thousand Niagras falling, and just before the eye, when the tempest is strongest, sky, sea and wind unite like one howling white demon and attack everything in its path without mercy."

There was silence in the cabin. His words hung in the air as the boat pitched and the rain whipped against the windows.

"Grandpa said the last thing he remembered was grabbing for his mother's apron strings as she screamed and the floor rose up and slid the whole family from one end of the house to the other. His father broke away to brace the front door against the wall of water bursting through."

"Wow," whispered Jimmy and Chuck. Preston unwrapped his sandwich.

"Yep. My grandfather is the only man I know who rode a forty foot wave on his own floorboards and lived to tell the tale. When the surge receded their house was a hundred yards from the ocean and that was fine with them. They had bumps and bruises, and they never found their horse or their buggy. They were stranded for two weeks and never stayed past Labor Day again."

Preston grinned. "So. Imagine a storm like that hitting Markisons, and all those bungalows along the boardwalk."

"I still think it would be neat," said Jimmy. Chuck nodded in agreement.

I asked, "What was that one's name?"

Preston replied, "Good question Sara, but that was before they started giving them names."

The Captain's voice crackled out again: "Land Ho! We made it folks! It's safe to go out on deck again. Thanks for coming, and pick up a ticket at the booth to sail with us again no charge!"

We stood up unsteadily. Clare moaned, "I don't think I'll ever sail again."

As we clambered onto the deck the rain was softening to a drizzle, the clouds were lightening, and pieces of gray sky were peeking through. The boat easily maneuvered the choppy currents and banked west into the inlet toward the welcome sight of home port.

"Elaine" never did land, she headed farther out to sea, generating awesome waves all along the eastern seaboard and ruining Labor Day weekend plans before she sputtered out and died.

My family, the Jordans, the Folgers and all the other 'summer people' spent the weekend performing different variations of the same routine; cleaning up and packing up a summer's worth of clothes and toys, dishes and sand, ready to head to our 'other' homes.

On Sunday night we said our final good-byes and loaded the station wagon with the same foot lockers and cardboard crates we'd come with in June. At 4am Monday morning my eyes were barely open as I was lifted from my bed and squeezed into the car between Jimmy and Nana and two pillows for the long journey home.

I savored my last breath of sea mist in the dark stillness of the morning air and fell back asleep dreaming of a little girl who lived in two different worlds. One was cold and gloomy where stiff clothes and tight shoes were required, hair and teeth were brushed twice a day and school rooms and homework filled the hours.

The other was filled with warm and endless barefoot days, where children and dolphins swam side by side in the sunshine, lived in sprawling sandcastles with blue sea glass windows and green sea weed trees, ate only ice cream and penny candy and slept at night on soft beds of dune grass with the melody of tumbling waves and fog horns drifting in and out of their ears.

CHAPTER THREE

The second I let the shell fly I regretted it and glanced up the beach to see if anyone was watching. I didn't think so but just in case I straightened my shoulders, put my hands on my hips, and stared intently at the horizon as if I charged onto the beach every morning to throw clam shells into the sea.

I never wanted to care what other people thought but I always found myself caring nonetheless. I constantly analyzed my actions and words, and often wished I could snatch them back. Age and circumstance had only forced me to better conceal my insecurities with a face of nonchalance I built up around me like layers of a clam shell. But every so often when I caught someone gaze at me as Elizabeth Morgan had that morning, and I saw myself as others did, it terrified me to realize that my shell wasn't fooling anybody but me.

Was my facade just beginning to fade without my consent or control, and what would be left then? A clam shell's beauty intensifies as its layers wear away and the purple lining deepens. The Indians carved the pieces into beads and used them for currency. They called it wampum and the darker the purple the more valuable the bead. But that was long ago. The only ones who value the shells now are beachcombers.

The sea eventually reclaims its shells and tosses them about until they disintegrate into tiny specks and disappear among the millions of grains of sand that shift with the tides. Who would reclaim me? I knew the answer to that, but how much would I have to answer for? Or would I sit untouched in my fortress on the shore, slowly shrinking away until I disintegrated and disappeared among the thousands of questions and memories shifting restlessly about in my mind?

I didn't want to shed my shell. I had meticulously applied the layers during endless evenings passed alone; each visit cancelled, every voice unheard, every letter unwritten, every overture rejected, and every forlorn holiday celebrated with other families playing along as if they belonged to me and I to them.

They all graciously included me; the Allens, the Morgans, the Hastings, Charley and his crew. On any given occasion I received no less than three invitations. And I was not ungrateful. I was a good actress and I knew my part. I never overstayed my welcome or whined about misbehaving youngsters. I was careful never to drink or eat too much, speak out of turn or be silent too long. I bore generous gifts and minded my manners.

I convinced myself that friends could be just as close as relatives, that even though for seventy years family had been the most important part of my life, that I could live and thrive, without it. Until I glimpsed Anna Allen's granddaughter climb onto her knee and giggle as she whispered in her ear, or watched a young mother rock her baby off in a corner, or heard the camaraderie of fathers and sons watching a football game on television, and those walls of insulation would silently crumble and fall around my heart and the ache for all that I did not have would not subside for days.

Being the youngest of a family only has advantages while the family is young. My immediate family was gone, as they should have been, in the natural order. I had twelve nieces and nephews, and lost count of the grand ones. Many of them still remembered my birthday and Christmas. Joann's daughters brought her children once each summer and I cherished those visits. Ever so often a young boy or girl would knock at the back door, the son of a cousin, or some relation or other, and I would welcome them in and offer what I could; a drink, a meal, a day on the beach, and enjoy their company.

I was eccentric Aunt Sara in the old house on Eastwind Island. I once laughed at the tales of Uncle Somebody and tried to figure out whose brother he was, and wasn't he the one who...? I was probably featured in numerous faded photographs on dusty dressers all over the country. Another role I played well. And yet, there were too many moments like this one when I stared out at the sea wishing, and wondering if it was too late for wishes.

I turned back to the house and followed my shadow to the steps. I looked up to see Charley Duncan, apparently asleep in my rocking chair. His arms were folded on his chest, head back, eyes closed, feet propped up on the porch railing. He didn't flinch until my foot touched the bottom step.

Then without opening his eyes he said, "So, how does it feel to be eighty Miz Sara?"

I climbed the steps. "You know the answer to that better than I do you old rascal. Let's see, what is it now, going on eighty five I believe..?"

"I don't count them anymore Sara. I only keep track for you because I know how much it annoys you when I do. Now be quiet and listen. I've been sitting here waiting for you to finish whatever it is you were doing out there, when I heard an odd noise."

I leaned back against the railing facing him and listened. The south wind stirred the buoy wind chime in the corner of the porch, a few gulls called, shouts and laughter drifted down the beach, a car engine started out on the street.

"I don't hear anything. What is this, my eighty year old hearing test? Are you going to revoke my license?"

Then I heard the scraping noise coming from the roof. "Oh that. I think it's the weathervane. I told you last summer I wanted to have it taken down before it gets loose and impales some innocent beachcomber."

Charley still hadn't opened his eyes. He reached his hands up and put them behind his head. "I remember the day Mike's grandfather put that weathervane up; women folk skittering about like nervous hens, sure he was gonna fall off the roof and break his neck. Mike and I watched him working on it for hours. We were itching to climb up there and give him a hand but nobody would go for that. When he finally finished he stood with us out on the beach to admire it. He got down on one knee, pulled us close and said, "That thing will stay up there until the house comes down."

I groaned. "Oh come on now Charley. Don't tell me you think it's an omen? You think this is going to be 'the big one'?"

He answered slowly, "I can't say Sara. I can't say. And even if I did you wouldn't listen so why waste my eighty five year old breath on you. It's too precious."

"Well, you're right about that. I wouldn't listen. All this hoopla is ridiculous. It's just something to fill up the papers with. Where was all this concern when they were building mansions on piles of sand? That's when somebody should have been worrying about storms. It's a little late now......Anyway. Let's change the subject...Where's this special birthday present you've been going on about? I hope it's not more asparagus seeds."

Charley opened his eyes and sat up, stretching out his khaki-clad legs, smoothing out his plaid flannel shirt. He wore the same outfit all year long, the only variation being the colors of the plaid and the triangle of white undershirt peeking out at the neck in cooler weather. He was a typical old salt; a bulky build with a sailor's step, skin tanned rugged from hours at sea or on the bay in his sundry vessels, and pure, unwavering eyes as blue as an island sea.

Charley had a smile permanently etched across his face. I saw him without that smile twice in all the years I knew him. Once at the end of a brief and disastrous marriage to an extremely beautiful and equally selfish woman, and on the day we buried Mike. Charley bore the weight of his life long friend's coffin down the steps of the church with a sorrow even deeper than my own darkening his eyes.

Charley and Mike grew up together on the island sharing and sharpening their love of the sea, the river and the bay; swimming, surfing, boating, hunting. They mastered it all together, following a long tradition of Duncan and Hankins men before them.

I had an inkling that history had something to do with my birthday present. I had been after Charley to get it down on paper. I was certain that the enthusiasm he conveyed relating his stories to after dinner groups in various informal gatherings could be captured in the written word.

His eyes sparkled with mischief as he said, "Actually I'm hurt that you wouldn't welcome my asparagus seeds, you certainly enjoy the tender spears when they arrive on your plate. But no, my gift is not in the vegetable family. And it's just as well, since you seem to kill them before they sprout anyway.".

I ignored that comment, along with the reference to 'whatever it was I was doing out there.' I realized he had been watching, but he wouldn't mention it again. Charley didn't delve into other people's business. He was a private person and assumed everyone else was too, or if they weren't they should be. After Mike died he slipped soundlessly into the role of my provider. I didn't need money, or need him to mow my lawn or drive me to the store, though he would have done any one of those things willingly. All I needed was for him to be my friend and Charley Duncan did better than anyone else I had ever known.

"Now Charley, don't keep me in suspense. Remember I am eighty. I could keel over any moment and you'd never forgive yourself for killing me with curiosity."

He stood and took my hand, opened the screen door and led me into the kitchen where he motioned to a manila envelope on the table. I picked it up, opened the clasp and peeked inside.

"Well, well, well," I smiled. "This is an extraordinary gift. And you've kept it a secret. How long have you been working on it?"

"Why, my whole life according to you. So now it's done and you can stop nagging me about it." Charley fidgeted with a button on his shirt, shuffled his feet, gazed out the window, focused on everything but me. I knew him too well to be fooled by his nonchalance, but I also knew better than to make a huge stir or he might grab his masterpiece and run away and I'd never see it again. I set the envelope back on the table and gave him a kiss on the cheek. He blushed like a school boy and gently pushed me away.

"Oh for heaven's sake. Don't go getting all excited, wait until you read it. You'll probably blue pencil it to death and it'll take me another eighty five years to fix it to satisfy you.!"

I looked straight into those blue eyes of his to let him know how proud I was. "I wouldn't dare change a word," I said. "Now go on and let me start reading."

"Actually, Miz Sara, I'm taking you into town for lunch at "Donna's". They're running a special; Hurricane Stew. I hear its pretty good if the shells don't break your teeth. Then again that's not a problem for us, is it now?"

"Very funny Charley, but speak for yourself. My teeth are in fine shape. And what is this, a date? Are you finally putting the moves on me? Was eighty the cut off or something?"

Charley ignored the sarcasm and gathered my straw hat and bag from the hook by the back door. "Well, I realize it's Friday which isn't your day for lunch in town, and that wavering from your schedule may set you off kilter for the entire month, but it is your birthday and we're going. After you my dear." He held the door.

Charley's dilapidated white station wagon was parked in the driveway. The passenger door squeaked when I opened it. Coffee cups, soda cans, and doughnut boxes littered the interior. I rolled my eyes at Charley as I made a space for myself in the mess. He rolled his eyes back at me and started the engine. He stopped the car half way down the drive, leaned forward over the steering wheel and squinted out at the bay. The man had an uncanny ability to recognize any sailing vessel and know immediately who was at the helm and who else was on board, even though he had trouble reading the menu in a dim restaurant.

"So, who is it? And why shouldn't they be out there?" I asked impatiently.

He continued down the drive. "I thought for a second it was Joe's boy out on his new Grady, but he's supposed to be helping out in the store. I expect to be real busy today."

"So how come you can take off and go gallivanting with me?"

He smiled. "Because I'm the boss, Sara."

I laughed. Charley was owner and operator of Duncan's General Store, a landmark in Eastwind. It survived economic, political, and weather related storms by staying one step ahead of the times. In a town like Eastwind certain items were in as much demand now as they were a hundred years ago, like boat supplies, kitchen staples, and the daily newspaper. Other items changed with the seasons; rakes or shovels, sunscreen or bug spray.

In the back corner a few oak tables were scattered in front of the original wood stove where locals gathered just as their ancestors had done. In the summer visitors who fancied themselves locals did the same; took their ice cream cones to the back and sat at the tables in the cool quiet.

For years local artwork was the decor; walls and shelves filled with paintings, old beach signs and hand carved decoys. But Charley's grandfather realized visitors didn't just admire the art; they were willing to pay premium prices to acquire it, and so another successful marketing venture began for the Duncans, and provided inspiration and a rewarding return for local artisans.

Charley steered the wagon out of the drive and turned right, up North Bay Ave. He drove slowly, looking from side to side checking everything out. "The Morgans gone?" he asked, surprised.

I didn't look at him as I answered, more curtly than I intended to, "Yes. They took off earlier. Jane and Elizabeth came and said good-bye. And don't even bother asking. I'm staying."

I waited a second then glanced over to catch his smile and the slight shake of his head. "Believe me, I wasn't asking. Looks like most everybody else is leaving though."

Many of the summer homes were already boarded up, others in the process; shutters pounded over windows, patio furniture stacked in garages, vans and wagons loaded up. It was the normal Labor Day weekend routine, only a few days premature due to the storm warnings.

We knew the owners of most every house on the Avenue. He tooted his horn at a few and they waved, as we cruised past. I rested my arm on the window sill, reached up and unclasped my hair, let the breeze send it flying back like a horse's mane. For a second I was a young girl again, riding with my fellow up the strip as he showed off his new wheels.

The wagon pulled to a stop alongside the Allen's driveway, shattering my fantasy. I straightened up as Roger Allen made his way down from his garage to greet us. Roger's family had been in Eastwind for generations, and he and Mike and Charley were friends since birth. Roger had six brothers, Mike used to say they were the fastest men alive; all seven of them earned four letters in high school and college. The anchor of the Eastwind lifeguard team was an Allen for as long as Mike could remember, and probably still was.

I felt a special fondness for Roger Allen since he'd introduced me to Mike. His wife, Anna, and I had a less endearing relationship. We might never have chosen each other as friends, but since our husbands had we made the best of it.

Thinking of Anna brought Virginia to mind again. Virginia and I met at the time in a woman's life when friendships are often fleeting; you become attached to the mother of whoever your children are enamored of at the moment and then move on as quickly as they do. And in that pattern you never really become friends with any, but acquaintances with many, and enemies with a few of the faces you sit next to at PTA meetings. But my boys were staggered in between Virginia's four children and so they became merely acquaintances, and we were allowed to enjoy a true friendship like little girls playing house side by side.

Five years after Mike died Virginia suffered a stroke strong enough to sink her into a coma but not strong enough to kill her. She lay in limbo in her hospital bed while family and friends watched and waited. Those were dark days. Virginia was gone, yet she was not. I didn't know whether to pray for her to live, or pray for her to die. After three weeks she passed peacefully away, allowing the devastating yet strangely welcome grieving to commence.

As I watched Roger approach the car, I wondered why my mind was wandering so. Because it was my birthday? Was I dwelling in the past because I had no future? What future was there for an eighty year old lady? I shook my head to clear my thoughts, forgetting my hair was loose and it spun around in front of my face and back again like a spinning top. From the look on Roger's face it must have appeared as if I was taking some sort of a fit and I laughed in a hysterical gulp which made it worse and by the time I got hold of myself both men were leaning toward me, staring, ready to do God knows what.

"Oh for heaven's sake. What's the matter with you two?" I asked, barely controlling my laughter. They immediately straightened up, deciding to ignore what they had yet to understand; women. Roger backed off and leaned on his mailbox, pulled a handkerchief out of his pocket and dabbed at his forehead.

Charley leaned across me to peer out the window. "So Roger, what do you think?"

Roger gazed up at the clear blue sky and answered slowly. "I think I wish I knew old man."

I sat back and pretended not to listen as they discussed the storm, and young Joe out on his Dad's new Grady in that old familiar code good friends share and tried not to think about how much I missed that.

Charley was saying, "Well I think I'll lose in the long run. Nobody seems to be staying around long enough to need much either way. The extra candles I

40

ordered will sit next to those flowered paper plates and cups 'til next year I'm guessing."

"I don't know, they sound like perfect ingredients for a lovely Labor Day picnic to me; flowers and candle light." I looked coyly from one blank stare to the other as if I didn't really understand that the paper goods were for the picnics and the candles for the power outages.

Once again they ignored me. I glanced up at the house. It was a magnificent example of classic Eastwind architecture sprawling here and there in wings they opened and closed as needed. I noticed a shadow in the sunroom facing the street and sure enough, Anna stuck her forever dyed brown head out the door and yelled something to Roger. He turned and waved her off, then leaned back in the car window. "Why don't you two come on up to the house for a cup of coffee? Give me an excuse to take a break from painting these damn shutters."

I answered quickly, "Well, thanks Roger. Aren't you kind to want to use us that way? But Charley here has to get to work, don't you Charley? What with Joe junior being a.w.o.l.?" I sent him a sidelong smile.

"Yes Miz Sara," Charley bowed his head, spoke in his best southern drawl. "Gotta be on my way Roger. Boss lady says jump I say how high. Maybe I'll see ya later for that cup of 'jo'."

Roger winked at him, turned to make his way back up the drive. "The fastest man alive." I mumbled shaking my head as I watched him go.

"What's that?" Charley asked.

"Oh nothing." I sighed. Roger suffered from arthritis and his pained steps made me cringe. I wondered how Mike would have handled the prison of old age, and then wondered why I saw it that way. Most would say Mike and Virginia were imprisoned by death and I was the one who was free.

I wondered what he would look like, how we would spend our time. As we pulled away I caught a glimpse of Anna, waiting for Roger impatiently, hands on her hips. In the blink of an eye change moves in. One second you're breathing the next you're not, one day you're the fastest man alive the next you're the slowest creature on earth. I reached over and took Charley's hand, held on tightly to him, to the moment, before it slipped out of the car window and was whisked away in the breeze blowing steady off the sea.

Charley pulled the car to a stop in front of the light blue store front; a faded white sign over the door spelled out: Duncan's General Store. Two display windows flanked the entrance, one already dressed for fall; orange and red leaves spilled out of an ancient wood and iron wheelbarrow surrounded by an assortment of rakes, rusty garden tools and gloves. The other window held an eclectic mix of old and new; worn wooden delivery crates were stacked up like shelves housing a collection of hand carved duck decoys, set against a marvelous water color beach scene done by a young Eastwind girl.

I paused to admire the painting and Charley went inside. I was vaguely aware of the hustle and bustle around me as everyone reacted to the threat of a hurricane. I thought briefly of Preston Folger and the infamous 'September Storm', remembering his eyes dancing as he spun the tale on that fateful excursion out to sea long ago. Storms were big news. Curiosity seekers travel for miles to witness their approach, fury and aftermath. I had witnessed a few, and in my experience the ones to worry about were the raging northeasters the weathermen never knew about until the rains were pounding the roof, the high tides licked at the front door and the wind was knocking down telephone poles and garages and ripping out the roots of hundred year old trees.

Island boys love storms. The bigger the better. Their adrenaline builds as the winds blow and the tides rise. A few outgrow it, or learn to hide it, but it's always there. Storms always led to adventures. Charley would come calling that somebody was stuck out on the bay or stranded on a roof top, a child was missing, or some old man needed his medicine and off they would go. Mike and Charley used to say they were born too late, and in many ways they were right. But they performed their share of heroic deeds.

Once a refrigerator repair man came to my house, and as I signed the bill he asked, "Mike Hankins your husband?"

I said he was. Then he told me a story about when he was thirteen, swimming with some friends after a summer hurricane and they got caught in a rip. His friends struggled, barely made it to shore, but he was stuck and nobody would come to get him. By the time they roused some lifeguards he was so far out they called the Coast Guard. He thought for sure he was dying and he went under never expecting to see the sun again. His friends told him later this kid ran out of his house, dove into the raging surf and swam out like he was shot from a cannon. He got to him, pulled him out of the rip and brought him into shore. He said he never came back to the beach since then and he never got the nerve up to thank Mike so he wanted me to do it for him. Then he tipped his hat and was on his way.

I cried when he left I was so moved. I cried again when I told Mike. He was comforting but nonchalant about the story. His only comment was, "It could have been anybody Sara." Just like that. But I knew it was him. And I got a glimpse at that moment of the chasm between people like Mike, compelled to respond and the rest of us who watch from behind the safety of tempered glass.

The town was alive with energy that morning as Islanders reacted to the threat of the hurricane. They were no strangers to storms. Almost by instinct they checked for batteries and candles, canned food and radios, and dragged the raingear out. As the storm moved closer and the warnings intensified, their preparations would expand accordingly. Outdoor furniture, tools and bicycles were secured, storm shutters went up, bath tubs and gas tanks were filled.

Over reaction was rampant; from visitors to islanders, and the reporters and weather experts who happily fueled the panic. Some listen to every weather report and believe every worse case scenario the media offers up. They talk incessantly about the storm, needing to convince disbelievers until it elevates to a religious fervor.

I encountered two of the worst offenders inside Duncan's. The inseparable and insufferable Eleanor Forman and Joan Johnson focused intently on the battery display. Their husbands had made careers out of selling family land on Eastwind and using that money to buy more land on the mainland and turning that over again, always fighting for smaller parcels and generous variances. And all the while they complained about the influx of newcomers, overcrowding in the school, and congested roads.

I tried to slip past them but Eleanor saw me. "Sara! Sara, dear! Have you come to stay in town?"

I walked over to them smiling. "Why yes…Haven't you heard? I'm putting the house up for sale, these storms you know…I just can't take it any longer. I'm moving in with Charley until I find something……" I winked at Joan, who could barely shut her shocked mouth.

Charley walked over and the women looked from me to him, wishing it was true because a juicy bit of gossip like that would be bigger than any hurricane.

I grabbed his arm and held him close, grinning at them. He said politely, "Good morning Eleanor, Joan. All set for the big storm?"

The shock slowly slipped from their faces as they realized it was a joke, and they'd been needlessly diverted from their true mission.

Eleanor shot me a stern look and spoke to Charley. "Yes. Charley, of course. But your boy there says you are out of "D" batteries." She waved over at the counter where Charley's clerk rolled exasperated eyes back at him. Eleanor continued. "Now, I'm sure that can't be possible, you know what with the hurricane almost upon us…" She raised her voice with each word.

Charley welcomed the escape, sensing the three of us were up to more than batteries and excused himself to check the storeroom. Eleanor scowled at me. "Really Sara. You should be ashamed of yourself." She took Joan by the arm and left me giggling.

I took a basket and roamed the aisles. I didn't need anything, though I talked myself into and out of a few items, bath salts, lavender soaps. I picked up a bag of chocolate chips thinking I might bake a batch of cookies in honor of Hurricane Iris. By the time I approached the counter a box of teas and a pack of fireplace matches had found a place in my basket along with some scented candles. Bits and pieces of conversation swirled around the store. Charley bustled about, taking care of customers. Eleanor and Joan wandered around attempting to engage everyone in morbid speculation about "Iris."

Two boys from the marina burst in searching for bulkhead rope. The ladies didn't bother with them, they might actually know something. A young woman was having a tug of war with her toddler over by the candy bars. I watched the battle, and was impressed that the child didn't win. I placed my basket on the counter and began to empty it, chatting with Joe. As he rang up my purchases he leaned over, shook his head and groaned, "Looks like they finally caught one, eh?"

I turned to see Eleanor and Joan zeroing in on the young woman and child. They had them cornered over by the paperbacks, interrogating the girl as if she was a criminal; demanding to know if she was prepared, bantering her with exaggerated horror stories of past storms.

I started over toward them when Charley appeared, lugging a case of the coveted "D" batteries. The ladies saw him and made a mad dash for the box, towing along the poor girl who was now convinced she needed ten of them, and every other essential she could get her hands on.

Charley tucked my purchases behind the counter and took me by the arm. "Trying to start trouble Sara?"

I started grumbling about Eleanor and Joan, but Charley interrupted me. "Hey, hold on! I'm not complaining. They'll boost sales higher than a banner over the beach on the Fourth of July. And they do it for nothing. Free advertising Sara."

We laughed all the way to "Donna's", a small sidewalk café that served the best crabcakes on the island.

"Order for me would you, Charley? I always admired a fellow who ordered for his girl." I sat back and watched Charley work his charm on the young waitress. He ordered two iced teas and two tuna melts.

As the waitress brought our drinks Charley asked, "So, have you heard from the boys yet?".

I stopped stirring for a second and I know he instantly regretted asking the question, as I instantly hated myself for the way I was about to answer but I couldn't help it.

I didn't look up. "No." I said slowly. "I'm guessing my annual birthday floral arrangement is sitting on the desk in Clare's apartment, where it will certainly remain since I have no intention of going to fetch it and she won't dare venture out here what with the imminent end of the world and all that."

Charley made no comment. I continued. "Of course, it would be just like John to call Clare again to see if I'd gotten it, and then send another one, this time to where his mother actually lives, not where he assumes, or hopes she is so that he won't have to worry about her being washed out with the tide."

There. I was finished. I resumed stirring and looked up at Charley, who was settled back in his chair staring up at the clear blue sky above us, waiting, I supposed for me to continue, or hoping I would stop, or simply wondering how to respond.

After a few minutes he said, "Well I'm no expert but I think maybe you best get out that old bubble you used to talk about cause at eighty I don't imagine you can ride those waves like you used to…"

He looked at me and I smiled. The sandwiches were delivered. I gazed past Charley at the parade of people marching through the town. Two boys rode by on bikes precariously balancing surfboards under their arms, followed by a group of teen aged girls, long hair flowing, laughter drifting. Shoppers scurried from the bank to the Post Office and in and out of the shops.

Suddenly I wasn't finished, I had more to say, even though I knew Charley didn't necessarily want to hear it.

"You know Charley, when I think about my two sons, I honestly don't know what I feel. I love them, more than it appears, I'm sure. I imagine it seems like I don't care. But I do. I'm just very good at pretending, but I've become so tired of it." I picked up my sandwich then put it back down. "I'm tired of the act, tired of the silent suffering. It sits with me night and day; anger, love, guilt, a sorrowful bulky weight that I can no longer bear."

Charley went on eating his sandwich. I knew he was uncomfortable, I rarely spoke with such candor, and it sounded so pathetic, spoken out loud. I was afraid to meet his gaze and see pity or disdain, but when he looked up the only emotion there was understanding. For the second time that day I was shaken at how wrong my perception was from reality and I wondered if I had ever really looked at the people I loved. Had I always been so busy worrying what they saw in me that I had not bothered to see them?

I went on. "You see, I always knew I would lose David. He was never really mine. He was like Mike and you, a child of the air and the sea. Can't you see him Charley, setting off sparks wherever he went? He never walked; he crawled and then he ran, and then he swam and sailed and surfed…day and night, winter, spring, summer and fall…can't you see his smile Charley? That electric smile, those clear blue eyes…I miss them so…"

My voice quivered but I cleared my throat and continued. "I thought the island might hold him, but for him it didn't have to be this island. It had to be the sea, but any sea. He wasn't like you and Mike that way, for you it had to be Eastwind, but not for him. And not for John either."

The waitress took our plates. Charley told her how delicious everything was, ordered a hot tea for me and another cold one for himself. When she'd gone I continued. "John. Strong, silent John. So like me, keeping everything inside. That's the trouble, as if the miles between us weren't enough, we have to overcome that innate inability to bare our souls, to reveal no truths, so we act on some superficial level where we think it's safe, but in the end we both wind up injured and alone."

45

I stopped. Charley cleared his throat as the waitress fussed over his iced tea. When she left he spoke.

"Sara. First of all nobody thinks you don't love your boys. And second of all, you need to tell them all this. Why don't you get on a plane this morning and go and see John. Get away from the chaos of the storm. Hell, maybe I'll go with you. Why not?"

I laughed. "I can't see that, Charley. You wouldn't leave today if somebody paid you a million dollars. We both know that. But it's funny. I was thinking this morning about calling John and David, and asking them to come out and see me. Do you know what I think would happen?"

"Don't leave me in suspense, Sara…"

"Well, I think they would both come. But David would be on the first plane while John would take two days to get here, and I don't mean that in a bad way. It just illustrates the difference between them. John would have to think about it; plan, pack, make arrangements, just like I would."

Charley leaned over the table. "Why don't you do it then?"

I thought for a second. "Two reasons. One, I don't need them. They have their lives to live, and for now that's just the way it is. If the day comes when I do need them, I'll worry about it then. Two, because in the darkest corner of my heart where those nagging fears lie, I'm not sure I'm willing to test them lest they fail, for that would prove that I failed miserably wouldn't it?"

"Well, since we're being so frank this fine morning, Sara, I'm going to say this once more and then I'll say no more. You should call John. Invite him out here, Mary too, insist they come, demand it, and have it out once and for all. Because though you don't realize it, or won't admit it, you do need John, and Mary. You need to get over the disputes between you before it eats you alive. You said yourself you're tired of it. Ten years is too long to let a wound fester. I can't even believe it's really been that long. But it is too long. It's past time to air it out and let the healing begin."

I sat back in my seat as if I'd been pushed. His words took me by surprise. It was so unlike him to offer such assertive counsel. I had to think about what he said and digest it slowly.

I started to tell him but I was interrupted by a voice booming from the street. "Hey Charley! Sara! What luck to find the two of you here!"

Edward J. Blackmore Junior sauntered over to the table and Charley whispered, "Any chance of avoiding him?"

Eddie didn't wait to be asked, he pulled out a chair, took my hand, planted a kiss on my cheek, shook hands with Charley and called the waitress over all in one clumsy motion.

Eddie Blackmore was a huge man. His face, hands, body, arms and legs, and especially, his disposition, was thick.

He immediately monopolized the conversation, rudely directing all his attention to Charley, discussing the storm and how the marina was in chaos and he jetted up here in the middle of a mean golf round on his private course down south to lend his boys a hand managing the whole mess, but he'd be back on the course before dinner. Oh Maria made him promise that. She didn't want her precious caught in any hurricane. Maria was about twenty, to Eddie's eighty five, as far as I could recall. Eddie had been through countless wives and twice that many mistresses over the years.

The longer I listened to his meaningless chatter, the more annoyed I became. From the moment I first heard the name Blackmore I had despised anyone or anything associated with it.

The Blackmore family moved into Eastwind when Charley and Mike were in kindergarten. Eddie Junior, a strange dark haired freak of a child tagged along after them constantly, determined to fit in and become one of the gang. They made games of avoiding him. By the time they were in high school Eddie's father had quietly acquired every available piece of property in town, particularly beach and bay front parcels. He put together enough lots on the southern end of the island to build a marina, which quickly became the only game in town. He started his own construction company specializing, it appeared, in tearing down older homes and building modern eyesores. Before anyone realized what was happening Eastwind was in a state of friendly take-over and E.J. Blackmore was at the helm.

Half the town thought it was wonderful, just the shot in the arm Eastwind needed to keep up with the times. But others were alarmed at the rapid development, and the changes on the quiet island. It all came to a head when Eddie Senior ran for Mayor, and won.

That was when the half of town against the Blackmore siege realized the danger of their calm approach and sent up the flare, rallied the troops, formed and joined committees, attended town meetings, started petitions, became actively involved in planning and voting and developing precautions to avert the disaster they saw taking shape.

The Duncans and the Hankins fell into the latter category and did their part to successfully ebb the tide of destruction. But the effort wasn't launched soon enough to save Sandy Point. And for that I would never forgive the Blackmores.

When I was in my last year of high school, the Markison complex and beaches were sold, and that launched a domino effect causing most of the owners of the bungalows lining the northern end of the island to sell as well, until the few hold outs, my family included, practically had no choice but to give up their properties. Once Markisons was gone, Sandy Point's allure was lost for many people, especially when EJ Construction, the company buying the land, unveiled their long term plan.

Who wanted a summer bungalow next door to towering townhouses, condominium complexes and nightclubs? EJ Construction was willing to pay top dollar, they didn't want any trouble, and they didn't get much as they gobbled up property like some monstrous machine.

The town approved the 'Gateway to the Sea', and behind it all was Edward J. Blackmore. The Blackmores had an entire network of family members to run the operation, but not the way the Markison family had. One never knew who was really who, or who owned what. I couldn't seem to stop my thoughts from drifting back again and I thought I might have a stroke if I continued listening to him. I stood up abruptly. The men stopped talking and stared at me.

Charley stood. "Sara?" he asked.

"I think I'll head home now Charley. I feel like a walk. Joe can send my things up later."

Eddie lumbered awkwardly to his feet. "Well Sara. Nice talking to you..."

I stared at the foolish lug and could barely contain my contempt. For years I had tolerated him and hated every second of it. Mike and Charley never seemed to let him get to them, they said it was part of small town life, good business to get along with your enemies. I wanted so much to tell him off, tell him what I thought about his family, his money, his lack of manners, but I couldn't do it. I'd only make a fool of myself. So I held out my cheek and as he planted another crude kiss on it I surprised myself by hissing, "You weren't talking to me Eddie, you never have and you never will you ignorant buffoon." I smiled at his dazed face, turned and walked away.

I strolled slowly along Main Street. The town seemed full of strangers. I didn't recognize one soul, nor did anyone to notice me. I was an invisible old lady.

I started over the Eastwind bridge, the only access to the island. I remembered when it was lined with white wooden rails, a wooden walk to cross by foot, two narrow lanes to cross by car. I remembered how it felt long ago to finally cross that bridge after a dreary winter's wait, into the land of warm summer days. I could feel the thump of the tires on the bumpy road, see the huge red lobster carved out of driftwood hanging over the Lobster House Restaurant, hear the excited shouts rising all around me, "Look! The big Lobster!! We're here! We're here!"

I stood at the top of the bridge and closed my eyes, recalling those peaceful, comforting sounds and voices, willing them to drown out the clamor of the present, noisy world. I imagined I could look north, and gaze upon the Sandy Point jetty as I remembered it, long before the hotels and the condos, when it was nothing but a long pile of rocks separating the sea from the mountains of sand. I could see weathered, splintery boards rambling along past inviting pavilions, and down sandy paths between rows of bungalows, and from every window and doorway drifted the familiar, quiet melody of a simpler time.

A voice startled me out of my daydream, and I turned to face a young boy, smirking at me, saying, "What do you see out there old girl, that makes you smile so?"

I peered closely at his face to see if I knew him. I couldn't imagine he would be speaking to me that way if I didn't, but then again I couldn't imagine he would be speaking that way if I did. He was a brazen young fellow, yet he had an irresistible charm that disarmed me.

"If you must know, young man, I was traveling back in time. You know all about that. It happens all the time in movies today. Well I was staring at my past, and I liked what I saw. And I'm reluctant to turn around to look at my present, and even more anxious about my future."

He motioned at the scene before us. "What's so bad about all that?", he asked.

"Nothing I suppose. But did you know there was a time when you could stand here and watch the waves break on the Inlet beach? They don't even call it that anymore, but you could, once upon a time. You could see the jetty, and the light tower, you could see Squan Beach and watch the surfers over there." I paused. I knew that would get him, he seemed the surfing type.

"That's right. You didn't have to dial any surfer's hotline. You could just come up here and see for yourself how the waves were. Just imagine. Erase that enormous townhouse contraption, and take away the beach club, and tear down those condos and what would you see?"

He looked, and he thought about it, and he turned to me and said, "Wow. Cool." And then he turned and walked into town, and probably forgot all about me and my past before he hit the surf shop. Whenever I walked my boys across the bridge I made them stop and look, and remember with me, the way it used to be. I wondered briefly if they ever thought about that, about those days.

I crossed South Bay and headed toward home on North Bay past the graceful beachfront homes. This part of the island hadn't changed much since the days when I was an outsider, admiring from a distance, though change was always in the air. Even now, with no empty lots left, there was talk of allowing the large older homes to be razed and parceling off the lots. Another battle to fight.

The yards were immaculate; neatly pruned rosebushes, tall and firm sunflowers, black eyed susans, purple and white coneflowers, plentiful daisies. Gardening was a popular pastime on the island. Most of the old timers tended their grounds themselves, planting only what they could manage. In most cases it's a matter of letting things be. The shrubs and trees and flowers that grew well had done so for ages and need little actual care or maintenance. But that is a lesson some learn the hard way. They rip out perfectly healthy and hardy specimens, then replant in grand schemes only to see poor results and wonder why. They hire landscapers to fix things and keep it up, so lawns and gardens become yet another form of competition along with the tallest boat, the fanciest car.

The sun beat down and I was glad for my hat and the cool breeze blowing off the sea. The surf was pounding strong and methodical. I was never afraid of the sea. I was aware of the fury it could unleash, the damage it could cause. I remembered the first time I was 'clobbered' by a wave. I had been careless, allowed myself to be trapped in the point of no return where it is too late to swim out, too late to run to shore. There's nothing to do but stand helpless as the wave curls above you, then breaks over you, pushes you down, spins your body, head over heels and then heels over head, as you suck in gallons of salt water and bounce like a rubber ball on and off the rough sandy bottom of the sea until finally, if you're lucky, it spits you out in the foamy wash, and you tumble up onto the shore in a tangled heap. Once was enough for me. I was never caught there again.

One block from home I stopped to watch the crazed weathervane high on the roof spin out of control, then stop and spin again. I turned up Hastings Street on an impulse. The side streets in town were named for founding families and the Hasting's home was another impressive specimen. The entire property was fenced in by ancient hydrangea bushes; deep Nikko blues, faint pinks and dark shades of red, each bloom brilliant in the September sunshine.

Rhea Hastings used to tend them religiously, cutting the best blooms to make dried arrangements and wreaths. She rode around on her bicycle delivering her creations to neighbors.

Rhea's husband Caleb, had passed away a few years before, and she had done her best to carry on. She took care of her flowers, her children and her grandchildren without much complaint. But she went a little batty along the way. She began gardening at midnight, sleeping on the beach in her raccoon coat at noon, making dates she never kept, and playing whole rounds of bridge all by herself.

Rhea's friends found her humorous at first, entertaining even; they laughed at her childish antics behind her back. But soon they became embarrassed by her behavior, and stopped including her in gatherings, ignored her in town, shunned her as if her ailment was contagious, or for fear of being labeled guilty by association. Fortunately Rhea was blissfully unaware of their betrayals.

I visited Rhea every Thursday afternoon; brought her a home baked treat, letting myself in and brewing a pot of tea. I would sit my old friend down at the iron table on the front porch and will her to carry on a conversation. Sometimes she would oblige me, and we would reminisce about the old days; when Caleb and Mike and Arthur would take the kids out fishing or crabbing, and she and Virginia and I would sit on the beach and read or have a shopping excursion on the mainland. We talked about our famous Labor Day clam bakes on the beach, fresh lobsters and clams cooking over a smoking sand pit.

The past year our Thursday afternoons had grown especially quiet. Rhea seemed to have slipped away for good. But I still went, and poured the tea and sat beside my friend as we stared silently out at our own sea of ghosts.

Her family kept watch of course, they had a woman come in, they took her to specialists, and eventually decided she shouldn't be on her own. I suggested a full time nurse, knowing she wouldn't want to leave her home, leave the island. They wouldn't listen, and who was I to fight them? When they came in August to take her up to the city, my heart catalogued yet another loss. I didn't come and say good-bye because I was afraid I might see a glimmer of awareness in her eyes.

As I neared her house I saw the garage doors open, heard rumblings inside. I walked up and called in, "Hello?"

Rhea's granddaughter Jennifer appeared, carrying a cardboard crate crammed with old tennis rackets, and ice skates. She called back to someone, "No, I've got it."

I looked at her, fearing bad news. "Hello Jennifer. Has something happened to Rhea?"

Jennifer smiled. "Oh hi Mrs. Hankins! No. Grandma is about the same. Mom just thought we should clean the place out a bit. Sooner or later, it's got to be done you know. So Billy and I came down for the day. We hoped to get in a swim but I heard they closed the beaches, water's too rough."

I stepped farther into the garage out of the sun. I nodded absently at Jennifer. "Yes. They are very careful now. Quick to close, better safe than sorry."

My eyes adjusted to the darkness. A life story lined the walls of the Hasting's garage; rusty bicycles, stacks of beach chairs and striped umbrellas, a rotary lawnmower, a well used stroller. In the corner under a sunny window stood Rhea's potting bench, assorted clay pots on the shelf under it, a pair of flowered gloves, a rusty spade and a collection of tin watering cans. I looked up. From the rafters hung a battered green canoe, surf boards and boogie boards, wooden oars and life jackets.

I fought back the sadness that nearly overwhelmed me. Jennifer was still talking, something about a garage sale in the spring. Her boyfriend Billy, came out of the house carrying a box filled with yellowed newspapers and magazines.

He groaned, "Jeez. Didn't your grandma ever hear of recycling?" Jennifer laughed and helped him with the box.

I stood in front of the potting bench and looked out the window at the beautiful hydrangeas. I picked up the clippers and put on Rhea's gloves. "You don't mind if I take these, do you dear?" Jennifer didn't respond, but I wasn't speaking to her anyway. I went out the side door into the yard.

I cut a bunch of her favorites, the deepest blues, and carried them back in, tied the stems neatly together with string, and placed them in the basket of Rhea's red bicycle.

I gripped the bicycle handles and rolled it out of the garage into the sunlight, passing Jennifer and Billy who stood gawking, not sure quite what to make of me. Billy was holding Rhea's cane in his hand and I motioned for him to give it to me. I hung it over the handlebars, lifted one leg gingerly over the frame, plopped my rear down on the seat, and started pedaling.

I yelled over my shoulder at the startled kids, "Some things should never be sold at yard sales!"

And I rode down the street laughing and crying and wobbling like a loose wagon wheel all the way home.

CHAPTER FOUR

I made my first and last yard sale purchase when I was fourteen years old; Mrs. Jameson's potted red geranium. Mrs. Jameson was dead. I hadn't really known her but I knew her house well.

Clare Jordan and I used the freedom of our teen years exploring the southern end of Eastwind Island. Ocean Avenue ran the length of Sandy Point then turned into Bay Avenue at the bottom of the bridge. Bay Avenue was a loop; South Bay took you to the end of the island on the bay side and North Bay led back out to the bridge along the ocean side. A narrow parcel of land, thick with trees and brush separated the two roads, and sandy, pebbled paths marked where islanders had crossed back and forth from the bay to the sea.

Clare and I circled that route on our bikes every afternoon, stopping for an ice cream cone at the Lighthouse Snack Bar. Sometimes we rode over the bridge and followed Main Street into town to window shop in the intriguing little stores, or cruised the quiet side streets picking out favorite houses.

Mrs. Jameson's house was on South Bay Ave, half way between the bridge and the Lighthouse. It was one of my favorites; facing the sea and backed up to Fishawk Bay. It reminded me of my bungalow; weathered gray shingles and white trim. It was a friendly looking house with cheerful red geraniums in clay pots perched on each gray step leading from the porch to the walk. Her house had a widow's walk on the roof. I imagined myself up there, wistfully searching the horizon for a sea-faring lover, my skirt billowing in the brisk offshore breeze, just like in the paintings.

The back yard was fenced in by tall green hedges with an opening framed by a white arbor seething with dark red roses. It was a brilliant oasis of color in a desert of driftwood and sandy yards.

Mrs. Jameson was usually on her knees weeding, or up on tippy toes watering, but she always stopped working to wave as we glided past. She was a tiny woman with childlike eyes and an impish smile that radiated out from under her enormous straw hat.

I always smiled and waved back and I often thought of stopping, but there was always somewhere to go, something else to do. So when I found myself standing on her porch step holding the geranium I felt miserable that I had never done it because now it was too late. Too late to be greeted by that kind smile, welcomed into her home and given a tour of her prized gardens. There were only strangers milling around the house and yard carelessly touching her things, bickering about how much the wicker furniture was worth, a fair price for the linen tablecloths. I felt the least I could do was save the geranium from the Memorial Day yard sale vultures.

I didn't want to ask the man in charge how much it cost, so I left fifty cents on the table and took it to the car to wait for my mother. She loved yard sales. She hustled me out early every Saturday morning with the choice ones circled in the newspaper.

Mom came out carrying her prize for the day; a blue striped mixing bowl. She placed it on the front seat and eyed the geranium.

"Well, isn't that a nice plant, honey," she said with a curious smile.

"How did she die Mom?" I asked staring straight ahead.

"Who?" she responded, startled.

"Mrs. Jameson," I said, asking myself her next dumb question. I didn't really know how I knew her name, I just knew it.

But she didn't ask. She started the car and put it in gear slowly, trying to figure out my sudden interest in this situation.

She started talking as she drove, "Well, I don't know really, but I overheard some women talking about a Nursing Home and how stubborn and unhappy she was about going."

I wished I hadn't asked.

She didn't read my silent cues, couldn't sense that I didn't want to hear anymore about it. Worse, she started a lecture about people with all the money in the world and nothing to show for it.

I interrupted her. "How do you know she had a lot of money?"

She looked at me. "Why, Sara, anyone who lives in Eastwind is rich, very rich." She was trying to be kind but she might as well have said I was a moron for not figuring that out already. "Just look at these homes, they're all beautiful, and enormous, and most of them are summer homes! Can you imagine what their winter homes must be like?"

"Well, Mrs. Jameson lived here all year." I said, and turned away stubbornly. I didn't know how I knew that either but I was sure it was true and it seemed important to establish that fact, in Mrs. Jameson's defense. And then as an afterthought I added, "And she had a wonderful family that loved her very much." But I garbled the last words because I was pretty sure it wasn't true and if I went on I would start crying.

Then my mother stopped the car and reached over to touch my arm. "I'm sorry, Sara. Did you know her, this Mrs. Johnson?"

And I stared out the window miserably as my confusion and sorrow turned quickly into anger at my mother the way any emotion tends to when you are fourteen and unsure of what is going on and then I turned and snapped at her, "No, but I wish I had. Now can we please go home?"

I stopped going to sales with my mother after that. I told her they were too depressing, and that was the end of that.

Clare and I didn't ride our bikes past Mrs. Jamesons' for the rest of the summer either. We were too busy working on our tans, our weight, our make up, hair color, clothes; the whole package. We spent hours studying fashion magazines, shopping, experimenting, worrying, eating and dieting, and boys became the focus of our daily existence.

Jimmy and Chuck were life guards at the Water Street beach. We made our camp on the inlet beach but we strolled every inch of Markisons every single day, rain or shine, no longer in pursuit of a pail full of clam shells, but collecting stares, greetings, and glances from any and all available males.

The warm days of June and July passed quickly as always. The first of August dawned hot, muggy and humid and carried with it the usual impending gloom of the approach of summer's end. But my fourteenth August proved to be nothing like any before it.

I took my morning walk to the boardwalk; surveyed the surf, bought the newspaper and continued out to the Inlet. I sat on the bench and watched the fishermen cast their lines from the jetty, waved to passengers on the charter boats sailing in and out of the channel. The scenic dunes west of the boardwalk had been flattened the year before. The tall grass and wild flowers, scrub oaks and bayberry bushes existed only in my memory. In their place stood a three story hotel, with a paved parking lot and a fenced in pool. The egrets, pelicans, rabbits and raccoons were gone too, forced to find homes elsewhere.

The gulls still came, squawking and pestering the fishermen, stealing fish from their buckets and their nets. The gulls would never go quietly. They made their displeasure known to the hotel owners by leaving droppings all over the building, cars, railings and decks, and no number of plastic owls would scare them away.

I stood at the rail and imagined I was a child on my father's shoulders, looking out over the island wishing it would never change. Sandy Point was clearly destined for change, had already been altered, but I was naive enough to refuse to acknowledge it for what it really was, and to believe that nothing would ever change my wish to live there forever.

I walked down the boardwalk to visit Dave. The older I got the more people like Dave seemed to stay the same. He was setting up his stand and talking to a man I recognized too late as Arnold Markison, or I wouldn't have gone over. They were in the middle of an animated discussion, but they straightened up when Dave saw me. I had never been formally introduced to Mr. Markison.

He reached out his hand, smiled warmly and said, "Oh, yes. I've heard about 'little Sara'. We're looking forward to having another Boyle on the payroll soon. Give my best to your parents, tell them there was no real harm done, it's forgiven already." With that he saluted Dave and strode away.

Dave was trying not to laugh. "Sara, I gotta tell you. This one will go down in history. That brother of yours…"

"What are you talking about Dave?" I asked.

He stared at me. "You don't? Oh my, I'm sorry." He shrugged. "Well you'll find out soon enough. It seems Jimmy and Chuck were out partying last night and had a little too much to drink. Around midnight they decided to take a joy ride on the beach...in Arnold's tractor!" Dave doubled over laughing. "And that's not the best part. They parked the tractor and went in for a dip, then passed out on the beach, tide came in, and when they woke up the thing was buried up to it's axles!"

I was thinking it wasn't so funny. "What happened then?" I asked.

"Well somebody called the cops and they hauled them both down to the station but Arnold bailed them out. So..." He finally stopped laughing and looked at me. "Now, don't look so concerned. Like the old man said, no real harm done. They had a crew out there early this morning and dug the tractor out, Jimmy and Chuck did most of the work, though they were sick as dogs. They're paying, believe me, up on that stand already sweating it out." He raised his face to the sky, wiped his brow with his handkerchief, "Yep, it's gonna be a hot one today."

I mumbled a goodbye and left. I was sure my parents didn't know yet, I hadn't heard any screaming earlier. There had been a lot of that directed at Jimmy lately. He was sixteen, learning to drive, learning to do all sorts of things my parents didn't approve of.

I closed the screen door quietly. Nana was sitting in her rocking chair at the top of the stairs in the sunroom. Her eyes were closed, hands folded in her lap. She was so still I thought she might be dead. Then I noticed the slight shift of the beads, the whisper of movement on her lips. This would be an extra rosary for Jimmy. They must know. I tiptoed over and leaned down, breathed in the clean scent of her soft wrinkled skin.

She opened her eyes and smiled at me. Mary Molloy was going on eighty-five but still woke each morning at sun-up, bathed and dressed and said her rosary. Then she cleaned and baked 'til noon when 'The Guiding Light' came on and watched it with lunch and a hot cup of tea. We had brought down a TV that year, mostly for Nana. Sandy Point wasn't the same for her since Preston Folger had passed away and Catherine gave up their bungalow.

Things had changed a lot for Nana; Catherine and Preston were gone and she only had Jimmy and me to look after. I thought it was a good thing that she didn't have that much to do, she deserved the rest. But sometimes I wondered, watching her sit in silence, if a rest was what she really wanted.

I could spend an entire afternoon away, each second filled with excitement, and when I returned there she sat, just as I had left her and I couldn't imagine how she had passed the same seconds doing nothing at all. I felt guilty often, and was tempted to hang around, but she was wise to that and shooed me off.

I knew she missed the others too. Joann married a Navy boy stationed down south and was expecting her first child at Christmas. Eileen was a History teacher up in the city and taking summer courses for her Master's Degree. Bobby had never really come home from California. He loved it out there. He was in Graduate School at UCLA, working as a teaching assistant, progressing toward his goal of full professor of Marine Biology. They came home to visit whenever they could, but it wasn't the same.

Nana said, "I guess you heard about that brother of yours. I can't understand what's gotten into him. He'll send your mother to an early grave."

"Where is Mom? Did I miss the fireworks?" I asked.

"She went into town. Your father will be down tonight, they'll deal with it then," she said wearily.

The telephone rang, and we both jumped. The phone was another concession to convenience that year. We laughed at each other. It still sounded foreign. It was Clare, inviting me to go to the pool. The Jordans still bought Beach/Pool Badges though we'd only gone once that summer.

I said, "Nah, I don't feel like it. I think I'll hang home for awhile."

Nana zeroed in on that. "Sara! You certainly will go up to that pool. I'll pack you a lunch. Better yet, I'll treat you and Clare, you tell her so right now."

I couldn't refuse. I squeezed her hand as she slipped me the money, hugged her and said "Thanks, love ya!", then went to get ready.

I had the big room downstairs to myself now. I went in and put on my navy blue speedo suit, white shorts and my favorite UCLA t-shirt. I admired myself in the mirror.

My tan was dark and even, my hair was streaked from the sun, and I liked the way the freckles across my nose deepened my hazel eyes. I tried not to be too critical of myself, Clare did enough of that for both of us. She was never happy with the way she looked. Clare's clothes cost twice as much as mine, and personality wise she was twice as outgoing, never afraid to say whatever came into her head.

I grabbed a beach towel and my knapsack, yelled good-bye up the stairs and cut through the rows to Clare's. She was waiting for me on her porch steps, and I joined her as we giggled and listened to Chuck getting bawled out inside. We were about to leave when a commotion started at the bottom of the row.

A gang of kids were carting suitcases and cartons into one of the bungalows on Lenape Lane. Clare said two families were sharing a house for the month of August. Her parents hadn't known that when they rented to them but they weren't going to bother stopping them now.

We noticed two girls in particular. They were about sixteen, skinny and gorgeous, and we hated them instantly. Sherry, had shoulder length brown hair styled in a perfect bob with deep brown eyes to match.

Her buddy was Brenda, with straight blonde hair swaying majestically down to her waist, and sparkling blue eyes, and a thick silver ID bracelet snapped around her impossibly thin wrist, signifying she had the most envied possession a girl could claim; a steady boyfriend.

We made note of every detail until Mrs. Jordan came out and scolded us for being snobby and told us to go and welcome the new kids. We said we would, waited until she went back inside and took off for the pool.

We swam, ate lunch at the Luncheonette and played songs on the juke box, then went back to the pool. We decided to ignore the new girls, they wouldn't be any real competition, and they'd only be around for four weeks anyway.

Jimmy and Chuck wandered into the pool on their afternoon break.

Clare started right in on Chuck, "Nice going idiot!"

He responded by nearly drowning her. Jimmy was too sick to speak. I said, "Great move Jim."

Chuck floated past us. "Oh come on. It's not so bad. By tomorrow all will be forgotten."

Jimmy moaned, "Yeah, maybe. You know it wouldn't have been so bad if that damn thing hadn't gotten stuck...I'll tell you, when Arnold walked into that jail I thought I was gonna pee in my pants I was so scared!"

"Come on Jim, let's show the girls our high dive routine," Chuck said, leaping out of the pool.

Jimmy tried but he missed and fell back, folded his arms on the side to cradle his head and moaned some more. "Sara, I don't know how he does it. I swear I'm never gonna drink again..."

Chuck performed a series of daring dives delighting the crowd. We sat on the side of the pool and watched him work his audience.

Jimmy said, "Hey, I hear there's some new babes down at the inlet. Have you met them yet?"

"What do you mean?" I asked slowly, nudging Clare in the ribs knowing exactly who he meant.

"Oh. The guys down at inlet reported some new girls in town, said they were staying on Lenape. Well, I better get Johnny Weismuler over there and get back to work."

Jimmy tore Chuck away from the admiring crowd. Clare and I spent the rest of the day practicing for the annual Markison Water Show, held every August. Half of the show was races, and we decided to enter the 50 yard freestyle. The second half of the show the Lifeguards performed diving stunts, swim and rescue exhibitions, and clown acts.

That evening there was a great football game. Chuck and Jimmy both played since they were grounded. The score was tied and Jimmy's team had the ball when Sherry and Brenda came and sat down on the edge of the boardwalk next to Clare and me.

Brenda said, "Hi! You're Jimmy's sister aren't you?"

I couldn't think of anything witty to say so I answered, as blankly as I could, "Yeah, that's right."

"Well I'm Brenda and this is my friend, Sherry. We just moved down today. We love it already though. What did you say your name was?".

Clare piped in rudely, "I don't believe she said her name."

Brenda ignored her and asked me again. I just looked at her. I was used to older girls using me to get to my brothers but this was different. These girls were competition for us.

I begrudgingly answered. "I'm Sara, and that's Clare."

Clare was busy cheering for Chuck, Jimmy, whoever had the ball. She didn't have a good understanding of the game.

Brenda said, "Well, really, we are soooo glad to be here. It's been soooo hot up home, not to mention sooo boring. We couldn't wait to get out of there. You guys are soooo lucky, being here all summer. Of course, I miss Bruce," she fingered her bracelet. "He's my boyfriend. Watching these guys makes me a little homesick, he's quarterback on the school team."

As she spoke it occurred to me that I could learn a few tricks from Brenda. I studied her golden locks pulled back in a perfect ponytail, tied just so with a plaid ribbon that matched her shorts, silver hoop earrings dangling from dainty ear lobes, smooth unblemished skin, just the right touch of make-up.

Sherry leaned forward and said, "Brenda, why don't you shut up for one second and let somebody else talk?" Clearly Sherry was the brains of the duo.

Sherry asked, "So, Sara, how old is Jimmy?"

I smiled. "Jimmy? He's sixteen, but I wouldn't waste too much time on him, he's got a steady girl up home. You know, like you and Brucie, Brenda." I watched that information sink in. It wasn't true but it made me feel in control, they were both all ears now.

Sherry smirked. "Really? You wouldn't know it the way he acts around here. I feel sorry for his steady." She was smooth. She went on, "How about you Clare. What's the scoop on that hunk of a brother of yours?"

Clare appeared oblivious to the conversation, swinging her brown legs over the edge of the boardwalk. She was listening to every word, she just pretended not to, then dove in with a killer wisecrack. It annoyed me, because I spent so much time worrying if what I said or did looked stupid, I couldn't imagine trying to act like a jerk.

Clare let the question hang for a minute then leaned over and gazed blankly at us. Finally she blurted out, "My Chuck? Why would anybody want to know anything about him? Basically......how shall I put this......OK, I know, yeah, he's a pig! He sooooooo lives to eat, sleep and drink and that's it. Oh and his major goal in life is being sooooo gross every second of the day.!"

There was a moment of silence, then we burst out laughing. And so began our mutually beneficial friendship. We taught Brenda and Sherry the basic elements of survival at Sandy Point, what to wear, what to bring and where to sit on the beach. They taught us how to smoke cigarettes, french braid our hair and french kiss a boy. We suddenly found our evenings occupied with more stimulating entertainment than steal the flag and monkey in the middle on the beach.

Brenda and Sherry didn't need us to attract Jimmy and Chuck's attention. That phenomenon started rolling the first night and Clare and I didn't mind because we heard about each tender kiss, every passionate embrace, every hurt and sweet reconciliation. Our brothers, not to mention our parents would have been appalled if they knew how intimately Brenda and Sherry shared the details of soft whispers, forbidden touches, and moonlit strolls on the beach.

We sat together on the beach every day. Our equipment was standard; a jumbo bottle of baby oil, lip stuff, assorted combs, brushes and hair clips, a radio, magazines, occasionally a book or a box of stationery. My instincts paid off when our camp became a popular hang out for all the Markison guards.

I had my eye on a rookie guard named Stewart. He had short black hair, long black eyelashes, and dreamy blue eyes. The day he came over and sat down across from me I thought I would die. Up close he was even cuter. The conversation was football that day, and Stewart's favorite team was the same one my family was crazy about so I totally impressed him. He loved to talk and I could listen forever gazing into those eyes dancing in the sunlight off the sea.

By the time he left I was completely infatuated. He stood up and I amazed myself by calling to him, "Hey Stewart! If you're such a football fan how come you never come and play in the game?"

He answered walking backwards down the beach. "I work at nights at The Lobster House. But maybe tonight, if we can get off. Sounds like fun!" He winked at me, turned to catch up with the other guards.

Clare, Brenda and Sherry started right in on me. "Well, what was that conversation all about?" and "Man, did you get a load of those eyes?" and "OOOH Stewie, why don't you come play with me on the beach tonight!?"

I couldn't stop smiling. I felt warm all over and I couldn't sit still. I ran for the water, shouted, "I think I'm in love!" They chased me laughing and screaming until we dove as one into a cold, clear, cresting wave.

The afternoon was endless. I couldn't eat dinner. It took me an hour to decide what to wear. I went to Clare's to meet Brenda and Sherry for an emergency make-up session. When we finally we took our usual place on the edge of the boardwalk I was visibly shaking, but the game took my mind off Stewart. The guards had challenged the hamburger stand guys and it was an exciting match. In the last play of the game, tied score, Jimmy threw a hail mary to Chuck and we all held our breath as the ball spiraled across the darkening sky. Chuck caught it and dove into the sandy endzone with exaggerated celebration.

Stewart didn't show. Clare and I walked to the pavilion for ice cream. Brenda and Jimmy, Sherry and Chuck headed off to a beach party that we were still too young for. We played our favorite songs on the juke box to drown out my sorrow, and talked about boys and boyfriends doubting they were worth the trouble, but convinced they must be.

The next day on the beach, no Stewart, another game that evening, still no Stewart. Clare and I decided to skip the game and head to the big pavilion. Half way up Clare stopped talking in mid-sentence and jumped smack in front of two kids careening down the boardwalk on bikes.

It was Stewart. "Hey! Sara!" he shouted. "Where are you going? Isn't there a game tonight?"

"I mumbled, "Yeah...oh yeah, ah...yeah, they started awhile ago. You better hurry, maybe you can get in on the second half..."

"Why aren't you watching?" His foot was poised over the pedal, his gorgeous eyes were staring at me waiting for the answer I wracked my brain to come up with. I left because he didn't show up, but I couldn't tell him that, and if he was going I'd love to turn around and go back but I couldn't say that either. I looked over at Clare for help but she was busy flirting with Stewart's friend.

"We're just going up to the arcade for awhile...," I hated how immature it sounded.

Stewart didn't seem the least bit disappointed. He called over to his friend, "Hey, Steve! Let's go." He called back to me, "Catch you later, Sara!"

Clare couldn't stop talking about Steve. "Wow is he adorable or what? And his dad owns the Lobster House, they must have big bucks. He says he can get us jobs there next summer if we want. Sara? What's wrong with you?"

"What's wrong is I blew my chance with Stewart. I can't go watch the game now and who knows when he'll show up again."

Clare smiled. "Cheer up girl. You might have another chance sooner than you think. It just so happens I told Steve we'd be at the arcade later and he said they were probably going to hang out after the game so I told him we would meet them there."

"Really? And he said they would meet us?"

"Well, not exactly, he was in such a hurry with Stewart rushing him off but I'm sure he heard me say it and he smiled and nodded."

I rolled my eyes. A typical Clare interpretation, but it was better than nothing. I put my arm around her and we continued up the boardwalk. We made ourselves sick on the tilt-a-whirl, lost some money on the wheels, pigged out on french fries, then snagged a prime bench across from the arcade so we could spot them, just in case.

By 8:30 I was losing hope. Clare was perched on the railing in front of me and we had our signals all arranged. Clare whispered, "Two guys approaching, wrong guys but not too bad, kind of cute."

61

They were locals. We had just started talking to them when Clare gave me the signal. I looked and sure enough, Steve and Stewart were walking up the boardwalk toward the arcade, each holding their bikes with one arm and a girl with the other one. The guys we were talking to turned and looked too.

The shorter one said, "You know them?"

Clare said, "Not really. We know Stewart from the beach. He guards with my brother. Why? You know them?"

The tall one piped in, "Sure, we know them. Everybody knows everybody on Eastwind. Those two are total jocks. Stewart is practically married to Judy and Steve is usually joined at the hip to Helen, the hot number hanging all over him."

My face burned with embarrassment. I wanted to shrink out of sight, but I couldn't take my eyes off the couples, the easy way Stewart's arm draped around her shoulder, the way she gazed up at those mesmerizing blue eyes and laughed. I finally turned away.

I said, "So if they're jocks, what are you two?"

"We're brains," the short one replied dryly.

The other one snorted. "Ha! That's a laugh. We are your normal, average, extremely cool guys. We defy classification."

Clare jumped off the railing and grabbed my arm. "I'll bet that's not what your psychologist says! Come on Sara, we're late!" We ran down the boardwalk.

The next morning on the beach we told Brenda and Sherry. Sherry was against going after either one of them. "Believe me, you don't need that garbage. There's plenty of fish in the sea my dears, plenty."

Brenda, lathering on the baby oil commented, "Besides, Sara. You should have seen him play, he was pathetic!"

Clare said, "I guess they're right, Sara. Anyway summer's almost over. It's time to start thinking about my options up home. Let's see, there's Andy and Kevin, and Nick…"

I didn't want to think about home. I buried my face in my towel. "Don't remind me summer's almost over. And I don't want anybody up home. I want somebody here," I moaned.

Brenda jumped up. "Well that's enough whining. Get this. Jimmy and Chuck entered us in some stupid swimming race in that dumb water show tomorrow night. You guys have to help us get ready."

That sounded like a disaster. Brenda and Sherry were not good swimmers. Brenda could fake a stroke but Sherry was a hazard to herself and anybody within an arm's reach of her in the water. She almost drowned me twice, and the guards went in for her so often we had to beg her to stay out when the ocean was even slightly choppy.

Clare and I tried to teach them how to handle the waves, we told them about the point of no return and when to dive or run, which ones to ride in.

Clare and I loved rough water, the rougher the better. Brenda and Sherry watched us maneuver the huge swells when a straight southeast wind whipped up powerful waves. It was all in the timing. We'd wait on shore, then dive in during a lull and swim out like mad past the crashing breakers. Then we'd drift, floating over the rising surges, and peer down from the dizzying height to watch the wave crest and break and send its foam careening up the shore as people scurried to safety.

The trick was getting out gracefully and you had to be prepared to wait a long time and tread a lot of water. Then you had to fight the panic when you made up your mind to go, never look back, and run like hell as soon as you got your feet under you.

We never let Brenda and Sherry go in on days like that. It was fun to watch the day people get clobbered by the churning sea, but not your friends. I couldn't imagine either of them swimming in a race, but they were determined to do it. We went to the pool and practiced all day. By the afternoon of race day they were as ready as they could be.

We packed our suits and a change of clothes and headed up to the pool after dinner. Our curfew was extended to 10:00 for the occasion which meant we would be able to go to our first beach party after the show under the watchful eyes of Jimmy and Chuck.

Clare and I were in the same heat of the 50 yard freestyle and we took the lead side by side in the first lap, then in the last ten yards another swimmer surged ahead and stole first place.

At the finish line Stewart reached down to help me out of the pool. "Great going, Sara!" He gave me a big hug.

Brenda and Sherry's race started out OK. Brenda held fourth place the whole time, but Sherry lost her sense of direction and set off on a crooked course, splashing aimlessly around the pool never touching either side where the guards were jockeying positions to help her out.

She raced around in circles at top speed. Half the crowd was laughing and the other half nervously gawking until Chuck grabbed his clown shoes and nose and jumped in with a fire hose to rescue her as if it was part of the act. He whisked her off to the lounge before anyone could see if she was laughing or crying. Chuck was always doing things like that. He was a quick thinker, but he was as quick to get into trouble as he was to end up the hero.

When Sherry came back the show was almost over. The lifeguards were sneaking among the crowd grabbing girls and tossing them in the pool. Jimmy grabbed Brenda and me and we went in screaming. Chuck reached for Sherry, thought better of it and grabbed Clare instead. He lifted her high over his head and twirled her around, as she shrieked hysterically until he dumped her with a mighty splash.

We changed in the lounge and told the guys we'd meet them on the beach at the party. We took our time, reliving the events of the evening, for though they had happened only minutes before, they were destined to become precious memories. The best memories happen when you aren't looking for them, and they pass quickly, even when we are keenly aware of their bearing as they unfold they can't be cajoled into lingering, they slip away like welcome wisps of cotton clouds in sweltering sunny skies.

When we stepped onto the beach a bonfire was blazing, the keg was tapped and pumping, and a steady beat of rock and roll flowed from speakers in the pavilion. The night was cool, with the unmistakable hint of approaching fall.

I felt a pang of unease with the crowded scene of kids until we spotted Jimmy and Chuck sitting in the lifeboat with a group of guards and they waved us over. Jimmy handed me a beer and said, "Take it easy on this stuff, Sara, and don't be a jerk."

I was surprised to enjoy the foamy flavor. Clare took a swig and hissed, "Yuck! How do they drink this stuff?"

Chuck and Sherry mingled for awhile then dragged a blanket off to the side and started making out. Brenda and Jimmy got involved in a rowdy game of thumper on the now over-turned life boat. Clare and I strayed over to the keg and refilled our cups.

"Hey Sara!" A voice called. "Nice job in that race!" Stewart refilled his cup and gestured for mine. I was aware for a fleeting second, that I was about to have too much, but the notion evaporated as Stewart gave me back my cup and our hands touched, our eyes locked.

I felt giddy, shaky, strangely sure of myself. "Thanks Stewart. Great show, huh? I didn't expect to go in twice though!"

He laughed, and his eyes sparlked in the moonlight.

Steve walked over. "Say Clare, that was some dive you did…You practice that routine every day?"

"Very funny Steve," Clare cooed back, playfully grabbing his arm.

I knew some other Sara had taken over my body when I blurted out, "So, where's your girlfriends tonight guys?"

And the response…It was great. Everything I said was funny and clever. Stewart assured us they didn't have girlfriends. They just hung out with lots of girls from school. Sure, it made perfect sense.

Everything was logical, and wonderful. Like the way Stewart gazed at me with those unbelievable eyes as he led me over to the life guard stand and put his arms around my waist, helped me climb up, the way we sat so close, how snug his arm felt as it slipped around my shoulder, pulling me close enough to smell his sweet clean scent, feel his strong body, his heart pounding. Or was that my heart racing fast enough for two?

The moon cleared a path from the horizon to the beach, shimmering across the black water and straight into those magical eyes, and they were piercing another path right into my heart. Stars were twinkling, and I couldn't believe how witty I was. I had so much to say, and he was so attentive. When our cups were empty again, he jumped down to refill them.

I looked around for Clare. She was lying flat on the sand behind the garbage can making out with Steve and I thought that was the funniest thing I ever saw. Stewart came back and before I could get the cup up to my lips, his were there, touching mine, his eyes closed gently, his arms around me, his body so close. I was afraid to breathe and let this incredible feeling disappear. I was hypnotized, in a trance, floating in a warm, dark sea of lips and tongues and caresses.

The spell broke suddenly as an angry voice cried out. "Sara! Is that you up there?! What the..." Jimmy's face popped up in front of me like a jack-in-the-box. He towered over us on the stand, yanked Stewart up by the collar of his shirt and hurled him down onto the sand, booming at me, "Sara! I can't believe you! Do you know what time it is???"

I didn't answer because I couldn't stop laughing. I stood up and tried to jump down but barely managed a belly flop on the sand. Jimmy leaped down after me and growled at Stewart who was scrambling away sideways like a comical cartoon crab, desperately trying to return to the sea. I laughed so hard I started choking.

Then Jimmy looked at me and the rage in his eyes sobered me up momentarily. He shouted, "We'll see how funny this is when Dad shows up looking for you. What the hell were you doing up there?"

I thought that was kind of obvious which got me laughing again, and he stalked over, picked me up and threw me over his shoulder like a sack of laundry. I blanked out for a second and then the boardwalk was flying underneath me and with each pounding footstep Jimmy took, my head spun, and bounced, up and down, and upside down and nothing was funny anymore.

The last thing I saw was the boards spinning wildly, twirling, taking flight, and my stomach along with them, and I heard Brenda say, "Jim, I think you better put her down...She doesn't look so good..." And then I was lying in my bed and the sun was shining on my face with such intense heat that I began to think I'd dreamt the whole night; that none of it had really happened and I was still spread out on my towel baking in yesterday's noon sun on the beach. I opened my eyes and searing pain instantly sealed them shut as a rush of thundering vibrations echoed in my brain. A car driving over stones in the driveway, waves breaking on the beach, gulls crying, children laughing, all the elements that usually mingled perfectly to create the hum of a lazy morning jangled and jarred and made my head throb.

65

I thought I was dying. Or already dead. I squinted at the clock on the nightstand; 9:00. I tried to lift my head and it fell back on the pillow. Then I remembered Stewart. Wow. That was nice. I smiled even though it hurt.

Someone knocked on the screen door. I listened. Nana yelled hello from the top of the steps, the door slammed, then footsteps approached my room. Brenda and Sherry appeared beside the bed.

Sherry shouted, "So, how we feelin' this a.m.?" She tousled my hair, I cringed.

I moaned, "Shhhhh. Stop screaming, whisper..."

They laughed. "We are whispering," said Brenda.

They sat down on the extra bed and filled me in on the last act of the drama of which I was apparently the star, how I barfed all over the boardwalk just after Brenda made Jimmy put me down, and how they cleaned me up and managed to sneak me into bed.

They said Jimmy was already laughing about it and we were lucky our parents had gone out for ice cream with the Jordans after bridge, so they didn't know anything about it.

They didn't know what happened to Stewart, he just disappeared, and he didn't show up for work either. "And Clare!" Sherry said. "We thought you and Stewart were bad but you should have seen Chuck when he found her and Steve. They were doing a bit more than you and Stewie, believe me. Thank God I got to them before Chuck did or he would have killed that kid for sure. Steve must be a track star 'cause I swear I've never seen anybody run so fast in my life!" She and Brenda rolled around on the bed hugging their stomachs and laughing.

I asked, "Did Clare get sick too?"

"We're going over there now, but Chuck said she was still passed out when he left for work."

I rolled over and peeked out at them. Sherry was fixing her bathing suit strap in front of the mirror. Brenda was brushing her hair, sighing. "Well, come on Sherry. Let's hit the beach. Sara won't be coming today, and we can't afford to miss a second." She put down the brush, picked up a tube of strawberry lip gloss and expertly applied it. "You know, we've only got ten days left..."

Sherry sat on the edge of my bed. "Go back to sleep Sara, you'll feel better this afternoon."

They left and I lay there and cried. I didn't know why I was crying and that made me cry more. Sherry and Brenda were leaving soon, I was leaving soon, summer was almost over, and I was wasting a gorgeous day laying in bed.

I fell back asleep until 10:30. I tiptoed upstairs. Nana was dozing in her rocker, her white head nodding back and forth with the motion of the chair. I lay down on the couch and fell asleep again.

A jumble of voices caught my attention. Nana and my mother were in the dining room discussing the night before; Nana persuasively insisting, "I heard the door at ten on the button Mary. I'm sure it's a touch of a bug, that's all."

My mother just as insistent, "I don't know. Evelyn and I will compare notes on this one."

Nana said, "Now Mary. Jimmy was there. I'm sure he was keeping an eye on her…" Then she changed the subject, "Now…about dinner? Why don't I try that new chicken recipe you found?"

My mother, distracted, "What? Oh, yes, alright…"

Nana again, "Look, here comes Evelyn. You run along. Sara and I will be fine."

I was wide awake but pretended to be asleep when my mother went past. She reached down and gently felt my forehead, brushed her fingers across my cheek, hovered a minute, waiting. Then she left.

Nana brought in two cups of tea and turned on the TV. I sat up gingerly, relieved to find Sherry had been right, I was feeling better every minute.

I spent the afternoon curled up on the couch watching soaps on TV and gossiping with Nana about Jimmy and Brenda, Chuck and Sherry, Clare and me and our imagined 'loves'. She didn't ask anymore than I volunteered about the night before, and if she was keen to the source of my 'bug' she never let on.

I recovered as expected, and spent the next few weeks trying not to think about the end of summer. Sherry and Brenda spent every second with Jimmy and Chuck so Clare and I were stuck with each other.

We didn't see Stewart or Steve for the rest of the summer, but they consumed our time as if they'd been present and demanding it. We dissected every detail of that night. Clare was convinced that she and Steve were in love, even days later when he did not appear to claim her. He was simply scared for his life, which only enhanced the drama of her fantasy romance.

I wasn't sure how I felt about Stewart. I was secretly happy he disappeared because I dreaded actually seeing him and figuring out how to act. I was certain I would never drink again, and I considered it extremely unfair that Clare had not even gotten a headache.

I loved Clare as strongly as I hated her for the differences between us. The last few weeks of August she would begin to actually look forward to going home. She pretended to feel as miserable as I did, she moaned and complained; we cried together over summer songs and memories, and though misery loves company, I knew it was an act.

Clare shopped for fall clothes with her mother and I admired them and told her how fabulous she looked, listened attentively as she went on and on about trying out for cheering, football season, all the friends and boyfriends she would return to.

I did my best to conjure up equally attractive boyfriends, and even said I would try out for cheering, sometimes convincing myself that I could become the person she assumed I already was, up home in the winter. In truth I was a bear preparing for the long sleep through dreary winter months. I had friends, I had my share of fun, but the girl who lived that life never seemed totally alive, the real Sara existed only in daydreams during that winter slumber, awakening only when summer dawned on the sunny shores of Sandy Point.

I lingered out at the inlet on those cool mornings of late August, when they sky is a piercing blue and the sea a calm aqua and the winds of fall gently tease. I sat on the bench and imagined what it would be like there on a crisp October morning bundled in a scratchy woolen sweater, to witness a blazing sunrise over a barren windswept beach. Or to brave bitter December winds and watch the fishing boats head out to sea against a gray winter sky as snow flurries mix and dance with smoke from their stacks.

I begged my parents constantly to move down year round, or at least to come for weekends in fall and spring. They tolerated my nagging to a point before losing their patience and exclaiming, "You should be grateful you come here every summer! You don't know how lucky you are!"

I hated that statement because it was true and it made me feel guilty and they never seemed to understand how I felt. But I was wise enough to realize my whining could backfire and eventually make them wonder why they brought me there if it made me so unhappy to leave. And ultimately I did know, and I did appreciate, just how lucky I was.

Still, on Friday of Labor Day weekend, I wasn't feeling lucky. It was my fifteenth birthday. Big deal. Chuck left a few days early for football practice. Sherry and Brenda were leaving on Saturday. My family and the rest of the Jordans were staying until Monday. In every bungalow the ritual had begun and would continue until every family had shut the last shutter, swept the last grain of sand, packed the last trunk, stacked the last beach chair, and said their last goodbye.

Friday night Sherry, Brenda and Clare gave me a birthday party on the beach. We sat on the jetty, drank a few beers, laughed, cried and reminisced. Clare gave me a new bikini for next year, Brenda and Sherry gave me a new stationery set. They left the next morning vowing to return next summer if they had to hitch-hike down and live in the jetty caves. By Sunday night I was almost anxious to leave and end the prolonged agony.

I set my alarm for 5:30 Monday morning, dragged my bicycle out of the shed pumped up the tires, and rode down Pilgrim's Path onto Ocean Ave. All the rows were deserted, silent sleepy bungalows reticent in the dark still air.

I passed Markison's Main Pavilion and the merry go round and roller coaster standing in eerie silence, creating shadowy silhouettes against the sunless sky. I continued down Ocean Ave, stopped for a second at the bottom of the bridge, glanced at the darkened Lobster House where a few hopeful gulls searched the parking lot for forgotten morsels; the red wooden lobster, our family landmark, swung back and forth in the faint breeze.

I tasted the salt on my lips, felt my hair plastered with dampness as I rode down South Bay Avenue toward the end of the island. When I looked up I realized I had gone too far. I was nearly at the lighthouse, but I hadn't passed Mrs. Jameson's house yet. I stopped to regain my bearings. Something wasn't right. Her house was gone. The garden, the trees, the whole yard was flattened; an empty lot with a sign poked up in the middle; "EJ Construction".

I couldn't believe it. Two dozen beachfront homes still stood on North Bay, the 'enormous' houses my mother had pointed out to me, but there had been other homes on the bay side, and they were gone. Flattened. The only thing left standing was the Hankins Boatworks.

I walked along the pebbled path that would have been Mrs. Jamesons, crossed the road and followed a sandy trail over a tall dune leading to the beach. The trail wandered through a tunnel of dune grass, reeds stretched across and entwined overhead. I shivered as I passed through the dark, cool enclosure and stood at the mouth staring out at the sea. It was staggering.

I studied the sea every morning in Sandy Point, but this didn't look like the same sea. The beach was shorter, the ocean closer, the waves softly breaking and gracefully spilling up and over the glistening sand. Magnificent dunes covered with grass swayed in the gentle morning breeze, rambled along in front of the homes, sloping and rising in no apparent pattern.

A hint of thin light spilled onto the horizon from the sky over the sea. Terns danced at the water's edge, racing the breaker's gurgling foam. I took off my sneakers and walked down to the water, wondering if my footsteps would break the strange spell.

A receding wave left me an offering; a perfect white clam shell. Looking closer I noticed dozens of them drifting in the wash. I picked one up and turned it around and around in my hand. I instinctively curved my fingers around it, preparing to toss it back into the sea. I looked around to see if anyone was watching and then I stopped.

I realized what was so strange about this beach. It was empty. In Sandy Point by now, fishermen would line the shore, beach combers, joggers, walkers, a stroller or two thumping along the boardwalk. This place was untouched. I peered at the huge houses and they stared back at me, challenging my presence. Their black and lifeless windows sent creepy chills down my back. I felt like I didn't belong there. I dropped the shell and walked back to the tunnel, taking one long look at the beach of Eastwind before I got back on my bike.

Empty lots with the same sign lined South Bay all the way to the Boatworks. I stopped to inspect that property, it appeared unchanged though I had never taken a close look before. A stone driveway led out to a huge weathered white warehouse facing the bay, and a smaller office building next to it, a sign above the door saying, "The Hankins Boatworks; Sales and Service with a Smile". The place was closed up tight, a little sign next to the mailpost on the road read, "Closed for Labor Day".

I rode past the lighthouse and headed back to Sandy Point as the sun rose over the sea. I hoped my dad knew what was going on with those lots. I pulled into Pilgrim's Path with a spray of stones and didn't notice Jimmy sitting on the back steps of the house holding his head in his hands.

I didn't focus on him because I couldn't look away from the flood of brilliant color framing him; rosy pinks and deep red streaks streamed out from the ball of flame rising in the sky, shooting across the horizon, spilling over the sea and onto the boardwalk, and spreading out to me like a red carpet.

A wind chime on the Folger's old porch stirred and I imagined Preston Folger's scratchy voice whispered, "Red sky at morning, sailor's warning...red sky at morning, sailor's warning..."

I put my bike in the shed, walked back around to the steps and then noticed with alarm that Jimmy was crying. I couldn't remember ever seeing Jimmy cry. He looked up with hollow sorrow in his eyes, and I knew something horrible had happened. All the possible tragedies raged through my mind; Nana, JoAnn, Eileen, Bobby? What? Who? Jimmy opened his mouth and only sobs came out.

My parents came out of the screen door at the top of the steps. It was 6:30 in the morning and they were fully dressed. They came down the steps slowly, holding onto the railing as if they might tumble, carefully maneuvering each splintery gray board with their heads down, faces intent.

My dad didn't look at me, he took Jimmy's arm and led him away. I met my mother's eyes and she avoided mine, drew me to her chest, our hearts racing wildly in unison. I was terrified. She whispered in my ear, "Sara, I have some bad news to tell you, and I'm just going to say it quickly. It's Chuck. He's dead, Sara. He was killed in a car accident last night up at home."

I smiled. It had to be a joke. I pushed her away. "Mom! Come on! You're kidding, right? This is a mistake. You'll see..."

She tightened her grip on my arms. "Sara. Stop it. It's true. I know it's hard to believe, we all loved Chuck, and we'll get through this together."

"I'm going to see Clare," I said, trying to break away.

She started to cry then and her voice cracked, "Sara, listen to me. The Jordans are gone. They left in the middle of the night, as soon as they got the call..."

She pulled me to her again and I let her, though I couldn't cry. I kept thinking if I could just get over to Clare's, everything would be all right. This had to be a dream.

She kept talking, "We'll get through this, and we'll help Clare. I know how you feel...Sara...say something."

All I could think to say was, "Can I go to Clare's?" And before she answered I said, "I...I just want to be alone...I know she's not there, I just want to think...I'm Ok...just for a few minutes, please?"

I felt her eyes on me as I walked away slowly and deliberately to hide my somersaulting emotions. When I turned the corner out of sight I ran blindly over the sandy walkways to Lenape Lane, a path I had traveled three times a day, every day of summer, since I was four years old.

Images of Chuck flashed before my eyes as I ran; Chuck racing for a touchdown in a twilight game, Chuck swimming out for a rescue in rough seas, Chuck up on the lifeguard stand, smiling down with the sun in his eyes, Chuck dressed in his clown outfit, lifting Sherry out of the pool, Chuck's powerful arms rowing the lifeboat out against the breakers, but the panorama that spread out and came alive, the one that finally unleashed my tears was Chuck and Jimmy, little boys in rain gear standing on the deck of the "JaneMarie' holding a bluefish between them that was bigger than both of them, their smiles shining as bright as daylight.

I sat on the Jordan's steps and cried until my stomach ached. When I looked up at the sky the sun had burned the colors away, erased the brilliant dye on the earlier canvas and left a deep September blue.

How could everything change so quickly I wondered? Why? It was so unfair...I wanted to go back, ten minutes, yesterday, last week, change it all, fix it. I held my face up to the hot sun and begged God to burn away the last day as he had the red sky of the dawn.

I sat there until my mother came and took me home. As we walked away I glanced hesitantly, hopefully back at the Jordan bungalow, but my prayers had not been answered. Nothing had changed. It remained an empty, dark wooden shell over which a dawn would never break, quite the same again.

CHAPTER FIVE

Friday, September 1
4:00 P.M.
National Weather Service Advisory
RE: Hurricane Iris
 Hurricane Iris is presently following a NNW course at 10 mph with winds sustained at 78mph and is expected to make landfall between the hours of 12:00 A.M. Sunday and 12:00 A.M Monday. A Hurricane watch is posted for all coastal areas, check local updates as the storm progresses.

I dozed in my rocking chair on the porch in the cool late afternoon quiet and only when the knocking faded away did I realize that it wasn't part of a dream. I peeked out at the beach, estimated the hour to be around four. I could tell time by the sun's shadows, and the behavior of the gulls and the humans, who were more predictable than they might guess.

I rocked in my chair every afternoon; in summer heat, spring rain, fall winds, and winter snows, though I wasn't likely to nod off if the thermometer slipped below sixty.

I watched the days fade, the seasons turn. Summer had always been my favorite, but it didn't take long to fall in love with Autumn once it was a continuum. Before Mike fall was the signal of the end of summer at Sandy Point, but with him it became a colorful bridge into the magical cycle of life on the island.

In September only the very young and the very old still come; and only the very old are truly aware of the fleeting nature of the lingering warm days. The gulls come in all seasons, and by four they seem tired too, napping on the warm sand, moving with the sun until all is shade and they fly off. I recognized a few of the birds that graced the shores and I wondered if they recognized me? There was one legged Sam and speckled head Fred, who had been around as long as I had.

Bobby told me once of an experiment that proved gulls were capable of recognizing humans they've become accustomed to. The birds knew them even when they wore elaborate disguises. If the Eastwind gulls knew me, they gave no indication and I was never curious enough to test them, but if the theory was true then if I had the audacity to walk out naked one day the birds wouldn't notice but the people might. On the other hand if I didn't come out at all, the birds might voice their displeasure, while my fellow humans would simply go on their way, unruffled.

I recognized some faces, could put a name to a handful, but the number dwindled each year. Most of my friends were lucky to get to the bathroom independently, a stroll on the beach was hardly an option. There was a time I would not have had a moment's peace on this porch, but now it held nothing but peace and quiet. There was a time I had been too busy, not a second to spare for a chat with some old bird perched on her porch. I realized some time ago that I had become Mrs. Jameson, and wondered if I had learned any important lessons in my life after all, but I never forgot that I had been granted my wish to belong here. I could gaze out at the sea through cool days of fall, bitter winds of winter and misty mornings of spring, and I would never have to leave again.

I leaned over the railing on the side of the porch to see the back door. No sign of a visitor. That's the problem with living alone, solitude becomes a hard habit to break. You want to want company, but you wonder sometimes if you really do.

Perhaps I imagined the knock. I went inside and turned on some lights mumbling about wishes granted and wishes denied. I talked to myself often, I thought it a form of prayer. I took a steak from the refrigerator, fired up the broiler, picked two small red potatoes and put them on to boil with some carrots.

I prayed the usual way too, every night in bed I held Nana's rosary beads, whispered the refrains I learned by her side. For a while after I lost Mary, I gave up praying. I needed someone to blame and He was an easy mark, but that only compounded the emptiness so I forgave Him. The blame shifted but refused to settle in any one spot for long, it lingered over and under and around me and there it hovered, barely acknowledged and mostly ignored.

While dinner cooked I put Rhea's bicycle in the garage. My garage was void of the remnants one would expect to see after eighty years of life. No old sails, strollers or surfboards adorned my rafters; I had gotten rid of them all, stubbornly reasoning that if I couldn't hold onto the living ones I would not be left with the wood and fiberglass remains.

I took Rhea's pruning shears and the hydrangeas into the kitchen, put the flowers in a vase and placed it on the table beside the manila envelope containing Charley's story. I had been saving that. The hours from dinner until bed were often long and I was glad to have something to fill them. I set out my meal, poured myself a glass of wine, sat down at the table, opened the envelope and began to read.

Untitled Manuscript
By
Charles Duncan

The story of Eastwind Island is the story of my life; the history of my soul. I am one with the trees that sway in the wind, the sands that shift with the tides, the fish that breathe in the sea and the birds that rule the sky; caught up in the struggle some call life, some call survival, and some barely even notice until it's over.

Each of us fights every day to stay alive, and though for some the only battles he fights are in his mind, they are as real as those he fights with his fist or his rifle. I have fought many battles in my lifetime; for courage and for dignity, for truth and respect, for money and for love, but now that I am closer to the end than the beginning, when I expected to be able to sit back and watch the young men wage their wars, I see that I cannot, because the outcome of the most important battle is still undecided, and I find myself fighting not for life itself, but for a way of life.

According to Funk and Wagnalls' definition, "the primary cause of a species extinction is the destruction of habitat by urbanization and suburbanization. Habitats become fragmented into "islands", the remaining populations crowd into smaller areas and cause further habitat destruction. Species in these small islands lose contact with other populations of their own kind, thereby reducing their genetic variation and making them less adaptable to environmental change. These small populations are highly vulnerable to extinction; for some species, the fragmented habitats become too small to support a viable population."

Man's struggles are entwined with the forces of nature, sometimes by clever design, occasionally by accident, too often by ignorance. Man is dependent on nature, but is nature dependent on man? That is the question few dare to ask. In the name of progress, man takes and doesn't give back, never seeing what was destroyed until it's too late. Was it always that way? Five centuries ago whaling was a respected occupation, today it is cause for arrest. The difference is those men were acting on a basic instinct; survival. They took what they needed to live.

Today man takes because he wants, and we are slowly destroying our own habitat. We are engaged in a war we can't win, though we celebrate small victories. We build homes around a lake and become disturbed by the excrement of geese who have lived there for eons, so we form a committee and hire specialists to rid us of the problem.

We develop the coast and become disturbed that the shore line is shrinking, so we form a committee and hire specialists to 'replenish' it. We encroach on forests and become disturbed by deer feasting on 'our' shrubs so we form a committee and hire specialists to develop sprays and devices to keep the pests away.

We fish the seas and when there are no more fish we form two committees, a formal one to find out if we have over fished an area, or even polluted the water ourselves, and an informal one that blames the birds for eating too many of 'our' fish. The formal committee studies the problem for months and then years with no conclusions, while the informal one decides quickly and conclusively that the birds are guilty and sets about disposing of them.

Where and how did it all begin? I can go back only so far, and I can take only so much blame.

I can go back to my Great-Great-Great-Great-Great-Grandfather, Joshua Duncan and tell you how it was for him when he happened upon the staggering beauty of Eastwind Island. I can tell you how he was captured by all he found there, just as I am, every day of my lucky life.

Joshua Duncan was sixteen years old when he left his family in the city to search for a simpler life. He appeared on the beach of Eastwind on a windy, cold March morning. Jonathan Hankins was on duty in the watchtower, scanning the horizon with his spy glass, searching for the spout that would make his job worthwhile. Jonathan, also sixteen, was the youngest member of the whaling crew from the village on the mainland across Fishhawk Bay.

Jonathan's eye was trained on the sea but caught a glimpse of the lone figure wandering along the shore. He was not easily distracted but as the stranger neared his curiosity mounted. Greetings were exchanged and before an hour passed Joshua climbed the pole and joined Jonathan in the tower. Just past noon, Joshua spotted a spout of white water streaking straight up into the blue sky. At first he thought he imagined it; he stifled the shout in his throat, but then the mighty creature breached, and there was no mistaking what he saw. A 35 foot, 40 ton sperm whale burst up from the sea and hurled his weight into the air, suspended for seconds before crashing back down and under, leaving only the wake from the splash of his majestic tail to prove he was ever really there.

Jonathan grabbed the glass and sounded the alarm. They climbed down from their perch to ready the boats, met by the men from the village.

The eldest member of the crew was Jonathan's father, Richard Hankins in whose name the whaling license was held. He was the founder of the village, a cluster of small homes of crude wood held together with salt hay and mud. The men and women farmed for essentials they couldn't get from the sea; fruits, vegetables and wheat, and harvested acres of salt hay in meadows along the bay. They raised sheep and spun the wool; dyed and wove it to make their clothes and blankets. The men and boys of the village were avid hunters; the forest of towering pine trees held an abundant supply of rabbits, raccoons, fox, pheasant, quail and deer, and the bay waters teemed with all species of duck; Dusky Mallard, loons and Black Duck. But the bitter days of late fall and winter their skill and endurance were put to the ultimate test determining if they would eat heartily or barely exist for the rest of the year, for that was when the mighty whales passed their shores.

Whalers farther north hunted the beasts with schooners and barks out on the open sea. Their lookouts were built high on the rigging and when a whale was spotted whaleboats were launched from the mother ship. Shore whalers launched their small whaleboats from the beach, limiting their range, but the villages and crews were small enough to be sustained comfortably by one or two whales a season.

They formed a close knit community, no room for waste, no tolerance for laziness or indifference. The people were physically and mentally strong and constantly called upon to prove it. A position on a whale boat was especially grueling and stressful, yet a coveted and hard won privilege. Expert seamanship was important, but the most essential characteristic needed was courage, because courage and determination were what brought those men safely home towing a prize of 40 tons or more, in mere 30 foot boats.

The Eastwind whalers had two boats, each with a crew of six men and young Joshua Duncan stood on the beach with their families, filled with awe, respect and envy as they set out in their vessels and the dangerous battle unfolded.

Richard Hankins commanded the first boat. He steered while the men rowed in rhythm, steadily shortening the distance between them and their prey. As they closed in, the harpooner prepared to strike. The whale lurched as the harpoon pierced its skin, then took off on a run dragging the tiny boat behind it. The men frantically put out line to keep up. One tangle meant a tragic end and an unsuccessful chase.

When the speed slackened the line was pulled in, then quickly recoiled for a second run. The men resumed rowing, neared the whale again, harpooner poised at the bow of the boat. Four times the men played out the drama, until the final spear plunged and drew a fountain of blood.

The creature rolled over and the group on the beach spotted the upright fins that signaled the end and sent up a cheer for the sailors, but it was a short celebration for they had to prepare to take in the whale. All hands immediately set to the task, with Thomas Isaacs in charge. Thomas had been the crew's harpooner until the spring before when he fell overboard and was tangled in a fishing line, dragged along with the boat and fortunate to escape death but rendered too crippled to man a whale boat again. Without much discussion or fanfare Jonathan Hankins took Thomas' seat in the boat and Thomas relieved an elder of his duties on shore.

Joshua turned his attention away from the sea to the scene on the beach and was amazed at the efficient chain of command. Long cutting spades were brought out and lined up on the sand, young girls gathered wood and lit the fires, women filled huge pots and readied them for boiling.

Thomas and a squad of young boys prepared the capstan; an enormous wooden wheel anchored deep in the ground, with spokes that turned like a ship's wheel. It was wound with the other end of the chain the men on the boats had secured to the fluke of the whale. It seemed an impossible task to Joshua, yet the determination on the faces of the young men left no doubt that they would accomplish the feat. As he watched, the bulky wheel passed him and he saw a boy, no older than eight, struggle, and stumble slightly. Joshua did not hesitate or wait to be asked, he grabbed hold of the worn wooden handle and pushed with every fiber of muscle and was overcome with a sense of purpose he had never known before.

The whaleboats rowed alongside their catch, an escort of tired, proud sailors. When they reached the beach they began cutting the blubber off the whale in long strips, then cut them again with mincing knives into smaller slices to be thrown into the boiling pots to melt the precious oil. All afternoon and into the evening they worked side by side, men, women and children.

Following tradition, the Eastwind whalers gathered with their families for prayers of thanks while the pots boiled over the fires. It was then that Joshua Duncan felt a pang of loneliness for the first time since he had left his own home as he stood alone, not belonging to any group. Thomas Isaacs had noticed Joshua first as a stranger,

77

then as a welcome pair of helping hands, and now saw him standing alone. Thomas embraced Joshua and drew him into the circle of his own family.

So begins the history of the Duncan family on Eastwind Island, the day Joshua was captured just like the mighty sperm. He was captured by the people and their ways, by the sea and all its glory, by the layered clouds against the clear blue sky, and the gull's cry harmonizing with the wind in the pines. But unlike the whale he was a willing victim who wasn't really captured at all but was, in truth, set free.

I was so completely immersed in the story that when Fred Allen knocked on the door I jumped out of my chair and the pages scattered across the table and onto the floor. Fred peered in the window. I motioned for him to come in and when the door opened a gust of wind sent the papers flying again.

"Gee Mrs. Hankins, I'm sorry," he said as we gathered them up. When we finished with the papers I sat down and Fred carried my dinner dishes to the sink. I was amused at the sight of him in his crisply pressed blue uniform, shiny black shoes, gun holster and radio hanging from his waist, rolling up his sleeves, washing my dishes. He talked as he worked. "I was beginning to worry about you. I stopped by earlier, but you weren't around. Then I noticed Mrs. Hastings bicycle out back and I thought maybe Jennifer was visiting. I heard she was down cleaning the place out."

He had the table wiped, pot scrubbed, plates and cup rinsed and drying in the rack. He continued, "Then I saw Charley in town and he said he's been trying to call you all afternoon and couldn't get through. He said something about you walking off during lunch?" He gazed at me quizzically, then turned to the window as he dried his hands and slowly rolled down his sleeves. "So I thought I'd come up and see if your line was down. It is getting downright blustery out there…" He faced me then, leaning against the sparkling sink. He said, "And I ran into Jennifer. She said something about you riding that old bike home yourself……?" He was still smiling.

I felt my face redden. If it was anyone else I would be furious at the implications of his comments, but Fred was an old friend. He was Roger and Anna Allen's grandson, a rookie on the Eastwind Police Force. He was two years older than Mary, they used to be thick as thieves when Mary spent her summers with me. Anna and I used to joke about what a nice couple they would make, the way grandmothers do. And why not? Their fathers had been friends, their grandfathers like brothers, it would almost follow, in the circle of small town life. But who could know what would be? Here were Fred and I, and neither of us had laid eyes on the girl for ten years.

But Fred had not forgotten me. He was one of the few young people for whom old ways held some meaning, and old timers were not a nuisance. When he joined the force he made a point of checking in on me, and others too, he made it part of his job. He kept me current on local gossip and details of his recent engagement to a girl from the mainland.

Fred knew me well enough not to think I'd gone batty in the past twenty four hours, but I was briefly thankful he hadn't run into Elizabeth Morgan who might have reported digging me out of a sand dune that morning, or a certain young boy whom I was time traveling with that very afternoon.

And then I thought of another disturbing image of me yanking out my phone cord earlier and leaving it disconnected where it remained in plain sight in the front room, dangling from the telephone table. My voice was shrill as I jumped from my chair and chirped, "Why Fred. I don't know what I was thinking! Don't dare tell your grandmother I sat and watched you wash my dishes! Imagine that! You sit and let me do some work now, would you......"

I took him by the arms and sat him down. I filled the kettle, droning on about a piece of apple pie I had for him. He watched me, suspiciously I imagined, or did I? I felt like a criminal under investigation. The harder I tried to act normal the stranger I acted. I was desperate to get into the front room and reconnect the cord.

"Tea, or coffee, Fred?" I asked.

He was momentarily distracted by Charley's papers. "Hmm? Oh, no thanks. I've got to get going. But can I use your bathroom before I go?"

"Oh Lord, no!" I thought I whispered it softly.

He looked at me sharply, concern etched in his frowning brow. "What's that?" he asked.

"Oh," I grasped for a logical explanation. "I was just, umm...let me run in and tidy it up first. I won't be a second!"

I hurried in and grabbed the cord, groped behind the table and plugged it back in. I closed the bathroom door behind me, trying to steady my nerves. I splashed water on my face, glanced in the mirror, giggling. "Well this is what you get when you stop caring what other people think! They think you're crazy!"

I returned to the kitchen and saw that Charley's story had saved me. Fred was absorbed in the pages of history. He looked up. "This is excellent. Can I borrow it?"

I laughed. "I don't know about that. I didn't even finish it yet. But I'll ask Charley if you can have it next. Bathroom's all yours."

He stayed for two pieces of apple pie and a cup of tea. Before he left he reached for his hat and with one hand on the doorknob he said, "You know Mrs. Hankins, this one is coming. I don't know why I think so, and I hate the media hype as much as you do, but I think this is one storm Eastwind hasn't seen the likes of it in my lifetime, or yours."

He held up his hands in anticipation of my protest. "I know, I know. Don't get all fired up now. I just want you to be prepared, that's all. Like grandpa says, "Don't be stubborn and don't be stupid.""

I walked him out and waved as the patrol car pulled down the driveway. I looked out at Fishawk Bay, darkness enveloping the rising waters. I listened to the surf pound the beach. The tide was coming in, the waves would reach the steps before dawn.

I went inside and called Charley. "Hello," I said when he answered. "Is there a Charles Duncan there; famous historian of Eastwind Island?"

He laughed. "What do you think?"

I sighed. "I think it is absolutely, positively wonderful. It's all I had hoped and more."

"Did you finish it?"

"Heavens no! I'm savoring it. I didn't get past Joshua. Fred Allen interrupted me. By the way, I left him alone in the kitchen for two seconds and he started reading it. He wanted to take it!"

Charley groaned. "Fred read it? Oh jeez. I'll hear about it now."

"You'll hear about it all right. You'll hear people begging for a copy!"

"Sure. We'll see about that. More like I'll be the joke of the town you mean." He paused. "So, tell me, did you really like it?"

I smiled. In so many ways he was still the shy boy I met sixty years ago. "Charley, I love it. I love every sentence, every comma, every single word. Now let me go so I can read some more."

"Ok, ok, but tell me. What did Fred say about the storm?"

"He said it's big and it's coming and subtly advised me not to be stupid and not to be stubborn. I guess he forgot who he was talking to because some say those are my middle names, 'Sara Stupid Boyle Stubborn Hankins'."

He chuckled. "Yeah. Catchy name all right. How does the ocean sound?"

I gazed toward the window. I couldn't see the sea but I knew what I would see if I could. Angry winds whipping white caps around a steely blue mass of water, sending monstrous waves pounding onto shore. "Sounds rough," I said. Then I added, "Sounds like a marvelous crop of purples being stirred up for tomorrow morning's beachcombers. You interested?"

"I'll be over bright and early. Listen Sara, if you need me, will you call?"

"I don't know Charley. That wind is howling pretty loud. If I call, do you think you'll hear me?"

"Ha, ha, ha. See you in the morning."

I hung up the phone, smiling. Charley could always make me smile. He was my best friend, the one person I still relied on. Many people relied on Charley, he had family all over the island; an elaborate network of, brothers and sisters, nieces, nephews and cousins, so although he was virtually as alone as I was, he was never farther than a sneeze from a family member. Charley was married once but it didn't last long, not long enough to produce children which I knew he regretted. Or did he? How could I be so sure of his regrets when I couldn't even define my own?

I turned out the lights, went upstairs, got into bed and resumed reading.

Thomas Isaacs had seven daughters. His oldest daughter, Mariah, with eyes of indigo and golden hair, met the gaze of Joshua Duncan across that circle of warmth and as the story goes their eyes locked as well as their hearts. Joshua accepted a bed in their home and spent the spring and summer helping and learning.

Thomas loved his daughters dearly but was thrilled to finally have a son to share his vast wisdom and skills with. Joshua was an eager student and he learned in one short season the trades some took a lifetime to master. He hunted, he farmed, he fished; he tanned hides and forged iron and did it all with a zest the villagers had never seen before. They loved their life, but it was a harsh life and they knew no other way. Joshua knew another way and he hungered to experience the lifetime he had already missed, to make up for lost time.

Thomas loved Joshua but before the whales passed the island again, it was clear he couldn't live under the same roof as Mariah. Joshua discussed the matter with his friend, Jonathan Hankins. They approached Jonathan's father for permission to build a hut on the beach near the watchtower. In return for the land Joshua volunteered himself as permanent watch.

Richard Hankins agreed, though he considered it foolish and had no doubt the boy would fail and return to the village with the first nor'easter. Whalemen respected the sea. It was their limitless provider, but a dangerous adversary too. They knew the price men paid and were grateful when their work was done and they could turn their backs on it and return to their homes in the village, safely across the bay.

When word spread of Joshua building a permanent home on the beach the villagers shook their heads in wonder. But it was paradise for Joshua. He and Jonathan spent their free time planning and constructing the hut. They set it behind the watchtower, nestled between the widest dune on the beach side and the thickest pine grove facing the bay.

By October the hut took shape and by the end of November Joshua moved in. Each evening the men dragged their boats up the beach and tied them together beside Joshua's hut. Occasionally they would linger and discuss the day's catch over a bottle of rum. Joshua spread wooden planks out behind his hut and built a lean-to so the men could sit and watch the sun set over the bay sheltered from the stiff north winds of early winter.

On Sundays Joshua joined the Isaacs family for service and meals, but in the darkest, coldest months of the year he spent days and nights alone. Except for the sighting of a whale and visits from Jonathan, nobody ventured onto the island. The winds came and the snows came and for weeks at a time Joshua didn't leave his hut. He survived on rations he stockpiled, and when the weather cooperated joined the villagers for hunting parties on the bay and in the forests of the mainland.

He courted Mariah properly, and promised her a decent home to live in if she would marry him the next summer. Being a sensible girl she told him she loved him passionately and ached to become his wife, but would not commit to a life on the lonely and desolate island.

The company landed four whales that season and credit was given to the permanent watch, Joshua. By the beginning of March he was confident he had survived the worst of winter, and was eager for the warm winds of spring.

The second week of March a furious storm blew out of the northeast without warning. Rain and sleet poured from the skies for four days. Melting ice and snow swelled the bay and the river and sent flood waters through the village roads. Three tides ran high pushing the bay from the west and the sea from the east and gale winds swept it all together in the middle of the island with a storm surge cresting on the immense pines.

Joshua was awakened in the middle of the night by a wave crashing his hut to pieces. He latched onto one of the boats that floated past him just as another wave broke and he was knocked out cold against the spar.

The villagers huddled in the choir loft of the church praying for their safety, for their homes and possessions, and for the soul of Joshua Duncan for they were sure he was long dead. Mariah sat alone in the corner silently praying for his life and vowing that if he survived he would never face another storm alone.

At daybreak the men pushed the boards off the windows and stared out at the village. Six homes were destroyed, six left standing. As the sun rose over the ocean they spotted a boat with a still figure strapped to the mast like Ahab himself. They ran down into the flooded street, cast a line out and reeled Joshua in.

He was unconscious for three days and when he finally came to he comforted a weeping Mariah and assured her he would rebuild on the beach, but only for summers. They were married in June, and in the process of rebuilding the village the shop keeper decided to move inland, so Joshua borrowed money from Thomas, bought the store and built living quarters above it. On the first of August Joshua and his bride hosted the grand opening of 'Duncan's General Store'.

By the second year they built a house for their growing family next to the store and restructured their old rooms into guest accommodations for members of hunting parties led by the whalers during duck season. By the third year they had the foresight to encourage female guests who wished to accompany the men to the island and enjoy the sights and invigorating salt air.

The store flourished, and housed an informal dining area where Mariah served breakfast and dinner every day. Her specialties; grilled lamb chops and mutton stew with cranberry bread, and fried eggs and ham with blue berry muffins, were raved over in cities north, west, and south, and brought patrons flocking back every season.

The Duncan family grew as quickly as the business. They had three sons and two daughters in seven years. The oldest boy, Franklin, inherited his father's independent spirit and his yearning for a home of his own on the beach. And he shared his adventures with young Richard Hankins, Jonathan's oldest son.

Franklin and Richard spent hours on the beach keeping watch and reconstructing the hut. Before their fifteenth birthday they moved out there together and once again the Eastwind whalers had a permanent watch.

Whales became increasingly rare then, and the younger men of the village had to develop other professions to survive. Many turned inland to farming, raising cattle, and work at the saw mills. Others concentrated on harvesting creatures from the water; clams, oysters, mussels, lobsters, crabs and fish. Salt hay was still plentiful and harvested for seasoning and preserving food. The demand for salt to produce gunpowder increased heavily with the start of the Revolutionary War.

A few whalers set their sights on a less noble profession; smuggling. Vessels sailing up and down the coast were easy prey for the young men who knew every cove and inlet and navigated them swiftly in their small whaleboats. The ships held tempting cargoes; rum, sugar and molasses that could be sold at markets inland for prime prices.

In Eastwind, as in most villages, a whaler who turned to smuggling was not welcome; he was a pirate, with no home but his ship, no companions but other pirates, and no loyalty to any port. Between the war, the lure of piracy, and wealthier occupations inland, the village of Eastwind lost a few young men.

The close knit group scattered without the common bond of whaling, but the village prospered; new homes were built, and a school, and the store officially became "Duncan's General Store and Hotel'.

Franklin and Richard made a good living running hunting parties. They were renowned for their skill and charged a hefty fee that city folk gladly paid to enjoy their expertise and entertainment and return home with prize fowl and game. Their home on the beach was a ramshackle project, always destined for great renovations that were never fulfilled but constantly echoing with laughter and hearty spirits. The winters turned mild, the storms of the past tamed, and they maintained their bachelor's quarters until destiny intervened and altered their circumstances.

As the war waged out at sea and along the coast, smugglers became privateers; men who raided British supply and warships. Their actions were technically illegal, but rarely punished, and they were often hailed as heroes aiding the nation's cause.

Eatwind harbored no criminals but the British received information that 'Duncan's Hotel' was a hiding place for a notorious band of local privateers. They staged a midnight raid on the building and in the melee Joshua and Mariah were both killed.

The village was outraged, and Franklin's brother, a peaceful farmer, sought revenge. He formed his own band of privateers and led merciless bloody raids rendering the waters up and down the coast a suicide run for the British.

Franklin was devastated. His heart told him to join his brother's deadly siege, but his head told him to channel his sorrow into continuing his parents work at the store. He moved back to the family home and picked up where they left off, raised his younger sisters and took a wife of his own.

Saturday morning I woke up confused. I couldn't remember how much of Charley's story I had read and how much I remembered and incorporated into my dreams. I knew the tales so well and he had done a fine job, though nothing could compare to hearing Charley's voice fill with raw emotion when he told of landing a whale, rowing the skiff and running the raids as if he'd been there himself.

I lay in bed remembering the first time I laid eyes on Charles Duncan. I met Mike in the fall of my senior year of high school when he was a senior in college. Over Easter break he picked me up in the city and we drove down to Eastwind for a party. He was anxious for me to meet his friends. The party was at the infamous Eddie Blackmore's home. I didn't know that he was the son of the man who planned to destroy Sandy Point. I only knew him from Mike's description.

"Eddie is a piece of work. When you first hear him talk you might take him for a local, but the harder he tries to hide it the more the city in him sneaks out until he sounds like some hollywood mobster talking about catching blues on the beach."

"He sounds fascinating. But tell me," I teased. "Is that what you told Charley about me? That I'm a city girl who can't tell a blue fish from a sunfish?"

He looked at me with those deep green eyes that melted my heart and said, "I told Charley the only thing he needs to know about you..."

"And what's that?"

He pulled me closer on the seat and whispered in my ear, "I told him it was too bad for him that I found you first."

A spring thunderstorm was brewing as we crossed into Eastwind that afternoon. We got out of the car to watch the storm advance from the top of the bridge. Dark clouds swirled in the skies around the island, whipping up whitecaps on the river, the bay and the sea. Boats hurried home to port, people took cover under store awnings, behind hastily slammed windows.

It was not our first trip to the island together but as I stood beside him I marveled at how lucky I had been to find this fellow, whose love for all I saw was even deeper than mine. I closed my eyes and made a new wish.

I cast it out over the windy waters of the island and squeezed Mike's hand as tight as I could. I knew at that moment, what love is. My father always told me I couldn't 'love' a sweater, or a book, or the island, because they weren't living things. And I was sure he was wrong. But now I realized he was right. Because I loved Mike, and it didn't matter if I was on Eastwind Island or another planet, as long as I was with him.

A bolt of lightning streaked into the sea, followed by a clap of thunder that shook the bridge under our feet and sent us scrambling for the car. We turned down a street along Fishhawk Bay and I picked out the Blackmore house from Mike's description of it as the only high rise apartment building on the island. It was a huge, ornate stone mansion. Mike pulled into the driveway.

"Nice place, huh?" He winked at me and I laughed.

The house was filled with music and noise. Kids milled around spilling beer on the garish tiled floors, feet propped carelessly up on the lavish furniture, racing up and down the spiral staircase. A rowdy pool game was going on in the den where an entire glass wall looked out on the bay.

Mike led me around, greeting friends, engaging in a few idle conversations. We finally found Roger Allen loading beer bottles from a well stocked refrigerator into a metal bucket.

"Hey! Hankins! It's about time you got here!" He put down the bucket, slapped Mike on the back and shook hands, reached over to hug me. "Sara. Good to see you again. How's it going? Pretty well I see..." He winked.

Mike asked, "Where is everybody?"

"Well, we waited for you guys for hours. We even took a spin in the newest addition to the Blackmore fleet, the "Leona III". You gotta see it, she's a beauty." Roger explained, "You see Sara, it's a private joke around here, that Blackmore Senior has hung onto his young wife Leona long enough to name three boats after her. Usually they're lucky to get one!"

He let go of me and slapped Mike on the back again, laughing "You should have seen it, Mike. Charley zipped that thing around the bay like it was a ten foot whaler! Eddie was on the dock screaming for him to stop! It was great, man, you would have loved it!"

"How big is it?" I asked.

Roger and Mike just looked at me for a second. Then Roger said, "Well, come on. I'll show you! That's where we're hanging out, and you're just in time. Charley's got a good buzz on and he's about to start story hour. You're in for a real treat, Sara. Follow me."

We stood aside and let kids shove past us, coming in out of the rain that was starting to fall. We ran out past the swimming pool, across the multi-level decks leading out to the dock where a magnificent 40 foot Sea Ray barely rocked in the choppy waters.

I had seen many, been on a few, and this boat was beyond compare. I looked at Mike. He stood back to inspect it, shaking his head, and he muttered under his breath to Roger, "Man...What a waste of money...about as useful as tits on a bull."

Roger stamped his feet and snorted with laughter. I wasn't supposed to hear the joke, so I pretended not to. I didn't get it anyway.

We boarded the boat and followed Roger downstairs to the cabin, which was larger than my summer bungalow. Roger slammed a hatch shut behind us and it was as if the storm ceased in mid-thunder.

A group of kids were assembled around the galley table, more at the gleaming mahogany bar along the wall, others lying on the immaculate white shag carpet, all eyes fixed intently on the storyteller; Charley Duncan. He was sitting up on a counter, one arm draped over the top of the refrigerator, the other gesturing with his beer bottle as he spun his tales.

Roger started to interrupt Charley but Mike stopped him and pulled me down to the floor. I nestled back against him next to Roger and the bucket of beers and was immediately drawn to the fellow Mike had described, oddly enough, as the strong silent type.

I couldn't argue the strong part. He wore a white t-shirt, out of which tan, muscular arms bulged. He looked top heavy, his broad shoulders took up more than their share of space, compared to the skinny brown legs dangling from his khaki shorts over the edge of the counter. He had perfectly straight blonde hair, sunburned cheeks and deep blue eyes.

Clare Jordan and I would sum the entire package up in one word; gorgeous. And certainly not silent. He was full of dramatic energy, it flowed out from him and into his audience. When he finished the crowd clapped and cheered. Charley jumped off the counter and moved through the galley joking, laughing, accepting back slaps and high fives. The group slowly broke up, moved outside, someone said the storm had cleared.

When he saw Mike he came over and the minute we were introduced I saw how aptly the word silent described the real Charley. That easy going friendly guy transformed before my eyes into a shy, fumbling little boy. The guys bantered jokingly back and forth, discussed boats and school, friends and jobs, in their own familiar way, but Charley practically ignored me.

Later, Mike assured me that he would 'come around', that he was always shy when he first met someone, and that he 'liked me just fine', which was one of those vague statements Mike made that I would go over and over for days trying to figure out exactly what it meant.

But it hadn't taken long for Charley to 'come around'. I realized right away that he and Mike were closer than brothers and I knew how to win brother's hearts so I just treated him like one.

I raised my old body out of bed and squinted at the clock, realizing Charley would be knocking at the back door and I would still be in my nightgown if I didn't get moving. I went to the window and looked out on the extraordinary sight of a crazed sea. A turbulent ocean always made me think of a mind gone mad. Swirling with thoughts out of control, raging currents pushed mercilessly by an unseen force causing mountains of water to build higher and higher until the pressure cannot be contained and the energy explodes in wave after wave of angry outbursts, landing with reckless fury.

The storm was not close by air but the depths of the sea were already overwhelmed by it. The day was dawning like any other; sun rising clear and bright over the island, but a thick mass of clouds to the south loomed like a persistent dread in the back of one's head. It was low tide but the water had reached the steps in the night. The swells rose to five feet or better, crested and sent the wash running high onto the beach. The sheer power of the breakers could be measured in their reach up the steep slope the high tide had created. Waves surfers wait for.

I turned from the window, washed, dressed, gathered Charley's papers and went downstairs. In the kitchen I prepared a batch of cinnamon rolls and put them in to bake. By the time I heard Charley's door squeak, the rolls were cooling, the coffee was brewing and I was at the table drinking my first cup of tea and going over the pages I had read last night.

Charley breezed in. "Good morning Sara Stupid. Was that it?" He helped himself to a cup of coffee, sat down and reached for a roll.

"Something like that," I said. "Let me tell you……I love your book."

He looked at me in surprise. "Book?"

"Well I don't know what else I'd call it. It's ten times better than any book I've read lately, say in the last thirty years!"

"I don't know about that Sara, it's just a story."

"Yes.. And a book is something else?" I helped myself to a cinnamon roll and put another on Charley's plate. "Anyhow, no matter what we call it…it's great. I'm not finished reading it yet, I'm taking my time. I fell asleep with it last night and dreamt I was a mate on a doomed schooner, then in the next convoluted segment you and Mike were running guns for the British in an old sneakbox on Fishhawk Bay!"

Charley smiled. "So you really like it, then."

"I like it so much I'm going to finish it today and then I'm making a copy…I'm assuming you haven't…And then I'm taking it over to Lillian at the library…She has connections in the literary world you know…And she is very interested in preserving the history of our little hamlet. Actually she's also been waiting for you to get this wonderful stuff down on paper for years."

To my surprise Charley didn't argue. "Whatever you say Boss. Far be it from me to interfere with the likes of you and Lillian. I'd be way out of my league there." He took his plate and mug to the sink. "Now if you hurry we might get to take that walk on the beach while there is still some beach left to walk on."

I cleared the dishes. Charley went out onto the porch, I heard him greet Henry and attempt to engage the stubborn creature in a game. I knew he wouldn't succeed. Henry was well beyond playfulness, but it was good to hear Charley in such a light mood.

I knew he was pleased with my reaction to the story. It meant more to him than he let on. Charley had three brothers who all had sons, and their lack of interest in the family history frightened and annoyed him. Even more alarming than their indifference about the past was their apathetic attitude concerning the future; they were nonchalant on issues of preservation, were satisfied with the status quo, and refused to acknowledge any need to become active in town planning and politics.

And the worst part was that Charley knew he had been the same way at their age. He and Mike had watched the changes on Eastwind, lamented the losses, debated the benefits, and eventually realized the only way to stop it was to become involved. Mike had finally gotten a seat on the Planning Board two years before he died, and became embroiled in and frustrated by the battles waged behind the scenes, and at the front. The issue of development was an ancient argument.

Many people, powerful people, favored development, encouraged it, in the name of tax ratables and progress, advancement and improvement. Many others disagreed, but those were typically the quieter voices, the less powerful, and they found the fight exhausting until it became an unwanted responsibility that was easier to ignore rather than face.

When I was young and naieve the answer seemed simple, stop building. I kept waiting for somebody older and smarter to prove me wrong but they never did, and then I realized it was the simplest solution, but an unpopular one. An endless debate. In an island community the debate is more intense because there is more to protect, or more to exploit, depending on which camp you fall into. But I could never understand the constant lack of foresight in the pro-development camp. Figuratively and literally.

And when development is allowed, the first thing they want to do is restrict access, keep it to themselves. They put up fences and signs and attempt to enforce arbitrary regulations on walking, surfing and swimming. No man will ever own the sea, and none should be allowed to think he owns the beachfront.

The screen door slam interrupted my thoughts. "Sara! Are you coming?" Charley called impatiently.

I took my beach combing sweater from the hook and followed him outside. The deep pockets held some sea glass from a week ago. When I was young I collected clam shells. I painted them, sold them, made games of tossing them into the sea. As a teen I was obsessed with sea glass, bits of colored glass worn smooth and frosty by the salt water, and left at the water's edge. Blue was the rarest find, then green, white, and the most common, brown. I filled jugs with it, made frames and jewelry, fashioned sea scapes and sailboats out of it against driftwood backgrounds. Aunts, uncles, cousins and friends grew tired of receiving my sea glass inspired gifts.

In my golden years I switched exclusively to the pursuit of 'purples'. My purple collection included various shades, sizes and shapes and the ultimate find, a heart shape. In all my days spent scouring the beach in Sandy Point I never discovered purples. They were added to the long list of wonders I would have missed if not for Mike. The first walk we took together along the beach he picked one up and played with it. I hardly noticed it. I was too preoccupied with his sandy brown hair drifting in the breeze, his shoulder touching mine, his eyes shifting from hazy aqua to turquoise green like the sea behind him.

He tossed his head back laughing, and tossed the purple up in the air and we watched it fall back down, spinning and sparkling in the sunlight, end over end and we reached out to catch it at the same time and his hand closed over mine and we stood face to face, and his eyes gazed into mine and our lips touched, and I wanted to stay like that forever.

Halfway to the crest I bent down and picked up a beauty; a solid purple the size of a quarter. The waves kept us high on the beach, a safe distance from the roiling foam traveling up and over the cliff. "We should be down there you know," I said, pointing over the crest. "That's where all the good stuff is."

"Yes, well, not today Sara. Ok?"

"I suppose they'll make a law against that next. ORDINANCE NUMBER THREE THOSAND THIRTY TWO: NO WALKING ON BEACH WHEN STORM IS APPROACHING!" We laughed.

"I see the surfers are ready to defy the law in "Iris' honor," Charley said as we approached the Hastings Avenue access.

I looked up and saw four young boys heading out with their boards, six or seven heads already bobbing out beyond the breakers. We stopped to watch. The sun slipped behind a cloud and I pulled my sweater tighter, turned my back to the wind.

I said, "The law won't be far behind them I imagine."

Charley chuckled. "I will never understand that one. If ever there was a law begging to be broken, that's it. If I was a few years younger I'd give it a try myself!"

"Well don't look now, but the law just arrived."

Two Eastwind patrol cars pulled up to the beach access. Four officers got out and approached the surfers, prepared to enforce the controversial ordinance forbidding anyone to enter the water when it was deemed unsafe by the powers that be.

They blew their whistles and stopped the four newcomers from going in, at least at this beach. They barely had to set foot on the sand to do that. The more difficult feat was removing the surfers already in the water.

Young men intent on taking advantage of hurricane surf were more than willing to risk almost any consequence and habitually ignored warnings to the contrary. The local ordinance gave the town the legal power to prevent them, but the physical enforcement was quite another matter. If the surfers refused to heed the officer's demand to exit the ocean, which they did, the officers then had to decide if the instance warranted Coast Guard intervention.

Fred Allen was one of the officers. His sergeant whipped out a radio and spoke harshly into it, seconds later a coast guard cutter with sirens blaring broke the Sandy Point inlet and headed south toward the bobbing heads off our beach.

The surfers now had a choice; pick the best wave and make the thrill worth the consequence of being slapped with a $500.00 fine, possibly even arrested for resisting authority, or sit and wait to be plucked from the sea by the coast guard and given a lesser fine for cooperating.

I felt detached watching the drama played out; the young boys perched on their boards drifting over the towering swells, the men on the cutter poised for action, and Fred Allen and his crew making their way briskly onto the beach. Each player anticipated his own role yet was keenly focused on the movement of the others.

The whole scene played out in five minutes, but it felt like hours in slow motion. I had time enough to conjure up images of my son David, a dedicated surfer in his day. Time to recall the many anxious moments I endured as he risked life and limb, or so it seemed to me, for the pleasure of riding those waves. I was so frightened by it I rarely watched him surf, especially on days like this. But I often saw him inadvertently, as I cleaned, or worked in the yard, or simply passed by a window. I would catch glimpses of a tiny body flinging itself into a giant wall of water and teeter along the edge, and recognize even from a distance the tilt of the head, his fluid stance, his confident demeanor, and my heart would miss a beat.

I had time to worry for Fred's safety; think of his parents, and grandparents and how frantic they would be if they knew. If they knew, as I did, and as Fred sensed, that one of the young men had decided to opt for the thrill. I knew Fred knew, because he was the first to kick off his shiny black shoes, undo his belt and holster, tear off his shirt, and throw them all down with a spray of sand behind him.

He did not hesitate, did not stop to see if he was going in alone, did not stop to consider anything or anyone; himself, his mother, his fiance. I had seen that determined focus in the eyes of men and boys I had loved many times before. Mike, Chuck, Jimmy, John and David. So even as my heart begged me to cry out and stop him, I knew better.

Charley reached for my arm, as much to steady himself as to comfort me. I put my other hand over his and we hung there, watching the men on the cutter lift the other boys onto the boat while one man stood on the bridge shouting into a bullhorn in vain; his words lost in the relentless wind.

The lone boy had caught a wave; a seven footer. He also did not listen to any warning or heed concern for himself, or anybody else. He was determined, and for a second it seemed as if he would be Ok. He crouched low on the board; steady and sure as the crystal wall rose behind him. For that instant we all took a breath. Fred, at the shoreline, paused.

But then the surge crested and sent an avalanche of foam crashing along in pursuit of the boy and he lost control. Suddenly he was gone, swallowed up in the turmoil of the breaking wave, and Fred was in the water, swimming out with strong strokes, then pushed back as the swells continued to form and rise and break. The boy's board surfaced and rode by itself into shore, finally coming to rest just south of where we stood.

A second cutter joined the effort and moved in as close as possible, barely balanced on the crests. Fred reached the point where the boy went down and attempted to catch a line thrown from the cutter. The Hastings Avenue lifeguards had arrived on the beach and prepared to launch their rescue.

Another collective pause, as everyone waited for a sign of the boy. He surfaced for an instant, and was spotted by a guard on the beach with a well trained eye who gave the signal to move. The boy was twenty yards north of Fred who was secured on a buoy and line from the coast guard cutter.

Two life guards on shore, secured to their own line, dove into the surf against the caution of the police officers on the beach. A curious alliance exists between surfers and life guards; they are usually one in the same and storm surf entices them either way.

The Eastwind lifeguards were known for their sense of pride in protection of swimmers at any cost and they took their obligation seriously. They had not lost a swimmer in more than fifty years and this squad was determined not to lose one on their watch. So Fred Allen was fed line from the boat and the guards from the beach and they all headed in the direction the boy was spotted.

I thought again of the boys caught up in this drama, as some mother's little boys. Because all boys remain little boys to their mothers. No matter how big they get, and how smart and independent. And perhaps especially, as they bear children of their own, they remain as vulnerable in their mother's eyes as when they were first held in swaddling blankets and laid at their breast. The urge to protect, to comfort, to make their hurts go away, is an inborn drive. And even when the little boys go away, the instinct prevails.

The boy surfaced for the third time. Fred and the two guards were no more than five feet from him but he went down. The cutter closed in as the guards disappeared into the swirling surf again and again searching for the boy. Then they brought him up, and laid his lifeless body over the buoy. The cutter moved in again and lifted the four of them quickly onto the boat, then sped away.

I sat down hard on the sand shaking, praying for that little boy to live. I closed my eyes and there was Mike. The first day I saw him, over sixty years ago, in a scene so like this one it was uncanny. A dramatic rescue, the coast guard and lifeguards, a crowd on the beach watching, waiting. A brave young man performing a revolting task, way beyond the call of duty. But on that day, sixty years ago, somebody's little boy was already dead.

CHAPTER SIX

The summer I turned sixteen, tropical storms were born and buried as often as the fish of the day changed from pollock to bluefish in the Lobster House Restaurant. None of the storms grew into full blown hurricanes but they transformed the seas along the coast into a raging mass of unpredictable currents that claimed the lives of seven people before the end of July and three more by Labor Day.

It was a season of many changes. Nana died in her sleep one January night with her shiny rosary beads clutched close to her chest. I missed her terribly, she was my friend and confidant and the void she left was a steady ache in my heart. At Sandy Point I moved her rocking chair away from the top of the steps so the emptiness would not cry out each time I passed by.

Dave, the inlet gate badge checker did not return that summer either. We asked around, but no one seemed to know what happened to him. We had grieved over Chuck the past summer, and adjusted to Sandy Point without him. Each loss piled on top of the one before and began to make me fear that phenomenon called change.

And one enormous change loomed over the island like a menacing storm cloud threatening to burst. Markison's was for sale. The entire operation; beach, bath houses, pavilions, and pool, was up for grabs to the highest bidder and that made my stomach turn. Sandy Point was an anchor in my life, another constant about to shift. I knew these changes were out of my hands yet I still believed that in the end all would be well, that no one would willingly disturb a haven as perfect as Sandy Point.

There was talk of condominiums, more hotels, an interested buyer from up north. And I knew how quickly transformations could take place. When we returned to Sandy Point the summer after Chuck died the southern end of the island where Mrs. Jameson's and twelve other grand homes had stood for centuries, a huge marina complex dominated the landscape; Blackmore's Marina.

The lighthouse was still there, but the snack bar had a new look and a new name: Eddie's. It was all wrong, plastic and neon instead of weathered wood and clapboards.

Clare and I worked as Markison candy girls the summer before, but Stewart and Steve convinced us that the Lobster House was the place to make money, so we started working as bus girls in June. By the fourth of July I was waitressing and Clare was a hostess.

Stewart and I had a curious relationship. Nothing ever became of that first summer's fling, but we did become friends. He was the broiler man, head honcho in the kitchen and he took me under his wing and made me a "cook's waitress" by his definition, one who kept both sides of the house happy; the customer and the kitchen.

Steve and Clare really hit it off. They had a lot in common; they were both rich. Steve's parents owned the Lobster House. She fell as naturally into the role of owner's son's girlfriend and glamorous hostess as I did into the part of the reliable, efficient, everybody's best friend waitress. It worked out well for me, the only better friend for a waitress than a cook in the kitchen is a hostess on the floor, especially when she's the boss' son's girlfriend. She kept me rolling in dough, sending the choicest parties my way. I gradually ceased to be surprised when a father of five with grease under his fingernails treated me with respect and a twenty percent tip while a well groomed 'gentleman' gave me a condescending tone and a lousy gratuity.

Jimmy finished one year of college at State, pursuing a major in Business and Finance, his goal being a future in banking. He was impressed with my income and I was impressed with his projections of compounding interest, so we formed a partnership where he took a portion of my earnings and invested it as practice for himself and savings for me.

Jimmy and Brenda were still dating. He was guarding at Main Beach and she was a guard at the pool. Her family rented the bungalow on Lenape Lane and Sherry came down on weekends. I had dated a guy from school briefly that spring and was awkwardly corresponding with him but the deeper summer slipped into July the less interest I had in poor Jason Kilmer.

Sherry was still convinced Stewart had a thing for me, but I was sure he didn't. She hadn't really dated anyone after Chuck, but I sensed she was ready to look around.

Saturday night of the Fourth of July weekend the Lobster House was hopping. I had a hundred easy bucks in my pocket as I headed out the kitchen door where Sherry was waiting to pick me up. Stewart grabbed my arm.

"Hey Sara," he said. "The Allen boys are throwing a big bash. You don't want to miss it, believe me."

Sherry chimed in. "Who the heck are the Allen boys? Some local yokel singing group?"

Stewart laughed. "Yeah. Something like that. Their place is on the beach, I forget the number but you can't miss it. Party's already started. Look for the house with twenty cars in the driveway and kegs rolling in and out the back door. And oh yeah, you'll hear the boys harmonizing on the front porch!" He winked at Sherry.

I looked at Sherry when we got in the car. "Well, what do you say?" I asked her.

"You're the working girl. You up to it? Sounds like fun, we'll finally see how the other half lives!"

"OK. Let's do it. We'll go to my house and I'll change," I said.

"How about Clare?" Sherry asked.

"They aren't around, remember? Steve's parents are away so they are home alone...you know...tonight's the night!"

"Oh my God. How could I forget," Sherry smiled. "I gotta get the details on that one!"

"Yeah, I can't wait either," I groaned.

Clare had developed a reckless streak the past two years. She had her driver's license, her own car, and the freedom to do whatever she pleased. That night she was hell bent on losing her virginity and the next morning she would tell us every gruesome detail.

I let Sherry into the bungalow and tiptoed up to my parent's bedroom. My adorable niece Margaret was sleeping soundly. She was staying with us to give Joann a break, another baby was due in the fall. My mother was lying fully dressed on her bed, also sound asleep. I nudged her gently.

"Sara. What time is it?" she whispered. "I must have dozed off. I've forgotten how exhausting a two year old can be!" She sat up. "How was work? You in for the night?"

I sat next to her on the bed. "It's only ten, and yes it was really busy but I made good money, and no I'm not in for the night, Sherry's downstairs and we're going to a party down in Eastwind, OK?" I brushed gray wisps of hair from her face, wondering suddenly when our roles had reversed.

She smiled. "OK. Not too late though. And no drinking, I'm sure it will be there, right?"

"If it is I promise I'll run out the back door. Hey, maybe in the morning I can take Margaret to the beach for a while."

"That would be nice honey. Be careful." She was already drifting back to sleep. I turned off the light and went downstairs.

Twenty minutes later Sherry and I were cruising down Ocean Avenue out of Sandy Point with the radio blaring, past the darkened Lobster House at the bottom of the bridge, into Eastwind on South Bay Ave past the lighthouse, and back up North Bay where we came upon a huge house showing all the signs of a party totally out of control.

We parked and walked up the street lined with hastily parked cars. A girl was puking into somebody's garbage can along the side of the road, a bunch of younger guys were noisily mounting bicycles, complaining about getting kicked out. A pickup truck pulled out of the driveway with an empty keg in the back. Stewart leaned out of the truck and yelled, "Hey girls, go on inside! We'll be back with more!"

Sherry and I avoided the house altogether and headed around to the beach. A bonfire was blazing, music blasting out of speakers on the porch railing. Someone called out to Sherry from the group assembled around the fire, she waved and we started over. Another keg was pumping out there so we grabbed two cups and sat down.

The group was mostly Markison Guards and their girlfriends with a few locals mixed in, including the two guys Clare and I had met up on the boardwalk two summers ago. We'd seen them again a few times and were definitely not impressed. I couldn't even remember their names, but they never seemed to take the hint. They came over to us.

"Hey, Sara, right? Remember us? Where's your buddy, Clare wasn't it?" They snuggled in between us before I could stop them.

Sherry, never much for tact, whispered to the one trying to move in on her, "No. It isn't Clare anymore nerdo. Now it's me. Get it? We're together and you aren't welcome so beat it buster. Comprende?"

He stared at her for a second then grabbed his friend and left. Joe Anderson, Jimmy's guarding partner was sitting directly across from us and he shouted over, "Hey, Sara. Everything OK over there?"

I laughed. "Yeah, Joe. Not to worry."

"Where's big brother tonight? I haven't seen him around," he called back.

"I don't know. But tell me if you see him and I'll get rid of this real quick." I held up my beer. A few in the group chuckled. My first life guard party after the water show two years ago was a well known joke. What most of them didn't know was that Jimmy wouldn't come near a party like this. He hadn't touched a beer since Chuck died. No one ever discussed the details of how he was killed but we knew he was driving home from a party and no one knew better than Jimmy what that meant.

The conversation around the fire shifted to the unusual rip tides plaguing the ocean and the remarkable number of saves carried out over the busy weekend, which led to an animated 'can you top this' discussion between the Eastwind and Markison guards. Sherry and I refilled our cups and listened to the stories. It was a beautiful, still night. A full moon shone over the sea, no clouds in sight. The commotion from the house eventually died down after two Eastwind patrol cars cruised by and a couple of the older Allen boys came home and kicked everybody out. But nobody disturbed the group around the fire. We talked past midnight, when the wind shifted and a cool southeast breeze blew in and rattled a few windows, stirred a wind chime and started some shutters banging.

At that moment, on a beach a few miles north three boys got up from a gathering much like ours and swam out into the deceivingly serene sea where they were caught in a violent current that pulled their powerless bodies farther and farther from shore until there was nothing to do but scream for help, and then nothing but silence.

The next morning the headlines said the kids had been drinking, they weren't good swimmers, that it was a tragic accident. It was very spooky. They recovered two bodies that night and found the third one at dawn. It was the talk of the town for days. I was forbidden to go to anymore beach parties. I reminded my mother how I hated swimming in the ocean at night,that someone would have to drag me in screaming and kicking, but she didn't buy it.

So to keep her happy I stayed close to home and helped out with Margaret. We went to the beach every morning and built castles, flew kites, chased each other in the warm sand. We collected buckets of shells and I taught her how to throw them. We painted them and sold them for a nickel on the edge of the boardwalk. I took her up to the 'big boardwalk', as she called it and we went on the rides and ate cotton candy.

The Boyles were spread all over, but still close. Bobby was a full professor at UCLA with plans to marry the following spring. He came home for Christmas each year, and a week every summer. JoAnn's husband got transferred all over the country but she came home at least once a month and I suspected that the more kids she had the more we would see them. Eileen was living with a fellow teacher. My parents hated that they were living together. They didn't discuss it and I was not allowed to visit her, but of course I knew all about it and thought it was intriguingly romantic.

When JoAnn came to take Margaret home my mother was ready for a rest, but I really missed her. When I seriously considered JoAnn's invitation to stay with them awhile, I realized maybe Clare was right about me spending too much time around the house.

Business at the Lobster House was slow as storms in the tropics continued clouding our skies and troubling our seas. In the middle of July four more people drowned thirty miles south of Sandy Point on a guarded beach in the middle of the afternoon. The Coast Guard picked up the bodies that night. The threat loomed over Sandy Point like the inclement weather.

The sun burst through at dawn one morning and Clare and I took a spin into Eastwind to catch some surfing action. Steve and Stewart and their friends surfed every morning off the lighthouse beach. Surfers love storm surf; rare swells and a sloping break.

We walked onto the beach and spread out our towels. Jimmy was just getting out of the water.

"Hey Sis," he called. "Bring any snacks? I'm starved." He stuck his board in the sand and stretched out on my towel. "Man, the waves are awesome. I wish I didn't have early shift today."

I sat next to him. "Here, you can have half of my bagel."

He accepted it gratefully. "So, are we looking for anyone special this morning? Or just looking?"

Clare scanned the horizon of muscular bronze bodies glistening on their boards like gods in the rising sun. "Well, I'm supposed to be watching Steve, but if you have any suggestions, I'm all ears."

"Stick with Steve, Clare. He's nuts for you. And I approve. So that's all there is to it."

She laughed. "Nuts for me, is he? I don't know about that James. I don't think I'm ready for nuts. There's many fish in the sea you know. Yes indeed, many gorgeous fish in the sea."

"How about you, Sis?" Jimmy asked. "When are you going to give one of these guys a chance?"

"Who's interested? I don't see anybody knocking on my door. You know something I don't know?" I asked with genuine interest.

He didn't get to answer. Clare yelled, "Wow, look at the beauty Joe's taking in."

Joe crouched on his board caressing the crest of a six foot wave and rode it all the way. He hopped off and ran over, totally syched.

"Man. Am I good or what?" he shouted.

He grabbed the other half of my bagel, yelled thanks, and he and Jimmy took off for work.

"What do you think of Steve, Sara?" Clare carefully applied baby oil to every inch of exposed skin. "I mean, do you think he's cool? Because sometimes I don't know. I think maybe I could do better. Now don't yell at me. I know how that sounds. Maybe I mean he could do better. You know he's so good, he never wants to do anything exciting, or risky or anything. And I know I should be glad about that, but, well, do you know what I mean or not?"

I didn't answer right away because as usual, I didn't have a clue what she meant. Just when it seemed like she was perfectly happy with a great guy like Steve, she wanted to start trouble.

"Honestly? I think Steve's great. Just think about it Clare. He's sweet, he's really rich, he's got a marvelous body, beautiful eyes...he's got everything. So, I guess what I'm trying to say is...if you don't want him, I'll take seconds. I'm not proud! Just send him my way."

She lay back on the sand and groaned. "Well now that you mention it, we do have to get busy on your love life. I guess I could put mine on hold for awhile. You know, do something as uncharacteristic as be happy with what I've got...You really think his body is marvelous?"

"Yeah, I do. And let's face it Clare, what could be more risky and exciting than dating you for God's sake? So, let's forget about you and find somebody for me."

"Well, actually, the other day Steve introduced me to one of the Allens. They own one of those huge houses on the beach. This one was Roger. He's too old for you, but supposedly there's a whole slew of them and they're all pretty cute. So I'll check it out. What ever happened with Jason from home? Did you officially cut the cord yet?"

I held my knees to my chest and gazed out at two surfers battling for control of a monster wave. "I don't know what to do about Jason," I said. "I don't feel much about him one way or the other. I guess I should end it, but I don't want to hurt his feelings. He's still writing to me like every other day. He actually called the house yesterday, so now my Mother is pressuring me about him. She likes him, he's just her type."

Both surfers wiped out, their boards shot straight up into the bright blue sky. I held my breath. An airborne surfboard is a loaded missile with a mind of its own. I heard once about a kid whose neck was nearly severed by his own skeg and wound up paralyzed. The two boards righted themselves and picked their own waves to ride in, landing gracefully in the wash and retrieved by their owners.

"Well, I vote for a royal dumping. I'll help you write the Dear Jason letter myself. It's not as hard as you think," said Clare.

"We'll see. Ooh look. Here comes Steve."

Clare sat up to watch Steve take the wave in. He expertly immersed himself in the watery tunnel inside the curl of the breaking wave that surfers call 'the tube'. He walked over to us with Stewart, who had been one of the wipe-outs. Steve laid down on top of Clare and they started moaning and thrashing. I made a space on my towel for Stewart.

"I hope you've been here long enough to see me do more than wipe-out," he said, pounding his head to one side to get some water out.

"Oh yeah," I lied. "Wasn't that you riding that giant a little while ago?"

He leaned close and stared deep into my eyes. "You're a lousy liar Sara Boyle."

I stared back at him for an instant before a voice screeched at us, "Stewart!!!!"

Clare and Steve jumped up at the tone. We all turned around and there was Judy, Steve's girlfriend, standing at the top of the dunes with her hands on her hips and steam coming out of her ears.

Steve murmured, "Better run Stewie, Mommy's calling..."

Stewart hesitated for a second, shaking his hung head and whispered, "Man. Am I in deep shit now."

He stood and grabbed his board, pretending not to hurry to impress us, but hurrying just the same for his own sake. "See you later Sara. You working tonight?"

"Yeah, I'll catch you later."

We were laughing before they stepped off the beach.

"Well that's it for Stewart. We won't see the poor slob for weeks now," Steve said.

"Why does he put up with that crap anyway?" Clare asked.

"I don't know. I think they've just been together so long, he doesn't know how to get out of it. She is too much. But I know one thing that might give him a little incentive..." Steve looked over at me, "some serious encouragement from a certain someone. Judy doesn't get that mad when he sits next to just anybody......"

"Oh please," I said. "I wish you two would give up on that. Stewart and I are friends. That's all. And even if I did like him, which I don't, I wouldn't want to tangle with that psycho!"

"Well enough talk about those two honey. Where were we?" Clare pulled Steve back down on the blanket.

I picked up my towel. "I can take a hint. I'm walking back to Sandy Point. I'll see you guys later."

I took my time, picking up sea glass. Eastwind was a magnificent beach. Once it had frightened me but now I saw only beauty in its barren loneliness. The houses were still intimidating but I grew to appreciate their elegance too. I had taken to walking on this end of the island and was beginning to recognize familiar scenarios, alien though they were to me. It was a different world here. People came and went, children played, dogs barked, but they all seemed indifferent to the beach outside their front door, as if it was just a backdrop for their lives and I couldn't imagine it ever becoming insignificant or taken for granted. What bothered me most about the homes on Eastwind was that they often seemed empty, even in mid-summer. I wondered how anyone could own homes like these and not spend every possible second enjoying them.

My pockets were full of treasures before long and I stooped over to pick up a clam shell in front of the house I recognized as the Allen's. At least their house was always brimming over with life. The wind carried the familiar early morning confusion of a large family out to me as I tossed shells into the sea.

A voice startled me. "Hey, could you give me a hand here?"

I turned to see a lanky teen-ager dragging an old wooden life boat down the beach. I stared at him.

"It's not as heavy as it looks. And if I don't get it out before my Mom sees me I'll never get out, so, would you mind?" He smiled. He was cute; blonde hair, blue eyes. I guessed it was true what they said about the Allen boys. I hesitated for a second, wondering if it was a good idea for him to take that old boat out alone in the rough water, but he seemed determined so I took a step toward him.

"Don't worry, he can handle it," a voice from somewhere answered my thoughts. I looked up to see an older version of the boy with the boat sitting on the bottom step of the porch. Same build, same eyes, same easy charm.

The boy with the boat seemed as surprised to see him as I was. "Roger! I didn't see you there or I wouldn't have bothered this beautiful shell thrower." He winked at me.

Roger walked over and joined me along side the boat. As we pulled he nodded to me, "I'm Roger Allen and this is my brother, George. I didn't catch your name..."

I smiled. "Sara. Sara Boyle."

As we neared the water's edge I worried what to do next. Again Roger read my thoughts. "We'll take it from here, stand back!" And with that they ran beside the hulking boat in the wash, until at some apparently predetermined point, Roger gave a mighty push, George jumped in and sat on the bench, grabbed two worn oars and was paddling out beyond the crashing breakers in seconds.

I watched with amazement. Roger came back and we stood together in silence. Then he smiled at me. "I taught him everything he knows," he said.

"Well he certainly seems to know what he's doing," I said.

"Oh, it's an old family tradition. That boat is one of the originals used by my great great great grandfather in the Eastwind Lifesaving Service many years ago. We just fool around with it now, pass it down to the next generation to see who will be the one to break his neck launching it, or sail out and be lost at sea!"

"Great tradition," I said sarcastically. "Won't your mother be mad that he's out there?"

"My mother knew he'd be out there this morning before he knew he would be. Not much gets past a gal who raised seven boys," he laughed. "God knows we try though. God knows we try."

I laughed. "Yeah. But that's just another family tradition right?"

Roger Allen turned and studied my face. "Did you say your name is Boyle? You related to Bobby Boyle?"

"Yeah. He's my brother. You know him?"

"Bobby worked with my brother Brian up at Markison's. They used to hang out at the house sometimes and I always tagged along. I thought Bobby was really cool. Tell me he became a marine biologist even if he didn't or I'll be totally bummed out."

"Wow," I said. "Small world, huh? He's a Professor of Marine Biology at UCLA. Is that close enough for you?"

"That'll do. You on your way home?" I nodded. "Mind if I walk along for awhile?"

"Still tagging along, huh? Be my guest," I said.

"I remember going to Sandy Point with Brian to watch him play football. The guys still play every night?"

"Not so much anymore. It's kind of a dying tradition." I hadn't realized until I said it and it made me sad to think of Bobby and those games, and how things used to be.

"Yeah. Change stinks doesn't it?" I was beginning to wonder if Roger Allen was a mind reader. He talked like we'd know each other forever. Walking on the beach can do that; your mind roams free in the scents and sounds that surround you, the wide open blue spaces of the sea and the sky. I sometimes found myself lifted into a trance-like state where I could be inspired, depressed, or both, so I understood how Roger found it easy to work through his feelings of grief with me, practically a total stranger.

He told me about a friend of his whose mother was dying. It was a matter of days, hours, and he felt helpless, for his friend and for himself. He kept thinking of his own mother and how he would feel if it was her.

"Wow. I can't believe I'm going on about this to you. I'm sorry. I just came home last night. I'm living up at school this summer, but I came home to see Mike, that's the guy.

"I was over there this morning and it broke my heart to see them like that. I mean, my family's close, but so are they. And that's the killer. It's just the three of them and now this…"

When we reached Sandy Point he stopped. He turned back toward Eastwind but before he left he said, "Thanks for listening Sara. I hope I see you around again. When you hear from Bobby tell him Brain's pain in the neck kid brother said 'way to go'."

I walked along Markison's Beach. The sun was beating down through a humid haze, groups of gulls lazed on the sand. The guards were setting up their stands, hauling down buoys, torpedoes, and first aid boxes. I stopped to talk to Jimmy and Joe at Main Beach. The surf hadn't died down and they were waiting for word on which flag to fly: red for no swimming, yellow for caution, or green for safe conditions. Mr. Markison wanted yellow, but the Guard Captain felt he should either close the beach or let them in, nobody paid any attention to a yellow flag. Jimmy and Joe were hoping for red, which would make their day slow, but easy.

Arnold Markison, business man didn't want red, because bathers would go over to Squan Beach. But Arnold Markison humanitarian, father and grandfather, wanted red so he wouldn't have to worry about anybody drowning on his beach. Yellow seemed the perfect solution to him, but he didn't like to question the advice of his head Guard, either.

By the time I headed for home, they still had not heard a decision. My mother was at the dining room table, so I ate breakfast with her and relayed the events of the morning. We laughed together about Stewart and Judy, and Clare's revelations about being too good for Steve. But when I told her the story of Roger Allen's friend her eyes darkened and I was sorry I mentioned it. Over the past year I sometimes caught a glimpse of a vulnerable, needy creature in my mother. It frightened me to see it, because it meant she had the same feelings and fears as I did and up until then she had known all the answers.

She had suffered many losses, both real ones, like her mother, and intangible ones, like her children growing up and moving away, and I felt bad about it but I was also resentful. Was I supposed to take care of her now? She wasn't done taking care of me yet. I felt cheated. And then I felt guilty.

I sometimes dealt with the guilt by picking a childish fight with her over some trivial issue, like money, clothes, or boys, or I would ignore her, or better yet just hate her. But every once in awhile we would slip into a state of suspension every mother and daughter cherish, where you accept that you are more alike than different. The daughter moves ahead and the mother falls back a bit, and you meet on a plane that only lasts a second in the big picture of your lives, but in those rare seconds, you dance in harmony with the best friend you can ever know.

I felt we could both use a friend that morning so I suggested she buy me some new school clothes and I would treat her to lunch. We went shopping on the mainland, then pulled into the Lobster House.

Clare greeted us at the door with a panicked look on her face. "Oh my God. Did you guys hear about Jimmy?" She loved melodrama and by the time she got the story out my mother needed a drink.

"Well. They put up the yellow flags, you know, even though everybody thought they should have closed the beach. So anyway, things were OK until about ten o'clock when some little kid got sucked out down at Water Street, and his mother went in after him, and then the father, and you know at ten half the guards are on break, so the Water Street guard went in without a line because he only saw the mother and figured he didn't need it. So Jimmy ran down from Main beach and took out the line, and Thank God Joe was just making out behind the stand, so he took off after Jimmy and they rounded up all five of them and the rest of the crew pulled them in safe and sound!"

I looked at my mother, her face slowly regaining color. "See what happens when I miss a day at the beach?" I said.

Clare went on, "And at about the same time they had a big save down in Eastwind, so the red flags are flying everywhere now." She checked her watch. "Well girls, you must excuse me. I have to go arrange some tables. We're expecting a busload of senior citizens in about twenty minutes."

Over our lobster salads we chatted about Clare, and about Jimmy's save, and my mother tried to quiz me about his relationship with Brenda. I was nonchalant. I thought they were getting serious but I wasn't going to be the informant. Then the conversation got around to Jason Kilmer.

"So, have you returned his calls yet Sara?" she asked over a shared slice of key lime pie.

"No Mother. And I don't intend to."

"Well you really shouldn't leave him hanging. I don't know why you aren't interested. He seems like such a nice boy."

I laughed. "Why don't parents realize it's the kiss of death to say that?"

She thought about it. "I see what you mean. Alright, you do what you want, I just think you should let him know one way or the other."

We went home, got changed and walked up to the beach. Jimmy and Brenda were walking arm in arm towards us from Water Street. He held up his hands when he saw us. "I'm fine. I'm fine. It was no big deal. OK?" But he held my mother's embrace just a little longer than he needed to.

The red flags were strictly enforced. No one was taking any chances, especially when news came that on a private beach just north of Squan Beach, a teenager and a lifeguard drowned in a failed rescue attempt around noon.

Mom went home, Jimmy went back to work and Brenda and I took a walk on the beach. We didn't talk much. I kept staring at the sea. It looked like the same old friend I'd always loved, but I couldn't help feeling differently about it now. Nine people had lost their lives. I knew they were accidents, but still...

I had humanized and romanticized the sea so much that I felt betrayed by it, like it was to blame, but when I began to wonder what reason the sea might have, anger, revenge, I realized I had gone too far. I didn't share my thoughts with Brenda.

We sat on the jetty rocks. The beach was a blur of colorful beach towels and umbrellas. A steady stream of boats sailed in and out of the inlet, the pavilion was bursting with families enjoying their candy and ice cream, and the south end of the boardwalk was a splash of brilliant colored canopies and arcades, bits of carnival music drifted in the breeze.

I lay back on a flat rock next to Brenda and whispered, "Do you smell that?"

She whispered back, "Smell what?"

"Summer," I said.

"How do you smell summer?" she asked.

"Close your eyes," I said. "I'll show you, and then you can do what I do. In the middle of winter when you're sitting in a classroom, you can imagine you're melting in the hot sun, listening to the water rush through the rocks and the train whistle in the distance, and you'll smell it. Summer: wet sand and clam shells, warm sweat and dried salty skin, with just a hint of greasy fries and cotton candy."

"Mmmmm," Brenda muttered.

"Jimmy drove me down here once last winter and I brought a tube of Coppertone and I walked out and stood on the beach, closed my eyes and breathed it in, and it was like I could open my eyes and it was summer."

Brenda sat up. "You're crazy, do you know that girl?"

"I was afraid you might think that," I said.

"Listen. Big beach party tonight. Right here on Inlet. Sherry's coming down, so we'll meet you."

Sherry picked me up after work and filled me in on a new guy she met at home. We were sitting on the jetty drinking our first beer by nine thirty. Clare and Steve were sitting off by themselves, I couldn't tell if they were making out or arguing. Joe and his latest girlfriend came over and sat with us. He said Jimmy and Brenda had made a rare appearance, and then left.

"Boy, Jim and I were pretty shaken up today. I guess he told you all about it," Joe said.

Actually he hadn't talked about it at all. "Yeah," I said and nodded my head knowingly.

"Hey, what's with your buddy Clare? She's totally gone you know. You just missed a huge scene."

The girl with him snorted, "Scene? More like a temper tantrum if you ask me."

"Well...Who asked you?" Sherry got in her face.

The girl took Joe's hand. "Come on Joey. Let's get out of here."

Joe winked at us, "Whatever you say dear."

Sherry turned to me. "So what is up with Clare?"

I shrugged my shoulders. "Who knows. I can't figure her out. Let's get another beer."

The night had clouded over with no moon to light the landscape. One group of kids was sitting on the jetty, another in a circle growing out from the metal basin holding the ever present keg. On our way around to fill our cups someone leaned out of the circle and into my path. I stumbled on top of Stewart.

He pulled me onto his lap. Sherry laughed and kept walking. Stewart was smashed. And obviously alone, or he wouldn't have pulled that stunt.

"Sara. Where have you been? I've been waiting for you," he slurred. I could only laugh. He pulled me closer. "I'm serious Sara. I have been waiting for you my whole life. But you appeared too late. Why Sara? I want to know why?" His voice raised to an embarrassing level.

I whispered in his ear, "Stewart if you don't shut up..."

He pulled me closer, searched for my mouth and planted a sweet kiss that I didn't want to stop. Something about what he said, his arms wrapped around me, I didn't think about it, I didn't want to think about it, I just wanted to keep kissing him and being kissed, and the next thing I knew we were lying on the sand kissing and groping and I wanted it to go on forever.

When we came up for air he propped his head up on his arm, and I realized he wasn't that drunk. I figured he'd pass out or throw up but he seemed eerily sober as he looked at me with those piercing blue eyes and said, "I meant what I said Sara."

I had no idea how to respond to that, so I said, "Yeah, right. You loved me ever since you laid eyes on me, and you're stringing Judy along to make me jealous, I know." As soon as I said it I felt awful.

We sat up. "Boy am I a jerk or what? I don't know what I'm doing, Sara. I'm sorry. Want a beer? I'll be right back don't move."

I sat there, debating whether or not to leave. What was I waiting for? I liked Stewart as a friend, and I was screwing that up if I let anything else happen. But I had always liked him the other way too, and if this was my chance, why not?

He came back with two beers. A couple guys came over and asked him if he needed a ride home. I got the impression they were trying to save him from the bad girl, and it was exciting to think I was so dangerous. It felt even better when he turned them down cold.

He said, "So, you wanna go for a swim?"

"Very funny," I said.

We drank some more and talked about Jimmy's rescue, and how weird it was with all these people drowning. I almost told him what I thought about the sea being angry, but I didn't think he would understand either. Sherry walked past and reminded me how late it was. I stood up to leave.

Stewart pulled me back down. "Can't you stay a little longer? I'll walk you home," he said.

"Oh, how cute," Sherry cooed. "Guess I'll see you later."

We drank and talked and made out until everyone else left. Then we stumbled arm in arm up the beach. The deserted boardwalk seemed insanely romantic in the still midnight air as we giggled and snuggled, unable to keep our hands off each other. When we reached the bungalow Stewart gently pushed me up against the wall of the shed and we started where we had left off on the beach.

A noise inside startled us and we reluctantly parted. I watched from the window as he skipped down the row, kicking up stones and whistling like a happy little boy. I fell asleep that night wondering if that was what love was like.

The next morning I opened my eyes to a dull headache and Sherry and Clare stretched out on the bed across the room. Clare was sound asleep and Sherry was quietly flipping through a magazine. She didn't look up as she spoke. "So, now, tell us again how Stewart doesn't like you. And then tell us how you don't like him. And don't even try the drunk routine, because when you two first started slobbering all over each other you hadn't even had your second beer."

Clare stirred slightly. I propped my pillows up behind me. This was new. I wasn't usually the one telling, I was usually listening. I hesitated, not sure I wanted to tell because I knew the second I opened my mouth the magic of the previous evening would be analyzed and picked apart and that incredible elixir I was savoring would lose its power and dissolve.

I stretched. My lips felt sore. Was that possible? I giggled.

Sherry looked up. "Well? We're waiting Sara."

"What's there to tell?" I asked innocently.

Clare lifted her head and feebly tossed her pillow over at me. "Come on Sara. Give it up. I missed the whole thing and I need to know what the hell happened!"

Sherry said, "Yeah. I want to hear what's up with you too, you lunatic. But first we must get details on the latest romance, correction the only romance of our little Sara."

"Well, alright. Let's see. Stewart confessed his true love for me and we made out a bit and, well what more is there to say?" I smiled at them.

Sherry threw her magazine on the floor. "Made out a bit? I thought you were going to give up your virginity right there beside the keg for God's sakes!"

Clare sat up. "Oh my God, Sara. Really? And I missed it. I can't believe it."

"You see, I never should have said anything. Now you're making it seem like it was awful or something. It was no big deal Sherry." I was beginning to feel sick.

Sherry softened. "Oh come on Sara. You know I'm exaggerating. Really. Probably nobody noticed but me..." She barely stifled her laughter.

Clare came over and snuggled under the covers with me. "Never mind her, dear. She doesn't understand. We'll have a nice talk later. After I sleep for about three more hours."

Sherry stood up and studied her reflection in the dresser mirror. "Well, it's a beautiful day and I don't know about you two losers but I need to work on my tan. It's August one and I'm still white. The least you could do is come with me. You can sleep on the beach Clare, I'll rent you an umbrella." She ruffled through my drawer, grabbed two bathing suits and threw them at us. "Here. Get dressed. We're going."

"So much for savoring my sweet love hang over," I mumbled as I got dressed.

We got Brenda, packed lunch, magazines, a radio, and chairs. We rented an umbrella, set up camp on the inlet beach and passed the morning as usual; soaking up sun, swapping love stories and secrets and admiring the scenery.

It was a clear August day. A thunderstorm had kicked up during the night and swept away the humidity, leaving an enormous deep blue sky spread out over the sea, clouded here and there with huge puffs of pure white cotton. A southeast breeze blew in over an ocean showing its muscle, strong and steady waves pounded the shore. Red flags flew unquestioned.

Clare slept under the umbrella all morning. I dozed in and out reliving the night before, my skin still tingling when I recalled Stewart's touch. Jimmy came and ate lunch with Brenda, Joe wandered over for a soda, other people drifted in and out of my dreams along with the music of surf and sea gulls.

Into that trance-like state Sherry whispered close to my ear. She startled me, and what she said sent an alarm that paralyzed me. My stillness surprised her and she repeated vehemently, "Did you hear me, Sara? Stewart is coming…He's about twenty yards away…you better get up and brush your hair or fix your face or something!"

I sat up quickly, grabbed a brush and gave my hair a swipe, wiped the sleep from my eyes, turned around and there he was. Walking down the beach all alone, windblown hair, looking sort of shy, yet ever confident, and so totally cute that I wanted to run over and hug him.

Of course I didn't. After checking him out I looked away and pretended I didn't see him, begging Sherry with my eyes to talk to me about something, anything, so I wouldn't have to think about what to do when he came over.

Clare woke up just in time to help me out. She picked up her head and called out, "Hey Stewart. Where's Steve?"

I think she saved him too. He seemed relieved to have some solid ground to start on. He held up his hand. "Hi guys," he said. "Steve told me to tell you he had to go to work. He'll call you later." He sat down next to me. I didn't move.

Clare said, "Well, how do you like that? Is he really working?"

Sherry stood up. "Didn't you ever hear that saying about shooting the messenger Clare? Come down to the water with me and splash some water on your face. You look like crap."

I silently cursed Sherry. With them gone, it was only Jimmy, Joe and Brenda engrossed in a card game on her blanket, and me and Stewart sitting awkwardly on mine.

He said, "Hey, did you hear that storm last night?"

"No. I missed it. Guess I was asleep. It must have been awesome."

"Yeah, it was. Especially when it came crashing down on my head while I hiked it on foot all the way home."

I laughed. The ice was broken. Stewart was still Stewart, except now I found it hard not to reach over and touch his smooth tan skin. He leaned back on one elbow so I had to turn to face him. The sun shone directly into his eyes and made them glisten like sapphires, casting their spell over me.

He squinted and said, "I didn't really mind the storm though. It was really cool, and besides, I had something to keep me warm." He smiled, and my heart jumped.

I smiled back, leaned closer and said, "Funny, I had the same feeling all night long."

He looked serious for a second, then stood up and reached for my hand. "I need to talk to you. Want to go for a walk?"

My heart was racing, but I answered calmly, "Sure," and took his hand.

I replayed the next few minutes over and over again for days, wondering if I could somehow have avoided what happened next. But I couldn't.

Stewart was gently holding my hand, after pulling me up he had not let go, an important detail I clung to. Sherry and Clare had come back, but their stares were fixed on something behind me, and before I could turn a voice called out my name. It seemed to come from very far away yet it was near, and in the same instant that I couldn't place it I knew exactly who it belonged to. I thought maybe if I didn't turn around it would go away. But then it spoke again, nearer, and I knew I had to respond since everyone was waiting for me and wondering what I was waiting for.

"Sara. There you are!"

Stewart's hand dropped away and I turned to face Jason Kilmer, my boyfriend from home who never got the word that he was no longer my boyfriend. And the first thought racing through my head was that my mother was right.

I might have saved the situation somehow if Jimmy, who had been oblivious to the Stewart scenario, hadn't recognized Jason, jumped up and shouted, "Well, look who it is, Sara's boyfriend Jason!"

I was speechless. Jimmy shook hands with Jason and his friend and introduced them to the group. I couldn't look at Stewart. All I could see was Jason and how out of place he looked. It wasn't any one thing in particular, he was just so...city.

He had day person written all over him and I despised him for being there. His skin was white as his t-shirt, I only hoped he kept it on because I knew his chest would be even whiter. I was embarrassed to stand next to him let alone have everyone think he was my boyfriend. I couldn't bear to look at Stewart.

Jimmy was looking at me quizzically. "Sara...Hello!"

As I opened my mouth to speak I heard Stewart say, "Well. I gotta go. See you later!"

I didn't turn around. I knew he wasn't waiting for me, and I didn't want to watch him go with the sun on his brown skin, walking away from me for good.

So I was left with Jason Kilmer, city boy who intended to spend the day and night thanks to my wonderful mother's invitation when he had appeared at the door of the bungalow.

He mistook my devastation for surprise. And I had to play along. Suppose Stewart had wanted to talk to me about how he really loved Judy and I was just a fling and he was sorry? Could I have run off with him and left Jason standing there only to find that out. In my heart I knew that wasn't Stewart's intention, but hearts can be mistaken, and if he wanted to tell me that Judy was history and I was the one, couldn't that conversation still happen? I hoped so, but I knew it never would.

As the day and evening wore on I continued the charade of enjoying entertaining Jason and his friend.

And Jason wasn't that bad. He was cute, in his own way, and smart and funny, and all that, he just didn't belong here. I avoided being alone with him, made Sherry come everywhere with us and when they left the next day I was totally confused.

Sherry was full of advice about not burning bridges. "Summer's almost over Sara, and even if you get together with Stewart, you'll be going home soon. He'll be here, and Judy will be here...Is he really worth the hassel? Jason on the other hand, is only attached to you, and you know what? There's ten months in the winter girl and only two in the summer. Maybe you should start thinking about that. What do you do all winter anyway? Dream of summer and what goes on here?"

"Pretty much," I moaned.

Sherry was in my room watching me get ready for work. "Is Stewart working tonight?" she asked.

"I'm not sure. I don't think so," I said. "I hope not. I don't know what I'll say to him. I feel like such a fool."

"You are not the fool, Sara. But you could wind up being one if you aren't careful. I never liked this Stewart deal anyway. It's not easy being the other woman, you know. And honestly, I don't think he'll ever give up Judy. Maybe for awhile but it would be a constant threat, and,"

I interrupted her, "OK! OK! I get the picture. Enough already. I'm late for work."

When I got to work Clare told me Stewart was not coming in because he and Judy were celebrating their fourth anniversary and they had reserved a table for eight o'clock. She also relayed a sketchy story Steve told her about Stewart and Judy having a big fight after the beach party and they called it quits but then Judy sank her teeth back into him big time. And then, true friend that she was, Clare closed my station at seven so I didn't have to watch the romantic celebration.

The next time I saw Stewart I was walking in to work and he and Judy were making out on a milk crate outside the kitchen door. Stewart mumbled hello, Judy ignored me as usual, but over the course of the shift we got past our awkwardness and wound up somewhere between strangers and friends.

It bothered me, but not enough to take Clare's advice and demand that we talk it out. I was content to let it be. I couldn't shake off that garbage Sherry said about living for the summer. And I wondered if Stewart and I got together, would he fit into my life at home or would he seem as out of place there as Jason had here? And where did that leave me? Unable of having a relationship in either place? Caught in limbo between two worlds?

Jason wrote to thank me for a terrific time and asked if he could come down again before summer was over. My acting abilities amazed me. I considered myself shy yet I was giving Oscar performances without even knowing it. He sent my mother a separate thank you note which impressed her to no end.

I wrote back and told him two lies, one that I had a great time too, and two that I was going to visit my sister for awhile. I knew that was a gamble. He'd probably come down and visit my mother and I'd get caught, but it was an easy way out.

Every summer for as long as I could remember, August heralded the peak of summer and with July's momentum close behind it a race ensued at breakneck speed to the bitter season's end. That summer was no exception. I wanted to freeze each moment before it slipped past.

I lay on my bed and listened harder to the rhythm of the breaking waves, singled out the sea gull's cries, memorized the pulse of the foghorn in the middle of the night. I took long walks on the beach, breathing in the sea air, spent hours sitting on the jetty.

I rode my bike around the island in the early light of daybreak and again in the setting sun of dusk, snapping mental photos to treasure. I was alone most of the time, and I welcomed the solitude. Clare and Steve were anticipating the end of summer and the end of their romance. They both knew what would happen when they went back to school, so they spent every minute together.

Brenda and Jimmy were in the same boat, though I was sure they would still be together by Christmas. And Sherry had fallen in love. She brought him down once, and proved to me that you can make one relationship work in both worlds. He fit right in. The difference was that he fit in because she wanted him to. Her explanation was that if you found the right guy, it didn't matter where you were, you would fit anywhere. It made sense, but I wasn't convinced.

By Labor Day weekend, I had, as I did every year, resigned myself to leaving. But this year was different as I began to realize life was too short to live in only one season. I was determined to enjoy my senior year of high school.

Steve left for school on Friday. I was surprised Clare didn't cause a huge scene, but all weekend she seemed strangely quiet, like a bomb waiting to explode.

Early Saturday morning we drove down to Eastwind. Clare crashed on the beach and I took a walk.

I passed a house I always liked, tucked between two sand dunes like a buried treasure chest. There was a lawn and garden in the side yard and I could tell it was not just for summer. I never saw anyone but there were always signs life; upstairs windows ajar, curtains blowing in the breeze, clothes on the line, beach towels on the railing, a surfboard laying at the bottom of the steps.

They were getting ready for a yard sale. Two men hauled out furniture, women carried suitcases and boxes of old toys, and arranged them on tables in the driveway. Curiosity got the best of me. I followed a path that led around the north side of the house. It was the kind of sale my mother would love, I made a note to tell her about it.

The people in charge didn't seem to be the owners. One of the women fussed with a bookcase and I overheard her whisper, "I don't know what will become of them." And the other woman shook her head slowly and replied, "So sad, so sad."

Sudden visions of Mrs. Jameson gave me chills and I decided to leave. On my way out a jewelry box caught my eye. It was out of place, everything else was impersonal, as if the box was an oversight.

There wasn't much in it; trinkets and costume jewelry. I fingered the pieces and wondered about the tale hidden in this house. My hand caught on a pile of tiny clam shells and I pulled them out. They were threaded on a strand of white yarn, clearly the product of hours of toil by some determined young child. When I held it up to the sun a large chunk of blue sea glass in the center weighted the necklace down so that it fell into a graceful V. It was fascinating. Each shell had a tiny hole punched in the top, I had crafted similar strands myself but the sea glass was the prize that made the necklace unique. Blues are rare but a blue that size with a natural hole in the center was a real find.

"That's not for sale, miss. I'm sorry," one of the women reached to take it from me.

But a man's voice spoke softly behind us. "No, don't. It's alright." He motioned the woman away.

I saw his story in the sorrow in his eyes, that he lost the woman whose necklace I held, that she had been his treasure, and the child's too, and the depth of his grief frightened me and made me want to run as far away from him as I could.

Our eyes locked and he seemed to sense my fear. He willed away the sorrow and the haunted gaze became one of gentle kindness as he smiled, took my outstretched hand, and closed it over the necklace.

"Take it please," and then he turned away.

My hands shook as I walked onto the beach, and ran into Roger Allen. He was heading toward the house I just left and it dawned on me that I knew the story all along.

He was surprised. "Sara! Hey...Do you know the Hankins?"

I hesitated. When I trusted my voice I said, "No. No. I didn't know..."

"What's wrong?" Roger asked.

"Nothing. I just...I was walking by and I saw the sale, but I didn't realize it was your friend...I'm sorry Roger."

I was glad he didn't understand since I felt like I had stooped to some lower life form, coveting dead people's precious possessions. I fingered the tiny shells deep in my pocket.

"Well, OK," Roger said. "I was just stopping by to say good-bye to Mike. I'm leaving tonight. You sure you're alright?"

"Yeah. See ya, around" I mumbled. I couldn't wait to get away. I looked back at the house just before it was out of sight and saw Roger, the man who gave me the necklace, and another figure sitting on the porch staring out to sea.

Clare ran over to meet me. "Sara! Where were you? I've been looking all over for you. I was just about to leave. Listen, some kid fell off the Sandy Point jetty late last night and there's a massive search for the body going on down there. Come on. Let's go!"

I followed her slowly. "Gee Clare. That sounds like something we really don't want to miss."

She was busy packing up our stuff. "What's wrong with you?" she asked.

"Nothing. I'm just not so keen on watching them pull some kid's body out of the ocean that's all."

"Well, actually Joe was just here and he was telling me if a body doesn't come up right away it usually stays under for three days. Gross, huh?"

"I'll say. What's this?" I asked, holding up an envelope with my name on it.

"Oh yeah. Stewart stopped down. He's on his way to school. He said to give it to you. Wasn't that sweet? He remembered your birthday was around now so I guess it's a card."

I stuffed it in my pocket with the necklace, marveling at the odd collection in there.

This drowning brought the total number of victims to ten. The papers were full of the story. The little boy came down from the city with his father to go fishing. Neither one of them could swim, but they had no intention of going swimming. The boy fell off the jetty and his father tried to pull him out but the current carried him away. The distraught father could barely speak English. The state police drove him home that evening to somehow explain to the child's mother why her little boy was not with them.

I was surrounded by sorrow. Everywhere I turned someone was grieving, dying, or leaving. The end of summer lurked like the bloated dead body floating out in my ocean, waiting to surface at any second. The sea itself turned calm and enticing, familiar, warm September surf.

My last two days at Sandy Point, I was reluctant to even set foot on the beach. I wouldn't go near the ocean. The body had not surfaced and I knew I would be the unfortunate one to find myself swimming next to poor Alfredo's lifeless remains. I was no longer concerned who the sea was angry at, I was angry at the sea. Why did this happen? I thought I had come to terms with death, I just didn't think it would wait for me at every turn.

I moped around the house, helped my mother clean and pack. I didn't toss my clothes resentfully into the footlocker like I usually did, I took time to neatly fold and arrange everything. I carefully wrapped the necklace in tissue paper and placed it in my jewelry box. I left the envelope from Stewart on my bed, worked around it, avoiding it. I was sure it would simply be one more good-bye, another sad ending, and I didn't think I could bear it. I dressed for work, my last shift, then sat on the bed and opened it. It was a birthday card, with a cuddly bear on the front. Harmless enough. But when I saw his note on the back I cried over and over, reading the words again and again until I knew them by heart and still could make no sense of them or why I could not stop my tears.

He said he was sorry, that he cared for me but he was committed to Judy. I wasn't surprised, or disappointed. I felt sad, strangely relieved, and mostly grateful to him for naming it, dealing with it.

Clare worked her last shift Saturday night too, but she left early and told me to meet her at Markison's Main Pavilion for their end of the year party.

I hitched a ride with another waitress. Clare wasn't around, so I drank a couple of beers with some Lobster House people and we reminisced about all the lunatic customers we had, like the regulars who come in every week and still insist desert came with the dinner the week before, and the guy who comes in once a month, orders a three pound lobster, eats it like an animal with melted butter dripping from his chin and leaves a two dollar tip no matter what the bill comes out to, and the kid who came in every Saturday night with his girlfriend, flashing a new fake I.D. and tried to order a bottle of Dom Perignon.

My gloomy mood was lifting higher with each beer and I was just starting to have fun when Clare burst through the Pavilion doors. She was arm in arm with a friend of Steve's which was bad enough, but the minute she opened her mouth I knew I had stayed five minutes too long.

One of the cooks commented, "Well if it isn't Tropical Storm Clare."

I mumbled, "Looks like she's been upgraded to a hurricane."

She was smashed. She saw me and staggering across the room, dragging her friend along. "Sara! You're finally here! Come and meet Tim..." She lost Tim's arm and he bounced backwards on the wooden floor and stayed there. She laughed so hard she lost her balance and joined him on the floor. I got her to her feet and dragged her to the door.

We headed down the boardwalk arms linked, and started laughing like two kids returning from a night on the rides. She turned somber halfway home and began mumbling incoherently about some secret and how sorry she was and how it wasn't her fault. I didn't pay any attention to her until she broke away, jumped off the boardwalk and ran screaming down the beach. I sprinted after her. All I could think of was she was going to jump in the ocean and I would have to go in after her, and with the thought of Alfredo still afloat I gained speed and caught her in the wash.

I dragged her back to dry sand and she spit out what I had completely forgotten, that the next day was the second anniversary of Chuck's death, and I felt bad that I hadn't remembered, and glad that was what was wrong with her, but there was more.

Her words sobered me up instantly and the more she said the more I felt like I'd been slapped in the face. She had known since the beginning of the summer that this would be her last one in Sandy Point. Her family was selling their bungalow, all the bungalows on Lenape Lane. But as awful as that was, it wasn't the worst, because what she said next meant that this had been the last of the kind of summers we had known and loved here all our lives, that Sandy Point was on the brink of enormous change and this was the end of it all.

She whispered, "I wanted to tell you Sara, but I was afraid. I'm sorry. I know how you feel..." She tightened her arm around my shoulder.

I bristled. How could she possibly know how I felt when I didn't? Emotions and ideas were piling up on top of themselves so fast I'd never sort them out. There was anger; a fury so deep and strong that I felt like lashing out at Clare, smashing her face deep into the sand to stop the words that kept spilling out of her mouth. Then disbelief. It wasn't real, it was a dream, a nightmare. Clare was lying, it was a pathetic grasp for attention, to be the star of the show, to know it all.

I played with the sand; built a castle with an elaborate wall around it as I had done as a child, hoping to protect it from the onslaught of a sea a billion times its size. Clare went on and on. I stopped listening, I was numb. What she said just couldn't be true; that Markisons had been sold to the same developer who had sought out and acquired the Jordan's property.

If that was true, a storm of destruction worse than any natural disaster had formed and was clearing a path straight to the doorstep of an old gray bungalow to wipe away a past and present I treasured, and the future I had wished for would be washed away in the gale.

She finally finished and we sat in silence staring out at the ominous water. When we stood to leave a wave broke and sent its eerie foam creeping up the shore, then another close behind it and the foam crawled faster, and then another, breaking down the wall, and then the castle too, crumbled and fell.

I slept late the next morning and avoided everyone, trying to forget it was my birthday. My parents knew something was wrong but were used to my end of summer blues. We had a silly celebration at the Lobster House and I tried to enjoy it. I kept looking for a clue that they knew what was happening, but they showed no signs of knowing. I went to bed early and cried myself to sleep.

Monday dawned like every other Labor Day, clear, cool fall breezes in a crisp blue sky signaling it was time to go. By ten the car was packed and ready. I walked through the house touching the cabinets and dresser tops, breathing in the salty cotton aroma of the curtains and cushions, rocked myself forlornly in Nana's chair.

My father called to ask if I was ready and I went out to the car. And then I walked right past him, like a ghost, my feet setting their own course up the row, onto the boardwalk, past the Pavilion and across the sand to the water's edge. The beach wasn't crowded, small groups of faithful sun worshippers sat in chairs, reading, playing cards, enjoying the last rays. Some kids were frolicking in the gentle surf, three or four guards were gathered in front of the stand, jackets on, laughing, ready to pack it in and shift gears to football and school.

I saw Joe talking to a guy I didn't know though there was something familiar about him. I walked toward them and the boy turned quickly and looked at me as if I had called out to him. Our eyes met and I thought I saw a flash of recognition in his startled green eyes. Beautiful green eyes, reflected in the sunlight and flecked with bits of blue sea and sky. He smiled at me. Then suddenly the calm scene was shattered by screams from the water. We all turned as the swimmers frantically clawed past each other to get out. Whistles blew, mothers jumped from their chairs, corralling and counting the fleeting children, huddling in a crowd on the shore.

There was a state of mass confusion, until the cause for alarm became crystal clear. And then there was silence, as what was left of the body of Alfredo rose on the crest of a wave in full view, its torn and mangled flesh hanging, then was tumbled in the wash and dragged back out again. Most of the onlookers turned away, only the morbidly curious able to watch.

The life guards were frozen, still as statues. Then the guy between me and Joe broke away. He shouted for somebody to call the Coast Guard, pulled off his t-shirt, grabbed the torp from the stand and ran into the water with a look of grim determination on his face. I couldn't stop watching as he put the body on the torp and swam out with it.

Joe sprang into action then, yanked the radio from the stand, made the call, barked orders to the dumbfounded guards to get the people away.

He looked at me. "Jesus Christ Sara...I can't even believe this."

I walked over to him. He kept his head down, trying not to look out at the body. "Jesus Christ Sara. Can you believe this?"

"It's OK Joe, it's OK," was all I could say.

"Holy shit, it's not OK. I should have gone in, not Mike. I can't believe he had to be in on this."

"Mike?" I asked.

Joe motioned with his head. "Out there. Mike Hankins. For Christ's sake, he was just taking a walk, and he had to get in on this."

"Mike Hankins," I said, as if I already knew.

"Guy just buried his mother for Christ's sake and now this," Joe paced furiously, shaking his head.

A Coast Guard cutter broke the Inlet and made the sharp turn, mercifully shutting off the grotesque view. In seconds it was gone again, racing back through the inlet, and taking with it all trace of Mike Hankins and the little boy, Alfredo.

CHAPTER SEVEN

Charley and I watched them pluck the surfer, the guards, and Fred from the water and leave.

I held Charley's hand tightly, too shaken to speak. Back at the house, I put the kettle on and took out a bottle of brandy. I asked Charley if he remembered that morning long ago, and he said he didn't. I was surprised Mike never told him, but then again Mike and I hadn't ever talked much about it either. I knew it was a traumatic experience for Mike, but supposed it was just another brave deed added to the list.

Charley's list was even longer, he'd had twenty-five more years to perform them, and you could never tell with Charley. He might have remembered it as clearly as I did and decided for one reason or another not to comment.

We warmed our hands around steaming mugs of tea. I offered Charley the brandy and we shared a silent toast, listening to the wind chime's frantic ringing on the porch and Harry scratching at the screen door. The air was raw, saturated with the approaching storm.

Charley took his mug to the sink and stared out the window deep in thought. He turned to me. "So, if you didn't meet Mike that morning, when did you meet him?"

"Why Charley, you romantic old fool. Didn't you ever hear the story?"

"I don't know. Humor me. Tell me again."

"Well maybe I will and maybe I won't. Perhaps I better write it down, eh?"

He jumped at that. "Now there you go. You're so busy pestering me to write my story and you've got one stashed away in that steel trap brain of yours that will probably die with you at this rate."

The words made me flinch. I knew he didn't intend them to be cruel. I stood quickly, refilled my mug, and started making sandwiches.

"You know, you're right. But I'd rather tell you the story and then you can write it down for me. Ha! Got you now smart ass!"

He groaned. "Go on, I'm listening."

"Well, that was Labor Day, so I went home and more or less forgot about the elusive Mike Hankins.

On Thanksgiving break Clare's parents were letting her come to Sandy Point for the weekend at their bungalow with some friends, as a last hurrah. Naturally I jumped at the opportunity to come down."

I paused with a buttered knife in my hand remembering clearly that bittersweet voyage across the bridge into Eastwind all by myself for the first time. I could picture it as if I'd done it the day before. A cloudy fall afternoon, air chilled and damp. Sandy Point was a ghost town; boardwalk rides dismantled,

117

arcades closed up tight, and rows and rows of silent desolate bungalows looking forlorn against the steel blue sky.

Charley cleared his throat. "Any time you want to serve that sandwich, I'm ready. And if I'm not mistaken, I think you were in the middle of a story?"

I served his sandwich, sat down and played with my own. "Well, I met up with Clare and her friends, and Steve came over and we got caught up with him. You knew him, right?"

Charley ate his sandwich, nodded, waved for me to go on.

"Steve told us the Allens were having a party. Thank God for the Allens, huh? Well, we girls had a few beers at Clare's then headed down to Eastwind. And it was the usual rowdy scene. But at some point I wandered into the kitchen, and saw Roger and Anna, sitting at the kitchen table with Mike."

The phone rang. "Oh, Roger......thank goodness. I'm glad you called. Yes, Charley's here, I'll tell him." I went back into the kitchen. "That was Roger. Fred's alright, the boy too. They're both shaken up, but everyone is fine."

Charley said, "Yeah. The boy's OK now but wait until his parents get slapped with a $500.00 fine for that little stunt. We'll be talking about this one at council meetings for a long time, you can bet on that."

"You know, I can't imagine how that issue will ever be resolved. As long as there are waves there will be surfers, and I believe it's their right to enjoy the ocean, but you can't stop someone like Fred from risking his life to save another, and what if they'd both been lost? All for a thrill of a ride on a six foot wave? If we'd been the only ones on the beach, I suspect it would have taken all my strength to stop your tired old bones from jumping into the wild surf to save that boy. So what's the solution?"

Charley took his plate to the sink. "I don't know. When you put it that way it seems some control is sensible, even necessary. But you know my feelings, the day any man stops another from enjoying that sea is the day any freedom worth having is gone."

"Well, I promise I won't go swimming today if you won't, deal?" I said.

He smiled. "Deal. Now I have to get back to the store."

"Hey! What about my story? I thought you were so interested."

"Sara, I know the story, believe me. But I do think you should write it down!" He went out the door then shouted back, "But first finish reading mine!"

I set the kitchen in order, let Harry in the front door, and stepped out onto the porch for a second, intending to go right back in and finish Charley's story. But the beauty of the advancing storm seized me and I sat down to acquaint myself with it, to see if my own rusty radar could foretell what kind of a tempest I would soon be facing.

I stopped listening to weathermen long ago. On my front porch I saw all I needed to know. The Eastwind sky was an enormous crystal ball, swirling with clues to the mysteries of the elements. A front moving in from the west, massive snow clouds brimming in the north, or high, feathery summer clouds floating like angel's wings over the sea, provided the only predictions I believed.

The southern sky was unmistakably threatening. Heavy, somber clouds mounted, descending over the sea inching closer and closer to the island. The southeast breeze was no longer a breeze but a steady, dominating force and the sea was responding with its own display of surging waves seven feet or better, cresting and tumbling onto the helpless shore. The hurricane was expected to hit at high tide and if it did it would be treacherous. But I was not afraid. What was there to fear? Death? Destruction?

Both were inevitable. I could flee the storm but I couldn't flee death. So why run? My home was the safest place, the only place I belonged, but I would have to be strong to stand my ground and stay. Some would try to make me leave. Like surfers willing to risk the ride others won't let them, they will risk their own lives to prevent them. Before I questioned their rights, now I was defending my right to do as I pleased, I just had to be sure no one would be put in harm's way trying to stop me.

And destruction? The fools on the island trying to protect themselves and their possessions amused me to no end. They were like children building walls of sand at the water's edge and like children, they believed their castles were safe.

I was resigned. My days of shuttering windows and filling bathtubs with fresh water were over. This house was built to withstand storms like the one bearing down on it. It was built by men who witnessed furious winds and seas, who knew the strongest winds blew from the north and the sea approached from the east, its waters flowing in the path of least resistance, no matter the tide or the height of the swells; the water simply must flow. That's why few windows looked out the north side of the house, and why the monstrous dune was allowed to build and grow and make its way around the northeast corner like a castle bastion.

They kept the frame low and solid, like a square box with a gradual curve in the hip roof, and no porch or step projecting very far from the frame as if just by keeping it all as close together as possible, a great gust of wind or a tower of foaming sea might skirt right past without even a glance at the simple structure nestled behind the ancient dune.

Nothing exposed to wind and sea is ever really secure, and luck plays a terrible game in severe storms. If a foundation is permeated by sand, and the sand is washed away by a destructive campaign of the sea, the wood and plaster will shake and shimmy under the simultaneous attack of the wind, and if luck isn't with you and the wind insists, and the sea doesn't flow past, the house will crumble from the inside out.

The men who built my house lived by the tale of Joshua Duncan, swept from his bed and washed into the town square. Luck rode with him but not his home.

They knew the day would come when its foundation would be tested again, and maybe that day was near.

I believed it to be safer than any of the supposedly "hurricane proof" monstrosities young architects bragged about. I scoffed at offers of "Disaster proofing" my home with insurance policies and devices ranging from the practical to the ludicrous. My house had been tested and passed, time and time again. Its very existence was the only proof I needed.

I asked myself a question I had posed many times over the years when facing dilemmas, "What would Mike do?" And the answer was obvious. He would stay. But if I rephrased it more accurately to, "What would Mike want me to do?" the answer wasn't so apparent, so I pushed the second question away.

I rocked and dozed and my thoughts wandered, and I worried, as I often did, if this was what it was like to go mad. But unlike other daydreams where whims and speculation drifted aimlessly in my head, these notions took shape, and became as crystal clear to me as if the storm clouds vanished into a stunning blue sky.

If I was staying I had to make a plan and I had to be very sure my plan would work. But there was more, I had to face something else first. Charley's beautiful family history, his advice the day before, and his earlier comment haunted me. I realized he was right. There were unspoken words and unresolved feelings I had avoided for too long. I couldn't let my story die with me. I had to tell it and hope that in the process the slate would be wiped clean and we could somehow start over.

I would write my story for Mary, and begin it with Mike. The grandfather she never knew. If I didn't tell her who would? Had John spoken of him, or me, in the past ten years? It didn't matter anyway. He couldn't tell my story, only I could do that.

My life on Eastwind did not begin the night I happened into Roger Allen's kitchen, but I often wondered if I hadn't walked in then, how different my life might have been. Would I have met Mike some other way? Our paths had crossed before, but who knows? I might have wound up with Jason what's his name, sweltering in the city for the rest of my life, visiting the island as a goofy day person.

I would begin with the moment our eyes met across that scratched and dented wooden table in the Allen's kitchen. The table was still there, I would tell her that too. I would tell her how Roger stood when I came in, and pulled out the chair across from Mike, and how I couldn't think of a thing to say to this handsome fellow who gazed at me with curious, warm green eyes.

I'll tell her how sweet he was. How he tried to make conversation and I avoided looking in his eyes so he wouldn't see that I already knew more about him than he thought.

All I could think about was his mother and the necklace, but my inhibition was no match for his irresistible charm; he smiled and joked and wore me down until the sad images melted away in his sweet green eyes and I was talking and laughing and falling in love.

I would tell her how we stayed after the party died, and sat among the empty beer cans, smelly pizza boxes, and passed out bodies, in the lingering scent of smoke and salty air and everything felt so right I wished the dawn would never come.

We talked for hours. I told him about my summers in about Sandy Point. I told him about Clare, who had left with her friends hours ago. He walked me home along the beach. On the dark stretch of sand we both knew so well he erased my uneasiness by telling me about his mom, how she got sick in the winter and the cancer she had progressed rapidly until there was nothing left of her by summer. He was thankful that he had time to spend with her, that he had the chance to say good-bye. As I listened it felt like he had walked beside me forever.

I toyed with a key in my pocket. I had secretly taken the key to my bungalow from the hook in the hallway at home. Just in case…This was it, the just in case…In case I needed a place to go, it was there waiting, but part of me was hesitant…As well as I felt I knew him, I had in fact, just met him. Did I really want to take him there? On the other hand did I want to take him back to Clare's either?

When we reached the jetty I hadn't made up my mind, but I learned a lot about Michael Hankins. He should have been starting his senior year at college, but he took the semester off after his mother died. He was flying south to meet his Dad the next morning to size up a new location for the family business. He said they built boats, like it was no big deal. But I knew all about the Hankins Boatworks, it was a huge operation down by the lighthouse. I hadn't put the name together before but I knew the Hankins' men and the boats they built were legendary. He explained that the main reason for the move was his Dad needed to make a break from Eastwind and all the memories it held. It wasn't until he said their house was for sale that I realized how final his plans were.

We walked up to the boardwalk and sat on a bench looking over the inlet, suddenly silent with our own thoughts. I put my hands in my pockets, he tossed a shell from one hand to the other. Finally he said, "You know, I've loved this sea my whole life, but last summer with all those people drowning I started hating it, and then when my mom died I hated it more, like I blamed it or something, and suddenly I wanted no part of it…how nuts is that?"

I smiled in the dark, watching the moonlit water flow slowly through the shadowy channel and then I looked into his sea green eyes expecting him to disappear into the dream I knew this must be.

121

He didn't disappear. He reached down and took my hand and said, "But now I don't feel like going anywhere." And then he spoke the wish I'd made a million times in this same spot. He brushed the hair from my eyes and whispered, "I wish I could sit here like this with you, forever."

The bungalow was cold and dark, but we were warmed with the tenderness of young love. I hoped Mary would believe her grandfather had been a perfect gentleman. It would most likely seem impossible to her, a woman of this new age, but it was true. When the sun woke us at dawn we were fully clothed but entwined in each other's arms and hearts more intimately than a couple who spent the night in the throes of realized passion.

It seemed so simple then, as I rocked in my chair watching the clouds gather and form, feeling the wind strengthen and moan, that I must write this for Mary now. I went to my desk, took out paper and began writing.

I had to introduce myself to my granddaughter. We had once been so close, and then so far apart. Ten years worth of Birthday cards, graduation cards and gifts were shuffled back and forth across the expanse between us; I had acknowledged each and every milestone and she had dutifully acknowledged my acknowledgements, but it was just an imaginary game we played.

I wouldn't try to justify mistakes of the past ten years, because what was done was done. I wasn't foolish enough to think words scribbled on paper could undo the damage. Yet I had to try. Running away had caused nothing but heartache. Maybe by facing it I could finally retrieve my uncertain soul.

If I succeeded then as Mary read this she would know me again, the me she would have gradually come to know, in a perfect world. And maybe it would help her know who she was. Perhaps she had already begun to search and didn't know where to look. She was twenty, a young woman. Had she fallen in love, for the first time, for the last time? Maybe she would recognize a little bit of herself in me, and that would be the miracle that would make it all worthwhile. Or she might toss the whole thing aside like a dirty dishrag, an old fool's desperate attempt to win her back. But somehow I didn't believe that would be her reaction.

I took a break and brewed a pot of tea. Wet wind whipped against the screens. The sky was ready to burst. My hands shook. I realized I hadn't eaten since lunch and it was near dinner. But something besides hunger was unnerving me. Now that I had delved below the anger, a new emotion surfaced and overpowered me, guilt. In all the years of anguish over my situation I had never fully considered or admitted that my actions, or lack of action, had kept the treasure I always cherished nearest to my heart out of Mary's grasp; family.

My family was as vivid a presence in my eighty year old heart as they were when I was twenty. I always knew where and from whom I had come. I looked in the mirror and saw my mother's eyes, heard the voice of Nana's wisdom, gained strength and comfort from my father's kind ways long after they had left my side. I had taken all of that away from Mary.

I wrote with a new sense of urgency, channeling my anger at myself into making sense of it all, for her as well as for me. The phone rang, I didn't answer it. My stomach growled, I ignored it. I needed to go on, fight the urge to make an excuse to stop, to second guess if it was the right thing to do. I wrote about the rest of that first weekend, how the next morning we woke up and went over to Clare's and how they made such a fuss over my handsome catch I couldn't wait to get him out of there. Then I told her how we got near his house and his mood abruptly changed and I didn't understand why. I kept trying to make him laugh and then he told me he didn't even have a key. The realtors had them and he was sorry he couldn't take me inside.

I went up onto the porch and there were two rocking chairs in the corner leaned up against the house, so I dragged them out and sat down. I leaned back and rocked slowly, and after awhile he came over and sat beside me, as I hoped he would.

I asked Mary if she remembered rocking on the porch and I told her those same chairs were still there, the ones her great grandmother and grandfather had rocked in, and Mike and I, and her father and I and she and I, and that maybe someday she could come and rock her babies in those chairs too. Yes, I had to make that clear, that she was always welcome here.

I put a pan of soup on the stove to simmer. The phone rang again, and this time I answered though I immediately regretted it, which caused me to hesitate with the phone at my ear for just an instant, and suck my breath in instead of out with the anticipated hello, as if I could still refuse the call.

That caused the person on the other end to speak first, and so the usually smooth voice of my son David, came through a bit disconcerted as he said, "Hello?" And then I thought that in those seconds of blank air time he had forgotten who he called, and my annoyance at that nearly caused me to slam the phone in his ear. Again I chided myself for answering it at all.

I didn't want to be annoyed at David, because then our conversation might wander in a dangerous direction and I would lose my resolve to finish my letter to Mary in the tenuous frame of mind I had found.

"Yes. Halo," I spoke in a convoluted southern drawl, both amazed and alarmed at my nerve and my invention, as I went on to tell my son that his mother had gone inland to sit out the storm with an old friend. "Clare?" he asked. Yes, I told him, I was pretty sure that was the name, but no, she hadn't left the number.

"And you are?" he asked.

"Miz LaJoy," I drawled. "I come in once a week now to help your Mama with the chores, didn't she tell you 'bout me?"

He paused, and I thought he was on to me.   I waited for the...what?...scolding...what does one say to one's eighty year old mother who misbehaves in this manner?

But no angry words came. His voice actually softened and he said, "Well, alright...Tell her I called. I've been trying to get a hold of her since yesterday. But I'm glad she's safe."

I spoke slowly so my voice wouldn't falter. "Oh, you don't have to worry about her."

He perked up then, the charm resurfaced. "Now how about you Miz LaJoy? Hadn't you better be getting out of there soon? By this time tomorrow nobody will care if you dusted that mantle when it's floating down the Squan River."

It was so typical, really. The range of emotions my children could bring out in me. This was precisely why I found it so difficult to talk to them. First he made me feel sorry for him, and then the zinger. What would he care if this whole house was washed out to sea? Not much apparently. As long as he knew I won't be tethered to the mantle, floating down the river. It doesn't seem to occur to him that without this house, and the life I have made for myself that revolves around these walls, meager though it may seem to him, that I would never be safe. It's all I have. What would be left for me without it? Where would I go? And what about the house, and all its history? Is that all it means to him now, that a casual comment about its destruction could roll off his tongue as easily as his middle name?

"Miz LaJoy? You still there?" he asked.

I cleared my throat, swallowed hard. "Yes, dear. I'm here, but I'd better be going, I'll tell your mama you called. Bye now." I hung up the phone quickly and once again reached behind the table and yanked out the cord.

I stirred my soup simmering in the pan, wondering how this had come to pass. That I would lie to my son to avoid speaking to him. It was ironic. Maybe I was really the selfish one. I wanted to be left alone, only I didn't want anyone to want to leave me alone. Maybe their whole lives they had been trying to figure me out and the only thing that rang true was that one thing, she wants to be left alone.

Young mothers utter those words in frustration, until, in the blink of an eye, they are left alone, and then they don't like it, and they complain, why don't they come, why don't they call?

The wind howled as evening fell. I probably should get the shutters up, but if this storm was what everyone expected it to be, what were those old boards going to prevent? Aside from the obvious answer of thirty broken windows, not much, but the shutters were probably the only precaution I should take.

I ate my supper and tidied the sink, swept the floor, and fed the cat talking to myself the entire time. I had been trying unsuccessfully to keep David out of my mind since his call. I could let it go, but he might just phone Clare, find I wasn't there, and then all hell would break loose.

I sat at my desk, eyed Charley's manuscript sitting next to the unfinished letter. "This is something," I said. "For ten years I haven't had a single pressing thing to do and suddenly I need to find a place to go and not really go there but convince everyone else that I've gone, finish reading this story and give it the full attention it requires, and write the most important and longest overdue letter of my life, and I must do it all as soon as possible."

I plugged the phone back in and dialed Clare's number and the second she heard my voice she started in, "Where in heaven's name, are you?...Did you disconnect your phone?...Are you coming?...Well it's too late...I'm going up to the city...I'm not waiting around for you..." I listened, smiling. My plan was inventing itself.

"Clare. Clare! Listen for a minute would you????" I shouted over her tirade.

"What?" she gasped.

"It's OK. Leave your key at the desk and I'll let myself in. I'll be fine. It's just for the night, I'm sure the storm will pass and I'll be back on Monday to sweep a little sand out of the garage."

She hesitated. "Oh. Are you sure you'll be alright? Because I could wait if you'll come right now, and we can leave together."

"No. I'm fine tonight, really, you go ahead," I said.

"Well, ok then," she hesitated. "You're not bringing that vile animal are you?"

I chuckled. "No, Clare, I wouldn't dare unleash my wild beast on your carpets. I'll ask Charley to keep him for me."

I marveled at the simplicity of it. I should have known it would be easy for me to vanish when for all intents and purposes I had disappeared a long time ago. But I had to be absolutely certain that the few souls who would miss me wouldn't be tempted to perform any daring rescues or twelfth hour heroics.

I dialed Charley's number. He wasn't home so I left a message saying I was settling in to finish his story. I told him again how much I liked it, and then added that it was getting a tad too windy for comfort so I had made arrangements to stay with Clare tomorrow night. I knew he wouldn't believe a word of it, that he would be the hardest to convince, and that I would have to give the performance of my life in the morning when he came over to see for himself what I was up to.

I dialed David's number and his machine picked up: "Hey. David Hankins here. Well, not here now or you'd be talking to me...So leave a message and I'll get back to you. Thanks."

I hung up before the beep. Not because I changed my mind, but because a message wouldn't do. I needed to actually speak to him.

I dialed his office number only to receive another message, this one in David's professional voice: "Thank you for calling Hankins Boatworks. We can't take your call right now, but leave your name and number and we'll get back to you within the hour. That's right, within the hour…without fail!"

I couldn't help but smile at his enthusiasm. Even at the age of fifty-two his positive energy came through the wire. A happy little boy, typical second born, free of the inhibitions imposed on the first. My two sons were so alike physically; images of Mike with his slight yet sturdy build, his light brown hair and warm green eyes. But they had opposite personalities.

David was an artist, an athlete, and an entrepreneur since the age of five when he took pictures he painted at home to school in his back pack to sell to his classmates. He rode his first wave on his father's back when he was six months old and from then on lived to surf and sail.

David was seventeen when Mike died and he grieved by rebelling against everything he had ever loved, including me. For three years I didn't know if he was dead or alive for months at a time. He hitchhiked back and forth across the country like a wandering spirit, never reaching either coast, then ended his trek with a hesitant knock on my back door one summer morning.

He embraced me and tiptoed through the house like a ghost in a trance, then he grabbed his board and ran into the sea. He frolicked in the clear blue water like a man reborn. He settled down for awhile then, but everywhere he turned he saw his father. Everyone assumed he would follow in Mike's footsteps, and that overwhelmed him. He admired and respected his father and grandfather, but felt he could never measure up to them. I tried to convince him he didn't need to, he just needed to be himself, and the rest would follow, but he was miserable.

When I met Mike, his plan was to finish school down south and make his home there. But sometime during that thanksgiving weekend he changed his mind. I loved to hear Charley tell the boys how I came along and reminded their Dad how much he loved this island, and that I was responsible for keeping Mike here, where he belonged.

Mike and his father made new arrangements, for Mike to finish school up here, and they kept the boatyard in Eastwind as a branch office for Mike to run. Mike's father didn't sell their house either, he kept the title himself and rented it out secretly for the three years we dated, then gave it to Mike on our wedding day as a gift from his mother and him. That gift was a staggering gesture for me. It meant I would live in a castle surveying the magical kingdom I had loved since a child. I was no longer a captive in limbo between two worlds.

Mike's father was an amazing man. Outliving his wife and only son did not daunt him as I had seen others daunted losing far less. He continued to command respect and admiration as a business man and friend into his eighties. He bestowed many gifts on our family, but the greatest for me was his support and guidance when David began to flounder after Mike died.

I recall a friend commenting that I should have been angry at him for taking David away. But I knew David was going one way or another, and when his grandfather offered him a place to live, and a job, I knew he was going in the right direction. He thrived with his grandfather. He made him work his way up the ladder and he rose to the challenge so eagerly that by the time Mike Senior passed away, David was running the entire operation; modernizing production and expanding markets.

His business career progressed successfully but his personal life was an explosive contrast. He never lacked female companionship, but rarely committed to anyone. He married once, to a woman with two children from a previous marriage, and when it barely lasted a year he swore he would never take the plunge again.

The answering machine beeped loudly and I realized I had done nothing but breathe into the phone. I was about to hang up when a breathless David picked up the phone.

"Hey! Anybody there?" he asked.

"David? Is that you?" I asked.

"Mom? What the hell has gotten into you? Disappearing like that. You should know better," he scolded.

I smiled. "What do you mean, disappear? I'm right here where I've always been dear."

He sounded distracted. He was probably pushing buttons, checking messages, reading notes. "So, you're at Clare's right?"

"Oh yes. We're having a lovely little visit." I spoke loudly, then continued in a whisper, "She hasn't begun to annoy me yet, but it won't be long."

He laughed. "Well, just make sure you sit tight until it's safe Mom. "Iris" passed by here this morning with a vengeance. I think Eastwind's luck has run out."

"Yeah, yeah, so say you and all the other doomsayers," I groaned.

"Hey, I called the house before, who is that Miz.Whacko you've got over there? Did you have her checked out? She sounded off the wall...And I tried to call you yesterday and wish you a happy birthday. I sent you something, did you get it?"

"No, I didn't. What is it? Let me guess...soap on a rope...stationary?"

"Hey, I can't help it you're so hard to buy a present for, but this time I think I did it. I kept remembering all those years I tried to beg borrow or steal to buy you something, and you would always say...He spoke in a high pitched old lady voice, "Honey, you know all I want is something from your heart, draw me a picture, paint a sea shell, that's all I want..."

I laughed. "Oh Lord, now you're scaring me, I'll be afraid to open the package..."

David was in a talkative mood. He told me about a new young woman in his life, very young; so young in fact that I almost got my dander up about it, but I held my tongue and listened some more and laughed and smiled. And I wondered why I hadn't done that in such a long time. Just listened. Without analyzing every word until I was bound to find a hidden sting somewhere.

Then he said, "Tell me what it's like there Mom."

He reminded me so much of Mike at times. The thrill of a storm.

"You're disappointed it passed you by, huh?" I laughed.

"How'd you know," he asked chuckling. "What about the waves, anybody out there riding them or are all the youngsters wimping out these days?"

I told him about the incident the day before. He was silent for a moment and then he said, "Wow that must have been weird for you."

I didn't answer right away. "Yeah, I practically had to restrain old Charley."

"No, Mom, I mean it must have reminded you of Dad." He paused. "I haven't thought about that in years. Did you know that is my favorite hero story about him?"

I was shaken, but I tried not to let him hear it. "Yes, it did take me back. I'm surprised you remember it though."

"How could I forget Mom? So it must be wild out there. You know I thought about hopping on a plane yesterday and heading up, just to see it, drag out my old board and ride a few kahunas. It's going to be a crazy forty-eight hours on our little island. I bet Fred's gearing up for some adventures."

"Yes, well, maybe the next one..." I whispered.

"Did you get the shutters up?" He asked.

"Not yet, I'll see to it in the morning......" I mumbled.

He paused. "What do you mean? You <u>are</u> at Clare's Mom, aren't you?"

I straightened up. "What? Of course. Where else would I be? I meant I'll call Charley in the morning and make sure he had Joe do them."

"Ok, so you'll be there until Monday at least." He sounded worried now and I cursed myself for causing it.

"I'll wait for Charley to give me the green light I promise." I said.

He laughed. "Just don't wait too long and miss any great photo ops."

We were both relieved. Then he said John called him three times to ask about me. I said he should pass the word that I was at Clare's, and that I would try to call John myself but communication would probably be sketchy for the next few days.

I didn't want to say good-bye, it was such a rare conversation. It took me back, before all the strife and complications we had been through. It took all my self control not to break down until after I hung up the phone.

When I hung up I still didn't let the tears flow. I wanted to call John quickly before I lost my momentum, for I wasn't at all sure that conversation would go as smoothly. I rarely spoke to John and when I did it was on that same artificial plane I shared with Mary. John did not possess the uncomplicated nature of his brother. David was like Mike, and John was like me. If David was angry with someone, his emotions manifested themselves fast and furiously and then were forgotten.

John was a grudge holder, and extremely sensitive, so if you slighted him you might not even know it, your only clue the almost imperceptibly cool reception you received for days, weeks, or years, depending on the offense.

In John's senior year of high school he visited Bobby on the west coast, and like Bobby, never really came back. He attended college there and decided on a career in law. Mike died in his junior year and John offered to come home and finish school here. I insisted he stay and then when he graduated, he took a position in a growing law firm, which cemented his future three thousand miles away from me.

I was sad but not surprised when both of my boys decided to live so far away. I knew all the sayings about boys growing up and away, I saw my brothers do exactly that. Bobby and Jimmy raised their children and lived their lives, connected to but not dependent on my parents, while my sisters and I nurtured and cared for the bond with them.

My mother struggled to build meaningful relationships with her son's and their families, and there were happy times when words and emotions flowed easily and other times when disputes erupted and flamed. But on the whole, the Boyle family remained intact with no serious estrangements, no unbreachable gaps.

I liked to think it was because we shared a bond strengthened and reinforced by our parents love and example, that branched through our own relationships, growing with each birth and marriage. But then when my family drifted precariously apart, I had to reevaluate that because when you assign credit for things that go well, you must accept blame when they do not.

My mother used to say I was lucky because I never had to share Mike's love with another woman. She often found it difficult to see her sons struggle as only mothers do. We see them try so hard only to be told it isn't hard enough, we see them grow into the men they are only to be told they aren't man enough. We know their weaknesses, and cringe to see them challenged; we know their strengths and loathe to see them wasted, we know their hearts so well, we cannot bear to see them bruised or broken.

I wondered what Mikes' mother would have thought of me. Did I treat him the way she would have wanted me to? Probably not and that's the point; in the eyes of either, the wife or the mother, nothing is ever good enough. That is where the struggle begins and usually where the cord begins to unravel.

The phone in my hand began to buzz obnoxiously signaling that I had to make the call or hang up. I hung up. I wasn't ready to call John. I glanced out at the bleak sky over the fuming sea. Fat drops of rain pelted the window, mottled the sand. A group of gulls were huddled together on the beach just beyond the steps. One brave soul attempted to fly, struggling time and time again to rise into the steady blasts of wind and each time failed and was blown back onto the sand like a weightless feather. Didn't he realize he was fighting a force more powerful than he could overcome? Did he think sheer will would lead him to victory? And what if it did? Was there some haven he yearned for, some zone of tranquility up above the storm clouds that instinct compelled him to seek? And if so, why him? Or why only him?

I picked up my pen and resumed writing. Maybe if I worked through it on paper, I would find the neutral ground on which to reach John, before it was too late.

I began again, with the first time I met Teri. John had dated her for nearly a year when they came out to spend Christmas with me. I suspected she was something special since he had never brought any other girl home, though I didn't dare voice those suspicions. I knew well the unwritten rules that mothers of sons usually learn the hard way.

I liked her from the start. She was beautiful, with long dark hair and deep brown eyes, an easy smile and a friendly laugh. And she made John so happy.

After I wrote the first few sentences about Teri I had to stop. I had pushed those memories away for so long I wasn't sure I could face them and end up with anything but a bitter sorry tale that wouldn't do anyone much good.

I hadn't even spoken Teri's name in the past five years, and for the five before that I spoke it only with contempt. Yet Teri was this child's mother, and the story could not be told without her, so I forced myself on, concentrating more on the pleasant times, for there had been pleasant times.

Mike had been taken from me years before in an awful but mercifully quick instant, a flash of piercing pain and then peace. Peace for him anyway. One second he was laughing, a shovel in his hand, not a care in the world save the mound of snow piling up beside him, and the question I had called out to him, coffee or hot cocoa? I blinked my eyes and he staggered backward, fell into the pile of snow, his shovel clattering down to the ground. I stood there, watching from the porch and thought for sure my heart would stop too. I remember clutching it, begging for it to stop so I wouldn't be left here without him.

I ran over to him, as if I could do any good, frantically pushing the snow off his face, his shirt, his hair, I tried to revive him sobbing hysterically, why couldn't I save him, he would have saved me. I needed him to tell me what to do. I prayed he would jump up and grab me, all the while knowing that he never, ever, would again.

So when Teri came into my life, I was anxious to put the years of grieving behind me I was eager to welcome her and begin a new chapter.

I wrote for two hours though it seemed like only minutes passed, and when I was done I felt foolish for wasting ten years on something that could be summed up so quickly. But in the course of eighty years, ten years isn't that long, and I was determined to get past it, and it was because of those seventy other years of building faith and trust that I could bury it and go on. For I saw clearly that what I had described was an ordinary life, full of beginnings and endings, imperfections and mistakes, some joy and some sorrow; not a horror story, not a fairy tale, just life.

And for the first time in a very long time I looked at myself and liked what I saw. I was content, but I knew there was still more to do. I straightened up my desk, put the letter in an envelope and printed Mary's name neatly on the front. I picked up Charley's manuscript, and walked through the house turning off lights, then headed for the stairs but found myself back at the window. I stood in the darkness and looked at the eerie stormy twilight. The gulls remained in the same pose as before. I couldn't tell what became of the lone courageous warrior. I wondered if he had indeed, broken through to a calmer plane, or surrendered and joined the dismal assembly of his comrades. Perhaps he had exhausted himself and perished in the effort, I would never know. All I knew for sure was that the struggle was over.

CHAPTER EIGHT

My twentieth summer was as hot and hazy as any other, but it emerged into a season like none before it. I graduated from business school in May, became Mrs. Michael Hankins in June, enjoyed a honeymoon cruise in July, and in August Mike and I settled into our sandcastle by the sea.

For the first time in my life, September brought me home to the island instead of away from it. Labor Day found me sitting idly on my porch, content to watch as one season of my life slipped smoothly into the next as effortlessly as the gulls in their sky, and the fish in their sea drifted from summer to fall. During those first bittersweet autumn days, I realized that sudden shifts, like death, devastate and destroy, while most change occurs subtly; weeks and days of imperceptible movement leading to a final result startles you, like fiery fall leaves that seconds before were a sea of green. It is the continuance of life, and as wondrous in the means as in the end, only easy to overlook.

I was always aware of the elusive nature of life, and tried to savor precious moments along the way, but they stubbornly flashed by quickly and quietly, drifting away in the passage of time. It seemed like a second ago I was a child, yet there I was, a married woman.

I was faced with the future of my dreams, and I was determined not to let that particular season slip by so quickly. But as usual, life got in the way; scattered my lofty intentions in the wind from the sea and time moved along with the lightning speed that constantly propels the present to the past and brings tomorrow to our doorstep whether we're ready for it or not.

The single thorn on the glorious rose of my new life was witnessing the annihilation of Sandy Point. A precious way of life with its own dialect, costumes and customs was irrevocably destroyed. The boardwalk from the inlet to the main pavilion was torn from its pilings and discarded like a can of pick up sticks, the rides were dismantled and hauled away, the pavilions razed, the contents auctioned off.

It took two weeks to flatten the bungalows, and I refused to even turn my head in that direction. The demolition crew finished up on a Friday afternoon in late fall. That evening I was preparing supper in the kitchen, when Mike and Charley burst through the back door.

"Sara! Drop everything, you're coming with us," Mike announced as he snatched the head of lettuce from me and tossed it back into the refrigerator.

Charley had a cooler under one arm and a sleeping bag under the other. Without a word or glance in my direction he began rummaging around, whistling some silly tune as he methodically loaded the cooler with ice, beer, soda, fruit and bread.

I looked questioningly at Mike. He flashed a mischievous grin. "Go upstairs and pull out the sleeping bags, Sara. I think they're in the front closet. And pack a bag...warm clothes, just enough for one night...I think."

"Hold on a second," I protested. "You two can't just barge in here and start barking orders at me!"

They answered in unison, "Oh yes we can." Then they debated whether or not to bring fishing gear.

I waited for an answer with my hands on my hips but they ignored me and continued packing, so I went upstairs, dragged out the sleeping bags and packed some warm clothes.

I carried my bundles to the driveway. Nobody was there, the car was still in the garage. I heard voices on the front porch and went around to see Virginia marching out of her house with a backpack slung over her shoulder, and Arthur right behind her.

We started walking down the beach, joined by Roger and Anna, and Rhea and Caleb. Mike and I lagged behind, and he explained the adventure.

"Sara, I know how much Sandy Point meant to you, and I know you've been upset about everything going on down there, but wait till you see it. It's amazing." He didn't need to go on because I looked up and saw for myself what had captured his and Charley's imagination and inspired this mysterious mission.

From the bridge to the inlet, and west to the Squan River, the only building standing was the Coast Guard Station, surrounded by seemingly endless acres of sand. Beautiful, clean sand, pushed up in piles resembling dunes. It was a halting vision from a past long before mine; the scene in a thousand paintings from days of whalers and pirates, an untouched, wild island. Gulls flew silently overhead, as if they too were fascinated with the wide open space.

When the sun set over the bay we had set up camp and were roasting hot dogs over the fire in the center of what a few months before had been Markison's Beach. As quiet darkness fell, with only the moon and stars to light the sky, the beer flowed and Charley spun his magical tales, and it was easy to imagine what it was like there, two hundred years ago.

We slept under the stars with the sea gently breaking and the buoys softly chiming. We laughed and joked like a gang of kids with a new yard to explore and no parents to call us home. But Saturday morning the sun rose again over the sea, and jobs and families called us back to reality, and Monday morning the construction crews commenced the battle in the war against nature.

Mike and I returned to a complicated task. When I married him I became his business partner. When Mike's father handed him the deed to the house he turned over the Boatworks property too. The production warehouse was flourishing down south so Mike had the option to sell the entire parcel and find a small office from which we would run the Eastwind Sales Division, subdivide the land, or develop it however we chose; homes, restaurants, commercial.

Mike saw the process as a challenge, a chance to prove himself. I found it confusing and overwhelming. I had no experience with a family business; my father had gone to work each morning and come home every night, and I knew very little about how he made a living.

Mike never knew anything but building, selling, and maintaining boats. It was discussed at every meal and he was included in the discussions from the time he could talk. He was involved in the office paperwork, sawing and sanding in the lumberyard, and sailing the finished product alongside his great grandfather, his grandfather, and his father.

I didn't know a boom from a mast, a brig from a dory, or a schooner from a surfboat. I couldn't seem to keep even the simplest definitions straight; leeward, windward, starboard or port. But I loved watching my new husband practice his trade. He rarely owned any boat for any length of time. It was the tinkering he enjoyed; diagnosing and fixing a problem, designing a special feature for a customer, negotiating a delicate sale. And Charley could always be counted on for a ready vessel, to captain himself or lend to Mike for a private cruise.

Sailing introduced me to a cosmos I had overlooked for years, Fishawk Bay. Listening to Mike and Charley casually discuss bluefish or striped bass, and whether or where they were running; snowy egrets, great blue herons, wood ducks, black ducks, mallards and muskrats, magnified the difference between me and them. They knew so much and weren't even aware of what a special gift it was. It was second nature to them, and I marveled silently each time I nodded my head and pretended to understand.

One evening Charley, his girlfriend, and Mike and I sat on our porch discussing the same thing we'd been discussing for weeks; the boatyard property. Mike relied heavily on Charley's advice on all decisions.

I shared an idea I had; that we could create some sort of museum or nature center on the property, so people could learn about and enjoy what the island had to offer.

Mike's reaction surprised me. He thought a minute and then said, "You know Sara, that's not a bad idea, but you can't teach kids in a day what it takes a lifetime to learn. And even if you could, then they all want to live here, and then they need to build a house, but there's no lots so they go and fill in another swamp and call it waterfront property and subdivide it and sell a couple more lots and before you know it they're all here and there's nothing left to appreciate but the house next door. And my biggest fear is that no matter what we do with that property, our kids won't have the lifetime I had, to learn all I did. The island is changing already and I don't know how to stop it."

We sat in silence then gazing out at the sea as the evening sky descended, and I said, "Well, then we better come up with an ironclad plan to keep that Goddamned Eddie and his clan away from it for the next three million years."

Charley nearly choked on his beer. "Wow! I never heard you talk like that before!"

Mike laughed. "Poor Eddie doesn't know he made a lifelong enemy in my sweet wife here, just because he was born a Blackmore!"

I blushed. "Very funny boys, very funny. We'll see who's laughing when he erects 'Blackmore's on The Bay' a few years down the road."

Charley stood, held up his beer and delivered a promise; "I Charles Duncan the hundred and twelfth, swear on my ancestor's graves, half of which are in the waves breaking on the beach that as long as there's a Duncan breathing this salty air, another Blackmore superstructure will not be built on Eastwind Island."

We drank a toast to that.

The next morning Mike and I made our final decision. We would renovate the warehouse into "The Sneakbox", a business complex consisting of twenty small offices and shops offering every supply and service a sailor might need, from insurance policies to sails, and keep one office for us to run as the Hankins Eastwind Sales Division.

We deliberately left ample open space. We designed a public boat access, and contracted a group of locals to maintain it to protect the natural habitat, and so wildlife displaced from other areas would be able to make new homes there. The south end of the island also attracted more tourists.

When Blackmore's "Gateway To The Sea" opened the units sold out quickly. The people of Eastwind didn't realize until too late that almost half the island's beach would be available exclusively to residents of the development. The beaches on the south end of the island had always been run by the town and open to the public for a nominal fee but parking was limited, and the only refreshment stand and restroom were at the lighthouse. There was a public outcry demanding access to the northern beach but the Blackmores stubbornly claimed that they 'owned' it and could determine who used it. The town council ducked the issue for two years as protests waged and tempers flared. Finally a group of locals banded together, sued, and "The Gateway" was forced to reopen their gates to the public.

Five years after we were married John was born, and two years later, David, and for the next fifteen years our lives zipped by in fast forward, a blur of diapers and bottles, then tricycles and skate boards, then surfboards and cars, girls and parties, until one day, everything stopped.

As in every other stage of my life where I fancied I could, I tried to hold on to those fleeting moments, good and bad and enjoy the laughter and innocence of my little boys. The feel of chubby brown arms around my neck, the toothless grins, the soft baby-fine hair, and then, the pride in watching them, when all you're allowed to do is watch as the little boys transform into young men; handsome, fearless and strong, and walk about in the world to take their place wherever that may be.

We sat at the kitchen table the evening of John's high school graduation, long after the ceremonies we had been a part of were over, and the boys had departed for the celebrations we were not a part of, and I watched Mike wrestle with the realization that our boys were grown. I saw that though I had lamented losing them from the day they were born, he was just then understanding it.

"You know, they aren't really gone, Mike," I said.

He stared off into the distance and sighed. "Yes, but it will never be the same, will it?"

"No. It will be different, but different is not always bad."

He smiled a weary smile. "But I keep wondering, why a college across the country?"

I had no answer to that. The obvious reason was that John loved California. What I didn't say was what he knew in his heart. John didn't love life on the island the way Mike and I, and David, did. John would never admit it, but his whole life he had simply gone through the motions; sailing and fishing.

John's world revolved around the written word. He was best at solving problems with logic and wisdom learned in text books and classrooms, whereas David was more like Mike, he needed to use his hands and thrived in wide open spaces.

"I think, Mike, we need to accept that part of our job is done, but we aren't finished. I read a poem the other day and it made me cry. It was about kids growing up, and that the little stuff was the easy part, three meals a day and homework, clothes on their bodies and birthday parties, that kind of thing, and that the really hard part is when they are gone and you stay up at night worrying, about their jobs and their children!"

"So. John graduated from high school, and you're trying to tell me to celebrate that before we blink our eyes and find we're worrying about whether he can support his wife and three kids?" Mike smiled, and reached for my hand across the table.

"Yeah. Something like that." I squeezed his hand back.

"Well, I guess it's true. When they're little everything is physical. You carry them here, there, wherever you go they're with you, and it's hard, but it's easier too. You put them in one spot and they can't wander very far away. If they do you just put them right back where you want them to be. But then they grow a little and they go just a little farther away, and then a little farther yet, and before you know it, they're the ones telling you where to stay and they turn around and walk off without a backward look."

I led him to the door for a stroll on the beach, and I whispered, so he wouldn't hear my voice cracking, "Yes, and if it happens that way it simply means we've done our job well."

Two years later, on the night of David's high school graduation I sat at the table alone and tried not to remember what it was like to have someone to share my pride and sorrow with, my hopes and dreams, my worries about my children's future and my own. I took a walk along the beach and then went back to my porch and rocked and stared out at my old friend the sea, the only constant in my life besides my being alive at all.

David left that summer, John was gone and I was a widow. I had Virginia, Rhea and Charley. I had the house and garden to tend, and "The Sneakbox" rentals, though Mike's father gradually took over the remaining accounts. For a time I didn't make any changes to the office. I would pack lunch and sit at my desk looking out on the bay and pretend to work. I watched the black ducks glide across the water, gazed at brilliant orange sunsets, and thought about Mike and our boys, and our life together.

I had no right to be sad, I knew how fortunate I was and it gradually dawned on me that the rest of my life was up to me and while that scared me, I discovered a new confidence. During those still moments looking out over the bay, I discovered something else. I realized I knew the difference between a black duck and a wood duck, an egret and a heron, where they nested, and where and when they breed their young, and I had a strong desire to share that knowledge.

One afternoon I packed lunch for two and asked Charley to meet me in the office. He let himself in and immediately drifted to the window and its magnificent view of the bay.

I gave him a sandwich and started my pitch. "Listen Charley, I've been thinking," I began.

He groaned. "Oh no. Whenever a conversation begins like that I know I'm in trouble."

I laughed. "Oh, no, it's nothing terrible. I've just been thinking lately about this office. You know Mike senior is really handling everything, and now that David's down there helping out, I don't see much point in my trying to hold on to things up here. It's really just a pretense."

He stood and walked to the window. "Well I'll be damned. Look at those kids out there." He pointed to a wooded cove where I saw nothing but trees and water.

He snorted and picked up the phone, dialed his neighbor and reported that his son and a few friends needed a friendly reminder to get their hides back in school. I was sure he hadn't heard a word I'd said.

"So, what do you think Charley?"

He sat back down to finish his sandwich. "I think it's a great idea Sara."

"Oh really? What idea was that?" I asked sarcastically.

"The learning center, or whatever you decide to call it, I think it's a great idea, and I'll be glad to give you a hand whenever you need it." He smiled at me.

I was dumbfounded. That was exactly my idea, but how he knew I didn't know. I hadn't mentioned it in years, but his approval was as good as Mike's as far as I was concerned, so I threw myself into a new venture; converting the office into "The Eastwind Nature Center", which quickly became a cross between a nautical museum and a library; a place where anyone could visit and touch a genuine whaling harpoon, read a bayman's journal, or simply sit and gaze out at the beauty of the bay.

It took long hours of organizing and cataloguing materials donated by residents. For years I was willing to lend the time and energy, but eventually I turned control over to the same local group handling the outside property and I was allowed to become just another curious caller eager to spend an afternoon perusing the past.

On my sixtieth birthday John and his wife gave me a lovely gift; a grand-daughter. John was thirty-five, a successful lawyer living happily in elegant style on the west coast. He and, Teri, had been married for five years, and visited me for a week every summer and once or twice a year on winter holidays.

Teri was a welcome female link in the Hankins family. I had become accustomed to the non-communicative style of my sons. They kept in touch, but kept their distance. I accepted that, even understood it better than others did, but Teri made me realize what I had been missing.

Before Mary was born she telephoned twice a week, after Mary was born she called twice a day. She had a tumultuous relationship with her own family and I often simply listened to Teri complain about them. Her parents divorced when she was young. She had three sisters, all with children of their own and they lived in a constant state of acute sibling rivalry. I was amused by her accounts of the explosive episodes they routinely engaged in.

Actually I envied their ability to vent differences loud and clear and then forgive, forget and carry on. Yet Teri envied my quiet lifestyle, and relished the individual attention she received. She told me more than once that she felt more at peace on the island than anywhere else on earth.

Teri was intriguing. She was intelligent, could not be stumped in any subject, yet she had very little common sense and 'a sharp tongue'. She was a lot like Clare Jordan; spoke her mind without care or conscience. She would meet someone new, size them up immediately, then let them know exactly how she felt, sometimes veiled in sarcasm, sometimes not. But she could be extremely sensitive and quickly offended by any off-hand remark directed at her.

I was fascinated as I always had been with those completely lacking the inhibitions I felt so keenly. But it was frustrating to feel that I didn't know the real Teri, when sometimes she appeared fragile and insecure, and totally dependent on John. I finally came to understand that her barbed nature wasn't that different from my reserved one. It was simply the defense she had developed, more creative and complex than mine.

David came to visit whenever they did, and enjoyed introducing her to island sports; surfing, sailing, and fishing. He brought various girlfriends home with him, and the four of them would occupy themselves much the way Mike and I had when we were a young couple. It was marvelous to hear laughter in the house again.

When Mary was born the good times got better. Teri gave up her job to stay home which allowed them to visit often. She and Mary came for two months the first summer, and John flew out to join us every weekend. The stroller and tricycle were permanent fixtures in the driveway, and beach pails and shovels lined the steps to the beach once more.

I fell into my role as 'Nana', as readily as David became 'Unca Dave', and Charley became 'Unca Chawee'. We doted on the child and watched her grow with each visit into a charming little golden-haired beauty. Teri had dark hair and brown eyes, John had brown hair and green eyes, but Mary had blonde hair and hazel eyes inherited from the Boyles'. She loved the beach and by the age of four was quite expert at riding waves, building castles, tossing shells and collecting prize bits of blue sea glass.

The summer Mary was six, John and Teri only stayed for two weeks. I sensed a change in them that I attributed to the transition they were going through. Teri had gone back to work, which was a shock to me. I expected to hear news of another baby, since for months she had spoken of little else than wanting a brother or sister for Mary. I didn't question or criticize her decision, although from the moment she told me about it she acted as defensively as if I had.

Our visit that year was strained and strange, as if another being had been created who lurked around every corner waiting for an opportunity to throw a jumble of conflicting and confusing emotions into the most innocent occurrence.

David drove up for Labor Day weekend with a new 'friend', Loretta, and they brought her two teen-aged sons who upon their arrival suffered visibly through introductions and then disappeared. Teri and Mary and I had planned a delicious barbeque, the sort we looked forward to every summer. Charley served the drinks while John cooked the burgers and roasted the clams. Crabs from the afternoon's catch boiled on the stove, corn on the cob was cooling on the picnic table. We gathered in the garden for cocktails and the conversation wandered and meandered from southern cooking to California rainstorms and back to Eastwind politics.

Loretta took an instant liking to Mary. She made a big fuss over her, lamenting how she had been stuck with two boys and would give anything for a little girl. David squirmed at that.

Loretta sat Mary on her lap and asked her about California. "Now, tell me sweetie, what are the beaches at home like?"

It was an innocent question, but Mary paused, deep in thought so long it semed she hadn't heard Loretta. Then she looked at Teri and the look on her face made me cringe. It was a hateful leer, the kind that devastates a mother even though its forgiven as quickly as it disappears.

When Mary finally answered Loretta, her words were steeled with the same contempt in her eyes. "I don't know. My mother never takes me to the beach at home."

Maybe if it hadn't been Loretta, or if one of us had quickly filled the following silence with something light, or certainly if John had read the situation a little more sensitively, and not commented that Teri was too busy getting her hair and nails done to take her daughter to the beach, maybe it wouldn't have gone so badly.

But it did go badly. Teri stormed into the house without a word. John calmly finished cooking the burgers and clams, placed them on the picnic table, and followed her inside, and we didn't see either of them the rest of the evening. David and his entourage left the next day, and John and Teri spent the remainder of their visit avoiding one another and everyone else.

The next few days I glimpsed a cruel side of Teri and began to wonder if I had ever really known her at all. She had the definite air of one who had been wronged, which might have been true, though I couldn't name what I had done wrong. Her anger was so subtle that I thought I imagined the slights, yet other times there was no mistaking the attitude that I was in the way, out of line, and intolerable.

The morning they were leaving I found Teri alone on the porch and sat down beside her. "You know," I said. "It's hard enough to say good-bye to all of you, but it will be impossible with things so unsettled. If I've offended you, won't you tell me how?"

She continued to rock in silence so I went on. "Well I'd have to be a fool not to see something is wrong, but whatever it is I'm sure you and John can work it out. And if there's anything I can do to help, you just let me know."

Still no reply. She sat in her chair staring straight out at the sea. I stood, leaned over and kissed her cheek, tasted the telltale sign of salty tears. I waited another moment, hoping for some response, but she said nothing. After they left, I found the nagging questions and worries excruciating. I remembered my words with Mike, and missed his confidence, his counsel, his hand to hold.

Teri calls dwindled to once a week, and our conversations became more and more impersonal. When I greeted her at Christmas she might as well have been a stranger. She was polite and friendly, she joined in all the usual activities, but it was an obvious act. We shared none of the confidences and laughter we once had, and I missed it more than I expected to. I saw the mask she wore, but I could not get past it.

The only common ground we had was Mary. We focused our discussions and energies on her, and it broke my heart to see that pressure on a six-year-old child. And even there, I knew that creature was lurking, waiting to pounce when I least expected it.

It appeared on Christmas morning. I gave Mary a doll I had Anna Allen pick up for me on the mainland after she explained that it was the most sought after doll on earth and she intended to wait on line hours if need be to get one for her granddaughter.

Teri sat on the sofa watching quietly as Mary opened the package. When the doll emerged Mary's face lit up with joy as brilliant as the lights on the tree. Teri's lit up with equal brilliance, but in fury.

She jumped from her seat and snatched the doll from the child's hands. "Well, won't your grandma back home be thrilled that the present she searched high and low for, and spent a small fortune on when she finally found one, will mean nothing at all to you because your NANA, already gave you one!"

Then she tossed the doll into Mary's lap and shot a spine tingling leer at me.

"But I suppose that was your Nana's intention all along, to save the day and steal the moment..."

I looked from Teri's hateful glare to Mary fiddling miserably with the doll, to John holding his head in his hands. It wasn't the best time to speak my piece, but I had no time to analyze anything. I was under attack and my anger rose instinctively.

I gripped the arms of my chair to steady myself as I returned Teri's scowl and spoke with the same laced sarcasm she had used. "Well, as a matter of fact Teri, I had no idea that particular doll was so significant, but you can be assured that if I had, I would have chosen another gift. I was not aware because you ABSOLUTELY NEVER shared that information with me. You have shared NOTHING but your annoyed attitude and icy stares for months now and I'm fed up. Also, stealing a moment was the furthest intention from my mind, but let me say that's all we've been doing lately, stealing moments from a young girl's life, and it has to stop."

I shocked everyone, including myself. John lifted his head, Mary turned nervously to each of us, and Teri held my stare, waiting for me to continue. But I was finished. I stared back at her and for a split second I saw her eyes soften. I eased my grip on the arms of the chair and leaned toward her. She took a step. We were so close. It would have been so easy. I was willing, I sensed she was too. A simple embrace. It was a footstep away. It was what we needed; to hug, to cry, to clear away the tension that didn't belong there, between us.

141

I stood up, took a step. But she backed away, her eyes blazed with anger again, the softness vanished. She turned away and announced bitterly, "Well then. I guess this is my fault too. Just like everything else always was and always will be. And you know what? That's just fine with me." And she stormed off to her room.

When they went home I was physically and emotionally drained, and utterly confused. I felt I had somehow failed them all, yet I still didn't even know what the real problem was, or if it was a symptom of many.

I was angry at them for putting Mary and me in the middle of their battle. Instinct told me to back off, think before I acted, but it was frustrating trying to find the balance between caring and interfering. I called John at his office soon after the first of the year and poured my heart out, explained my concern for Mary and Teri, and for him. I told him how difficult it was for me, being so far away, and feeling so helpless.

He listened, and assured me I was overreacting. He said it would take time to work things out. He was as anxious to get off the phone as I was reluctant to let go. He finally made an excuse to end the conversation and I held the buzzing phone in my hand for a long time trying to understand. I tried to convince myself that this was typical, that I shouldn't take it personally, that I shouldn't have expected more from him, that he was the one going through this, not me. I tried not to think that they were both being extremely immature and cruel, tried not to feel sorry for myself, tried not to be angry and resentful. I waited for him to get back to me, I was sure he would, and then we would talk it out, and I would be able to listen, to help.

John didn't get back to me, but Teri did. She called me a week later and blasted me with a biting lecture. She said I had no right to go to John behind her back and beg him to come back to her. She told me that I didn't know a thing about her life, about real life; that my whole life had been a fairy tale and I should mind my own business. She didn't give me a chance to speak. She raved for five minutes then hung up with a dramatic click.

So I was not surprised to be informed a few weeks later that John would fly out with Mary, leave her with me for the month of July, and then come back to take her home. John also told me that I shouldn't try to contact Teri, he said the marriage was over and it was all his fault. I instinctively jumped to his defense, which he just as promptly rejected.

The details were sketchy, and made no sense to me. There was nothing I could see as cause for a marriage to end. Lack of communication, falling out of love, irreconcilable differences; all bewildering phrases that belonged on television, not in real life. I never expected, or wanted, to know the whole truth. Whether it's your best friend, your next door neighbor, or your own marriage suffering, the facts are different in each player's mind.

The only indisputable fact was that Teri and John were separated, and would share custody of Mary. I couldn't imagine a more horrific state for a six year old to live in, though it was not unusual. Divorce was a common occurrence from the quiet shores of Eastwind to Hollywood Boulevard, but it was not an easy concept to accept.

I was torn. It would have been easy to blame the carefree lifestyle of the west coast, easier still to blame Teri. And what about John, who was so eager to accept all the blame? I thought and thought some more. I had no one to confide in so I talked to myself furiously as I weeded the garden, swept the walks, rocked on my porch.

By the next Christmas David and Loretta had been married and divorced and I was forced to question how I had raised two men incapable of the ultimate commitment. Anger piled on frustration and my sons and I were caught in a viscous circle of unspoken guilt and blame that weakened the bonds we'd shared until the actual miles between us were less significant than the emotional expanse.

I tried writing notes, full of uplifting encouragement and pledges of support. Teri sent hers back unopened. I was back to the non-communication days before Teri, and I realized I probably hadn't appreciated her nearly enough. When John and David resisted my advances I retreated even more until my own words began to lose their sincerity, and hung withering in the hollow phone wires, leaving me feeling alone and foolish.

My conversations with John revolved around welcome news of Mary, and the chance to speak with her. Soon even that became awkward and alien. I had to adapt to the new schedule, was it John's week or Teri's? I couldn't bear to let Mary slip into that unreachable void too.

When July finally arrived and she ran into my arms, her merry chatter and laughter bubbled forth spontaneously and melted my worries and fears. She was seven, and gracefully becoming a young lady. I was pleased she was not too grown up to collect shells and sea glass, be thrilled by a monster wave, or share quiet walks along the beach. At first it was a struggle to ignore the nettling strife surrounding us but her childish innocence and my desperate need for her, allowed our relationship to thrive and flourish like a tender rose amid prickly thorns.

We basked in two more remarkable summer visits full of laughter. Mary had no shortage of summer friends; the Allens, and a steady supply of grandchildren and cousins spewing forth from Virginia's house. The only sorrow each year was our goodbye, and I was reminded of my childhood summers. I knew how real her grief was to leave the island, yet I was grateful to be part of the precious experience.

When Mary was nine John and Teri finalized their divorce. John saw her every weekend, but by the next summer there was a noticeable strain in their relationship. He was seeing another woman, and apparently Teri was also dating, and comments from Mary left no doubt she was unhappy about it. So in December when John suggested I go out and spend the holidays with them, I accepted reluctantly, dreading what I might find.

I had visited them before, and the west coast seemed like an alien, though beautiful, environment to me. The rocky coasts and pristine blue waters, lush greenery, tropical florals, and eternally clear skies, were a contrast to the ever changing climate of the east coast.

The visit was a disaster. The tender rose Mary and I had nurtured during our summers on the island was snipped off the bush and left to wilt. We spent Christmas day with John and his girlfriend, which was awkward for me, and Mary's displeasure manifested itself in a display of intolerable behavior. The mood spread like poison through each of us and I couldn't wait to get on the plane and return home.

I never saw Teri again. I felt we knew each other at least well enough to respect one another's feelings, to recognize and seek to protect our frailties, but instead she actively attacked mine.

In the beginning I thought that what we shared would overcome the superficial differences; our basic love for the same two human beings. Even if her love for John had suffered her love for Mary would not. But I was wrong, and as the events of the next few years unfolded I was forced to realize just how mistaken I had been about Teri.

I knew that Teri had been hurt, but by what means and how severely, real or imagined, or what part she herself played in it I would never know. Never hearing her side, her questions, her fears, or worries, and only hearing loud and clear her anger and bitter resentments, I was left with no choice but to rely on my own perceptions, and they were not kind.

In a short period of time she had gone from savior and friend to vindictive enemy. She gave me no outlet for confrontation, sealed herself off entirely so the only way to confront her was through the hearts of Mary and John. And hard as I tried not to be drawn into that, she constantly challenged me through them, in bitter comments, sudden plan changes and irrational demands.

If I had been a sea gull, soaring overhead watching with detached interest the events of those five years I might have foreseen the dreadful outcome we were heading towards, and avoided it. But I was a mere mortal caught up in a chain of events, blindly living each day the best way I knew how, dealing with each situation and bracing for the next. We were seeds of moisture whipped about in the days before a storm hits, bouncing back and forth in electric air, hot and cold, around and over and smack into each other, stupidly unaware of the violent tempest waiting to unleash its mighty power.

But the storm never hit. If it had the damage would have been done and the air cleared. Instead we continued to drift blindly under the hovering dark clouds, tossed in the persistent rain and echoing winds with no clear beginning and no definitive end.

When Mary arrived for her tenth summer, she did not bound up the steps and dispel my anxieties of the previous months with her usual sunny greeting. She was courteous, she was polite, she hugged me and said she was happy to see me, that I looked well.

I saw in her a new child, or rather not a child at all, but a young woman wearing an uncomfortably familiar mask. It hurt to look into her dusky blue eyes and see pain there. I saw the forced bloom of a delicate flower, the turmoil of one who lived in a constant state of stops and starts, with no real opportunity for emotional adjustment.

I wanted to chalk her attitude up to normal development, but occasionally I noticed a sharpness in her voice that jarred my nerves. I did my best to give her room. I realized at seventy years of age I couldn't possibly recall what it was like to be ten going on eleven, and even if I could, a ten year old in my day lived quite a different life than one in my granddaughter's. She kept her distance, which I could understand, but it was more than that. She was distant, distracted, often seemed on the verge of boredom, and I wondered how I would keep her interest for a month.

She sunned on the beach with her friends, walked into town or to the lighthouse. We had spent many afternoons at the Nature Center, but now she did that by herself also. She was invited on outings with the Allens; sailing, crabbing, and fishing, and always had enthusiastic tales to report.

Her last week she seemed to have settled in. She joined me out on the porch, read, or rocked silently beside me. One afternoon I dozed off and was awakened by her quiet sobbing. I reached out to put my hand over hers and she held onto it as if she were drowning.

She stumbled over onto my lap and buried her face in my neck. I was not startled by this as much as I was relieved. When she stopped crying she stayed on my lap, snuggled like an infant, staring out as the late sun shadowed the sand. And then she whispered, so softly I barely heard her, the same question I had asked my mother, my grandmother, and myself, "Why does everything have to change Nana?"

Of course I didn't have the answer, but the fact that she asked it comforted me. I told her what everyone had always told me. I said, "I don't know Mary, but I know how much change can hurt. And I also know that while some things constantly change, others never will, like how much I love you, and your father and mother love you. And when you're feeling down and nothing is going the way you wish it would, remember that change sometimes comes along when you aren't looking and fixes everything, like a colorful rainbow in a blue summer sky after a frightening storm."

John came at the end of August and delivered Henrietta the mysterious Manx cat. He packed up his daughter and they flew home. Sometime before Christmas I learned Teri was no longer pleased with the extended summer visits. By the first of the year John's custody rights were being challenged, and with my Easter flower arrangement came the news that Mary would not be visiting that summer.

I sat alone as the dawns rose and the afternoon shadows danced and one evening faded quietly into the next and wondered if I would ever see Mary again. And I wondered if my words of wisdom to the child had been an utter lie.

Change. What did I know about change? As I dozed on my porch in the warm breezes of September I realized change had crept up on me once more and caught me off guard.

Mary's letters became scarce and John became more uncommunicative than ever. I received most of my information second hand, from David, who sensed how unconnected I felt and tried to keep the lines open.

As days and weeks turned to months and years, the reasons and excuses came at me like silent blows to my fragile ego and I took them all without flinching, like a boxer without arms in a surrealistic match against a powerful champion. But my opponent was never really more than circumstance, jealousy, good lawyers, and a war of words.

Statements of fact, such as "The child's father should not be allowed to pawn off his responsibility on his aging mother. The child's father's judgement and morals are questionable when he persists in co-habitating with a woman with no intentions of marrying her. While visiting her grandmother the child was allowed too much freedom, too many sweets, excessive material purchases and extravagant, unsupervised privileges."

It was funny, really. All my life I wanted to stop time; grasp those rare seconds of joy and taste them over and over, and those summers with Mary were no exception. Only I had no way to know those moments would prove to be the most fleeting of all, for when they were gone, they were completely gone; vanished, erased, obliterated. Not gradually or gracefully, in the normal progression from present to past, from real to remembered, but harshly, with the sudden realization of all that was lost, because I had no desire to recall those tender images at all.

And from that time on, as a sunrise colors the sky and the day to follow, so my life and all the moments gone before it and all the ones yet to be were colored by an underlying feeling of bitterness, resentment, and hopelessness, and the shell hardened still more.

CHAPTER NINE

Saturday, September 2
10:00 P.M.
National Weather Service Update
RE: Hurricane Iris
   Hurricane Iris has been upgraded to a Category II storm, sustaining NNW winds of 100 mph, moving at 12 mph. Landfall is expected in approximately 24 hours.
   A Hurricane warning has been issued and evacuation is recommended within two blocks of the shore line.

The raging wind and pounding surf outside my window were perfect compliments to Charley's story. I became totally immersed, imagining I was the soul inhabitant of a deserted island bravely facing a dangerous gale with no electricity or telephone, armed only with the steely resolve in my soul to survive and tell the tale.

Richard Hankins continued his hunting parties and lived alone on the beach until he met Alexandra Tucker. Her father brought her to the island to enjoy the beauty of the wildlife and natural surroundings, but she became more intrigued by the wild and charismatic nature of Richard Hankins, so her father returned home without her and she became the first woman to set up a year-round home on the beach of Eastwind.

Richard bought the property from Franklin and built a sturdy home, nestled between the same immense dune and towering pine grove chosen years before by Joshua and Jonathan. Alexandra wanted at least seven children and urged him to make the house big and strong enough the first time because if a storm ever washed her babies out to sea he wouldn't get any second chances.

They had ten boys who roamed the beaches as wild as the dune grass, half of them took to the bay and the other half to the sea. The baymen focused on hunting parties and boat building. They constructed the first rendition of "The Hankins Boatworks" on the south end of the island and set about perfecting their craft. There they developed the blueprint for the famous "Sneakbox" that would become the most popular sailing vessel on the bay.

The seamen focused on lifesaving, a new occupation that sprang up when the shipping lanes off Eastwind were traveled by scores of schooners, steamers and barks and were often caught in storms, stranded, and run aground.

The Hankins boys started out with an informal lifesaving station, a simple wood frame building on the southernmost end of the island. They took turns bunking in pairs during storm months with a candle burning constantly in the window facing the sea as a guide for lost souls. They stocked the station with firewood, blankets and bedding, clothing and food.

They devised an alarm system to alert villagers when a ship was in distress, using flags to relay their messages, and people would come from miles around to lend their aid, or simply to witness the scene. Survivors were well cared for. If there were no survivors, there were often no claims made, and the wreck was fair game. A few men made a living by salvaging alone.

There were stories of other islands, of ships lured onto shore with false beacons, hoping for human tragedy, but on Eastwind the only business was saving ships and lives. Many on the Eastwind crew were the grandsons of the original village whalers, and they carried on the tradition of earning a seat on a lifeboat much the same way their forebears had on a whaling boat.

Franklin Duncan, my great-great-great-great-grandfather, lived to the age of 95, having fathered six children. His sons ran the store and the new hotel which had been built closer to the bay. When Franklin passed on he divided the original Duncan family property evenly among his children. My great-great-great-grandfather, Charles, was given the store, the house of Joshua and Mariah, and five lots behind it. His older brother got the hotel and adjacent properties and the four others each received parcels of rich farmland, much of which was sold off, but some remained working and profitable farms for another century.

Looking back now, it seems that was the time where my ancestors made the decisions that set the course of history. They willingly opened their doors, sold their land, and never really concerned themselves with the consequences of the choices they made. Can I blame them? They did what they were compelled to do; for economic and personal reasons. They are only guilty of what we still are today; not considering how our actions today will affect the future.

It was also at that time that the government began to notice what was happening in coastal towns and imposed a new order superseding the rules of small villages. As more people settled in the area, new lifestyles fostered differing opinions, new ideas brought new solutions as well as new problems, and the old ways slowly and soundlessly disappeared. The life saving service was the first to face the future and fail, or at least be altered so dramatically to seem as if it had.

In one respect it was good when tales of the magnificent shipwrecks spread to cities and towns inland, and the courageous men along the coast received welcome recognition and payment for their heroic efforts. But when newspapers got hold of other information, of pirates and looters, those tales were exaggerated and glorified, and prompted investigations.

The eventual outcome was that strict rules and regulations were enforced requiring literacy tests and physical standards, and suddenly men like my great-great-great-grandfather, Charles Duncan, were deemed 'unqualified' to officially man the boats some of them had built themselves. It must have been a bitter pill to swallow when a college education and the right political connections held more weight than experience and honor.

The old life saving station was torn down and a new one built, with government issued equipment, and supplies were efficiently catalogued and maintained. But before long that too, became outdated and inefficient and was razed, and the state purchased the property to erect the Eastwind Lighthouse. On the northern end of the island banking the shores of the Squan Inlet, land was acquired for the Coast Guard Station.

Once again, the men had to turn their attentions inland for occupations, and there was no shortage there, for the town was incorporated and growing, a land company had been formed and lots were sold and developed on the mainland and along the beach. The Hankins family continued to grow. The ten sons of Franklin and Alexandra spawned another forty between them, and the Hankins Boatworks expanded and prospered, evolving with the times and trends. The boating business was booming; building, selling, fueling and maintaining them, and catering to the people who sailed them was a never ending source of opportunity.

The next major influence on the island was the automobile. When the bridge to the mainland was built some say prosperity drove over it, cementing the future of the island. The Eastwind hospitality that Joshua and Mariah had first provided now beckoned vacationers every summer. Roads were paved, a yacht club was built, and my great-great-grandfather turned the family farmhouse into a storage shed and built a new home on one of the back lots.

My great-great-uncles varied their business ventures in Eastwind and at that time a Duncan ran most every enterprise in town; Duncan's Pumping Station, to Duncan's Bait and Tackle, Farmer's Market, Restaurant, Tavern, and Tailors.

The northern end of the island, long considered a wasteland of infertile and unbuildable sandy acreage was purchased. Pavilions were erected for entertainment with a rickety plank of boards laid down between them inJune and put away in September. Summer bungalows sprang up seemingly right out of the sand and the thriving seasonal community known as Sandy Point was born.

My great-grandfather, another Charles, died when he was 95, as had his father, and his and so on, until we Duncan men anticipated that particular age with a mixture of relief and dread. Every one of them died from unnatural causes, unusual at such a ripe impasse, but not when you consider the hard-working lives they led. My great-grandfather was no exception. He broke his neck when he fell from an apple tree that still stands in my back yard. He was picking some choice beauties for his daughter, my grandmother to bake an apple pie for my fifth birthday.

I didn't know my great-grandfather well, but I think he and I were alike in many ways. His actions are evidence of that; he halted growth of the store beyond the original four walls, squashing an expansion his father had planned, and restored the home of Joshua and Mariah. He moved his wife and children in and converted the house where he had grown up into the store warehouse. He was also a strong believer in the written word and I am forever grateful to have thoughts and ideas from his journal to substantiate the connection we share.

I quote, "I watch our shores shift and change and I am helpless to halt it. Some ask why I would seek to and I'm not certain enough of a viable response to even begin the discussion. Yet my heart tells me something must be done, or the day will dawn when the folly of our ways is clear and it will already be too late."

Such telling words, from so long ago. Is this the day that is too late or do we still have miles to go in the wrong direction before we wake up. One man can only do so much, but I can at least contribute to the discussion.

There is no lack of discussion or debate today, preservation is big news that makes headlines at least once a week. What we lack is action; enforcement of control. We don't seem to have the will to enforce controls, and most important, a consensus on which controls to enforce. Nothing will work until the will comes from the hearts of men, until it becomes common sense and not imposed regulation. But how do you accomplish that? How can you convince someone that your way is right and theirs is wrong? Who determines which argument is sound?

The state has no less than ten active commissions on the subject; three of my favorites are The Beach Erosion Commission, The Beach Replenishment Commission, and The Beach Preservation Commission. I want to head The State Common Sense Commission that abolishes the others because they waste time and money and will continue to do so until they realize that erosion has been happening for eons and won't be stopped no matter how costly and extensive the 'replenishment'. Every time man gets involved the problems multiply. There is a persistent rumor circulating that sand from a replenishment project is clogging up the inlet channel, which will make a dredging project necessary soon. Replenishment is unnatural, it disturbs reefs and sea life, alters surf breaks, and most significantly, it doesn't work. The sea washes sand out with one storm and brings it back in with another. Can we stop storms, halt waves in mid-break? Think about this: the only avoidable encroachment is from the west, not the east.

The solution is obvious, though painful. The only answer is the removal of man. That's right, man; us, you and me. We are the ones refusing to accept what nature is repeating over and over again. I think she has been trying to tell us for a long time; when the whales stopped swimming past the island, what did the whalers do? Send out enormous boatloads of bait to lure them back, study the dilemma, sail farther out to sea? No. They accepted it and they adapted.

We refuse to do that. Our environment is changing and we are trying to fight it, expecting nature to adapt to us. We demand that our homes be constructed sturdy enough to withstand her wrath, we expect the sand we pile on the shore to protect what we build there even after they're destroyed again and again. We try to eliminate the creatures that were here long before we were, as in the geese and the deer.

Twenty years from now our children will realize the part those creatures played in the chain and lament their loss, devise some scheme to attract them back. And who will be next? Will the sea gull's cry become too disturbing, their dropping intolerable; how long before we turn a resentful eye on him?

We measure, we monitor, we debate; we calculate the cost of everything but the priceless beauty we destroy on a daily basis. I think of Joshua Duncan walking along the beach those many years ago and I can imagine how breathtaking it must have been; the rising sun sparkling over the sea, the air filled with misty salt. I think of my great-grandfather and the changes he saw wrought on this island, and I look around me today and feel no less helpless than he did.

I walk along the beach, sail the waters of Fishawk Bay, drive along Ocean Ave to the inlet and I realize that their island, and even the island I remember from my childhood has vanished, existing only in my mind. Homes clutter the streets now, over-sized houses squeezed onto under-sized lots, obstruct the once magnificent views, and block the fresh ocean breezes. The sun still rises each morning over the sea but now its rays sparkle and ricochet off windowpanes and rooftops.

There is a word, used sparingly in those commission's discussions, a word everyone fears, afraid to stand behind it, to support it, to enforce it, because it is such an unpopular word. The word is 'retreat' and it strikes terror in the heart of beachfront homeowners, in the heart of leaders of coastal communities, in the heart of developers and politicians.

Property owners have rights to use their land within the limits imposed by their towns, but they do not have the right to push those limits to the utmost extreme. They should not be allowed the often ridiculous interpretations, and to use money and influence to find loopholes in restrictions and guidelines as quickly as they are implemented. Time and money are wasted fighting those skirmishes and the real issues are lost in the shuffle. But those same individuals are quick to enforce their own regulations on walking, surfing and swimming on 'their beach'.

One initiative that makes sense is for the state to buy properties damaged by storms and leave it undeveloped. The opposition is astounding. Where will the money come from to maintain it? And who will be responsible? The answer to those questions seems clear to me. A beach doesn't need man for maintenance, mother nature will do that for free.

I make my living supplying the people of this town and the visitors that pass through it every season of the year, as do my brothers and sisters and their families. I realize there wouldn't be much profit selling paper plates in a ghost town. But I don't believe it would ever be a ghost town. People will never stop coming to the sea. Unless of course they can't get near it; if they have to look over someone's rooftop to glimpse a breaking wave or get a breath of salt air.

And what about those beachfront homes, many of which have stood for hundreds of years? I say put them to the test; the stone's throw. My grandfather passed this advice on to a child sitting on the shore with a shovel in his hand and grand designs in his mind. He told him to stand at the water's edge with a handful of stones. With each stone thrown take a step back and wherever you stand when your last stone barely reaches the sea, build your castle there. And maybe, just maybe, it will still be there tomorrow.

I was the child and Mike Hankins' great grandfather was the wise old man who counseled me. The Hankins family still lives in the house Franklin built for his bride, Alexandra, and it has weathered countless storms. But there is a glaring difference between people like them and people who build homes there now and the difference is that they accept the danger, and the risks as the price they pay for the pleasure of living there. They expect no less, and they seek no more than what nature has to offer. They do not try to change it to suit themselves, or try to exclude others and keep it to themselves.

So the debate continues every day, in town halls all along the coast, and in county, state and national arenas far from the shore. And still, every day all along that same coast mountains of sand are trucked in mobilizing the fiasco titled 'beach replenishment'. Crews pile up sand like little boys building castles. Then other crews measure it, monitor it, and watch it wash out to sea in the next storm. And on the next lot another crew is hard at work. A wrecking ball smashes an old beach house to splinters, hundred year old scrub oaks are ripped out to clear the lot for a new foundation, roots that held sand in place for ages are tossed in a dumpster, and a crane digs mercilessly into an ancient dune to sink the footing for a 12 x 24 foot deck.

Then more machines roll in for the ultimate rape. They pound their monstrous beams deep into the heart of sand and clay that has been settled there for eons and the echo of each thud resounds for miles. I listen to the sandy earth groan, resisting the horrific invasion, but eventually it gives way, it shifts, it moves, and the

pilings are put in place. The inspectors come and report that it is good, the foundation will be sturdy and storm proof, and old sailors like myself shield our eyes from the sun as we stand watching, then shake our heads sadly and go home.

THE END

Sunday, September 3
7:00 A.M.
National Weather Service Update
RE: Hurricane Iris
Hurricane Iris is maintaining Category II status, sustaining NNW winds of 106 mph. Landfall expected within 20 hours.
Hurricane Warning is in force and evacuation is mandatory for all areas within five blocks of shore line.

Charley let himself in the back door quietly. I sat at the kitchen table in the dark gloom of the dawn, watching him. He saw my suitcase by the door before he noticed me, and picked it up to weigh the contents.

I broke the silence with a chuckle. "Now Charley," I said. "Give me a little more credit than that. I would have at least stuffed it with socks and books if I was trying to trick you. Have a little faith, would you?"

He flicked the light switch on and stared at me, smiling. "Sorry Sara, I just know you too well." He hung his rain slicker on the door, went to the counter and poured himself a cup of coffee. He said, "All dressed and ready to go I see."

"You know, Charley, if I didn't know better I'd say you're disappointed that I'm going. And if that's so you better not let on any longer because it won't take much convincing for me to unpack that silly bag and stay put..."

Again he stared at me. A sudden pounding made us both jump. "Oh," I said. "That must be Joe. I called him earlier and asked him to come and put the shutters up."

Charley sat down. "Well, I see you've got everything under control......It's a good thing too. Fred was giving you until noon and then he was coming over to personally evacuate you."

He stared straight at me looking for the flicker that would give me away. "Are you ready now? I can give you a lift over to Clare's...That is where you're going isn't it?"

I stared straight back at him, revealing only serenity. "Yes, of course I'm going to Clare's. But I can drive myself, thank you. You will allow me that small dignity won't you? I'm going to 10:00 mass, that is if they haven't canceled it, and then I'll head over."

I reached for his hand. "Listen Charley, I want to tell you I finished the story and it is wonderful. While I'm on the mainland I'm going to make four copies. One for Lillian like I told you, but I also want to send one to David, and John and Mary."

His eyebrows raised quizzically. "Really?" he asked.

"Really." I said. "I thought about what you said yesterday, and your story got me thinking too, you know there is so much in there...anyway...I loosely quote: 'species in small islands lose contact with others of their own kind, becoming highly vulnerable to extinction.' I don't want to sit by and watch the Hankins family become extinct. It's much too precious and I realize I've been allowing just that to happen. Maybe it's the impending storm, or turning eighty, I don't know but it is time for a change. Time for me to initiate change instead of letting change rule my life. Come with me, I've got something to show you."

I led him into the front room where a package was propped up against the couch. I pulled off the covering and stepped back with him to look at it.

He kneeled down and lifted it up for a closer look, stunned, as I had been, by its beauty.

It was a breathtaking painting of the view from the bridge many years ago, with sand dunes and bungalows dotting the seascape.

Charley examined the signature. When I opened it, I could barely make it out through my tears: David Franklin Hankins. He put it down and put his arm around my shoulder.

I contained my emotions long enough to say, "It's my birthday gift from David. And it means more to me than anything has for far too long because it shows that it meant something to him, and that makes all the difference."

He looked at it again, and then turned to me and said, "Well that explains it then."

"Explains what?" I asked.

"It explains this whole new attitude of yours. I was beginning to think the calm front was subterfuge concealing a secret plan. But now I see why you seem so......I don't know...at peace? Sounds stupid I know, but that's it."

I smiled. "There's more," I said. I went to my desk and showed him the birthday note David had written. He explained how it was John who had found an old photograph taken from the bridge and suggested David paint a scene for me. "Imagine, those two collaborating on a project like that......"

Then I showed him the three envelopes; one addressed to Mary, one to John, and one for David. I've written each of them a letter, pled my case if you will, set the record straight, and I feel overwhelmingly relieved. I know it's no wonder cure, but it's a long overdue step in the right direction."

Joe burst in the back door, shouting, "Mrs. Hankins? Is Charley there? I could use a hand out here."

Charley gave me a hug and whispered, "Good for you Sara Boyle Hankins, good for you. You're not so stupid and stubborn after all." He went out to help Joe with the shutters. I stood at the window and watched the sea. The sky was bleak, the clouds hung so low you could touch them. High tide was approaching; the swells were cresting eight feet or better in an intense procession breaking with determined reach and overtaking what was left of the beach in front of the house. The wind was whipping wetness through the air, with little distinction between sea foam and sky mist. I turned away before Charley and Joe finally won the struggle with the shutter and my view was blocked.

They came in for coffee and a sandwich, full of storm related news and gossip. They were anxious to be out in it, preparing, rescuing, watching. Before Charley left I asked him to take the picture with him for safe keeping, and he agreed to keep Henry overnight.

He said, "I'll call you later at Clare's, maybe even stop in and check up on you."

I had worried about that, but it was a safe bet phones would be out by evening, and an even safer bet that he wouldn't leave the island during this storm, any more than I intended to.

He waited while I got my things and together we checked all the lights, switches, and plugs. We walked to the garage, Charley threw my suitcase in the back seat and watched as I pulled the car out. I rolled down my window and blew him a kiss that got lost in the wind, and I thought for a second he knew. He took a step toward the car with an odd look on his face, but just then a siren sounded and Fred's cruiser pulled in. I gave him a smile, he turned to Fred and I rolled up my window and slowly started down the drive.

I didn't have time to feel guilty or sad or think twice about what I was doing. I had to concentrate on driving and keep to my schedule to carry out my plan. Town was dotted with yellow rain slickers scurrying about under the gray sky. I sat in church with the few other brave souls who had ventured out. I prayed for my safety and for all those who would face the storm, I said prayers of thanks that I had faced my own private storm and for belief that I could weather it, and for the strength I would need to survive it and begin anew. But mostly I prayed that they wouldn't close the bridge before I could get back across it.

As we received our blessing and were told to 'go in peace', the heavens opened up. Rain pounded the wooden roof and pelted the stained glass windows. The priest raised his voice over the din and noted that the only peace any of us would find for the next twenty four hours would have to come from within. We responded 'amen' to that. Then he half jokingly invited us to stay, calling to my mind Mariah in the choir loft praying for Joshua and for an instant I felt doubt and was tempted to accept the offer.

I pulled my rain slicker over my head and fought the wind to get to the car. Each step I took I was pushed back and it took two more to recover. By the time I grabbed the handle I was exhausted, but undaunted. I drove carefully to Clare's, parked my car, went inside, called a taxi, and set in motion the most treacherous leg of my journey.

The driver gave me a dubious look when I told him my destination, but I paid him handsomely to follow my instructions; drive and keep his mouth shut. I sat hunched over in the back seat feeling like a cross between a criminal and a secret agent, hoping we wouldn't be stopped, but prepared to hide under the seat if we did as the driver would explain he was going onto the island to evacuate someone.

A crew was readying roadblocks, another frantically sandbagging the banks of the perilously high waters, and in the confusion the yellow taxi cab miraculously escaped detection and sailed over the bridge, up Bay Ave and into the driveway. I got out quickly, looking nervously over my shoulder.

I didn't have to wave the driver on, he was gone before I got the key out of my pocket.

As I turned the knob the wind pushed the door in with such force it was nearly torn from the hinges.

I moved quickly inside, pressed my full weight against it and finally wrestled it shut. The darkness of the house startled me and the sudden realization of what I had done overwhelmed me with shame, regret, and fear.

I hung my dripping slicker on the back of the door, slipped off my soaked shoes and socks. To calm my nerves I reached in the pantry and took out my secret cache of supplies; candles, matches, a flashlight, a book, and some food. I found the bottle of brandy I had impulsively included, and took a generous swig. I lit a candle and looked around to regain my bearings. The pitch darkness created by the shutters was unnerving, and the tempest raging outside was muffled but powerful. The shutters banging repeated in echoes, the windows rattled, the wind howled angrily through the cracks, and the sea pounded the shore.

I changed my clothes and busied myself preparing a cold supper. I was hungry and tired. The night before I had slept very little; plotting my strategy, reading Charley's story, and writing letters.

My letter to John was a difficult task, but I would never have been able to bare my soul to him on the telephone as I did in writing. I told him we had to put the past ten years behind us, that it was just that simple and I would accept nothing less. I told him I forgave him for anything he sought forgiveness for, for all the words he felt he should have said, the deeds left undone and I asked his forgiveness for the same. I reminded him of all the years of happy times and how insignificant these few of strife would seem, if we started over again.

My letter to David was more a simple thank you note for his lovely gift and all it symbolized to me. He and I had nothing to forgive, and I told him how thankful I was for that.

I ate my supper and risked boiling the kettle for a hot cup of tea. I blew out the candle, gathered my little crate, and turned on the flashlight to guide my way. The electricity was still on but I didn't dare risk someone spotting a light and investigating. I walked through the dining room, glanced my beacon on the framed photos on the breakfront and smiled at them as the light passed over them. They would haunt me no more.

I stopped at my desk in the front room and checked the letters, closed the rolltop, and locked it securely, tucked the key in the drawer. My footsteps echoed in the hollow silence. I straightened the lace dustcover on the table, stifled the impulse of habit to turn on the shell filled lamp.

As I passed David's room a deafening noise made me open his door. One shutter had loosened exposing a slice of window. I cautiously approached and peered through the opening. What I saw was a world gone mad; evening had fallen but the dark sky was indistinguishable from the black sea. The wind was in control, screaming through the wooden shutter, hounding the glass, searching for entry. I left the room and shut the door behind me.

I lit a candle in my room and changed to my nightgown. I expected to be afraid. I had prepared myself to feel it but it didn't come. I took Nana's rosary beads out and fingered them. I pictured her in my mind and called upon her faith, to help me sustain my newfound courage.

I fell into a sound sleep but was awakened just before midnight to a sound like crashing thunder. I thought immediately of Joshua Duncan but when I opened my eyes my bed was still on the floor, no water rushed under the door. I tiptoed from my room with my candle in hand and opened the door to David's room. The loose shutter was gone, ripped from its hinges, and the glass vibrated like a sheet of wax paper as it braved the assault. I went closer. All that had been black earlier was now white; sky and sea wrapped together in turmoil like a great ghostly beast rising from the depths of the earth.

I felt fear then. It gripped my heart as I surveyed the enormity of nature unleashing her wrath. I turned away and shut the door, returned to my bed and my rosaries and prayed even more fervently than before.

As I lay listening to the battle rage it seemed to me after some time, that the wind suddenly ceased its roaring and all but the surf was still. I briefly wondered if it was the end or the eye but I closed my eyes and slept in the calm of the storm and in peace with my soul and the sound of my sea. The restless haunting symphony that had inspired my dreams since childhood released me into a deep and welcome slumber.

I saw my life, but only the best parts, the brightest moments, the ones I had always tried so hard to keep, and I realized that this was what we save them for.

I saw the dearest souls, the kindest eyes, the ones that had always shown the finest reflection of me. And then I saw Mike, and I knew this was no ordinary dream. He reached out to me, I held his hand and together we climbed into the bluest sky above an emerald sea. A single gull led our way to the lofty plane above high white clouds.

CHAPTER TEN

Mary sat at the counter in the airport snack bar waiting for her father. A television set above the coffee machine droned on and on about the hurricane but Mary wasn't listening. She was thinking about what she wanted to do with her life in general, and the next year in particular. She had taken a semester off from school to get her act together and if she didn't find a job soon her father would totally flip, maybe even cut off her monthly allowance, which would be a disaster.

She watched the waitress pour a seedy looking guy two stools down his third cup of coffee and thought, "I could do that." Then the guy grabbed the waitress' hand and said something Mary couldn't hear but from the look on the girl's face she knew it was crude and she thought, "No way could I do that."

A reporter on the TV screen was interviewing some idiot who had supposedly 'braved the storm of the century; Hurricane Iris, and apparently intended to capitalize on his "amazingly awesome" experience. Mary mumbled to herself, "Yeah, buddy, did you sell the movie rights yet?"

After a few minutes the camera guy got bored and panned back to the reporter, who began his own commentary on the situation. "The President has declared the northeastern seaboard a disaster area. The National Guard has moved in to begin initial clean up. Structural damage is estimated in the millions, beach erosion is extensive, and four people are known dead from the storm that will not soon be forgotten, Hurricane Iris. This area of the coast has been spared time and time again in the past century, and last night, for awhile it seemed their luck would hold as Iris hovered off shore for what seemed like an eternity, undecided, like a woman choosing a new pair of shoes. But she made up her mind just before the midnight high tide and unleashed a swift and ruthless fury; nine inches of rain combined with a storm surge estimated at ten feet. The eye passed at midnight and then the worst of the storm hit with 115 mph winds and gusts clocked at 130, and luck ran out as they faced a Category 3 Hurricane."

"They had been warned, they were prepared; most residents obeyed the mandatory evacuation order and spent the night at designated shelters. Those residents are being cautioned not to attempt to return to their homes for at least twenty four hours due to serious flooding and downed power lines. Now back to the studio where our hurricane experts are standing by to give you an update on: 'The Storm of the Century; Hurricane Iris'.

John heard the tail end of the report as he took the stool next to his daughter. He shook his head. "Where do they get those reporters from anyway? Like a woman choosing a new pair of shoes."

Mary looked at him. "I think it's kinda cool. Maybe I could be a news reporter. They said four people were killed."

John stared at the TV. "Wow," he said. "Come on, let's go. I rented a car, it should be ready."

Mary flipped on the radio when they got in the car. Another news report: "Rescue attempts are still going on in some remote areas hardest hit by the storm. Particularly devastated were the outlying islands along the coast, some entirely cut off as bridges were washed away or are impassable. The storm created new inlets, closed existing ones, and altered the already precarious condition of the coastline. The death toll is expected to rise when those areas are…"

John snapped off the radio, avoiding his daughter's eyes so she wouldn't see the panic settling in them.

Mary didn't notice. She sat quietly on the front seat, deep in her own thoughts. She was trying to remember all she could about Sara, but as usual, she couldn't get past the anger. Anger at her parents, and herself. For a long time she had no desire to come and visit her grandmother. Her mother made it clear that was how she wanted Mary to feel, and at that particular time, Mary only wanted to keep her mother happy, because if mother wasn't happy, nobody was. And then, when she began to think she would like to come and visit there seemed no easy way to do it. She could have asked her father, he would have loved it, for years he had begged her to come, but at that particular time the last thing she wanted to do was make him happy because she hated him. She blamed him for the divorce, and for the mess her life had become. So for ten stupid years she had avoided the whole deal, and punished herself, and Sara, for no good reason at all.

She sighed, shifted in her seat and stared out the window. It was a bright clear day, brilliant sunshine bounced off the cars on the highway. It was hard to believe anything so horrible could have happened in weather like this. Maybe it was all hype.

She didn't dare say that to her father though. She looked over at him. He was acting like a madman, hunched over the wheel as if he were driving through a raging storm. She would never understand him. For years he practically ignored his mother as far as Mary could tell, and now all of a sudden he was so concerned. He'd spent the past two days trying to call Sara on the phone, frantic when he couldn't reach her. Then he called her friends, and his brother, Uncle Dave, who told him she was fine, but he didn't believe it, so he made all these crazy arrangements, and dragged her all the way out here to see for himself. He was such a phony.

She knew what was really bothering him. Guilt. She knew because she felt it too, and it almost made her feel sorry for him. She was no better than he was, she hadn't written to Sara in months. Not because she didn't want to, just because…why? She couldn't think of one good reason. She'd spent the entire summer hanging around with Frankie, her new boyfriend. Her Dad hated him which of course made him perfect. She had dyed her hair black, and that had

161

driven her dad crazy too. She got her belly button pierced and she came this close to getting a tattoo, but that was way over the line even for her. She had done a lot of partying, had a ton of fun, but hadn't done anything that should have prevented her from writing to Sara, or calling, or even hopping on a plane and coming to see her.

"How much longer, Dad?"

"About an hour," he responded tersely.

Mary sat back again and tried to remember the last time she had spoken to Sara. She couldn't. She tried to remember Sara's last letter to her. She couldn't. It seemed important but she couldn't remember a single thing of significance about her grandmother. That wasn't really surprising though. Mary wasn't big on memories. She believed in living for today, not wallowing in the past. There wasn't all that much back there to think fondly of anyway.

She could barely picture what the old woman looked like. She hadn't seen her in ten years. There were no pictures of her in their house. It was as if Sara didn't exist there and that's just the way Mary's mother wanted it. Again the anger stung.

Mary loved her mother, they had been through thick and thin together, but lately she didn't like her very much. The past few years Mary had begun to question her about how she fell in love with her dad, and then out of love, and what it was like in their happy years together as a family, and Sara's name would come up but her mother never wanted to talk about her and that bothered Mary. When she questioned her more, her mother would get totally annoyed and Mary could tell there was no specific reason for her dislike of Sara. She knew that because if there was her mother would have said so in no uncertain terms. Her mother always said what she thought. It was something Mary both loved and hated about her.

Her mother said that Sara took her precious son's side in the divorce, and told some story about a silly doll Mary could never remember even though her mother claimed it was a huge trauma, but nothing sufficient enough in Mary's opinion to warrant the strong feelings her mother seemed to have against Sara. And Mary was finally beginning to realize that her mother had used Sara, and Mary, to vent her anger at John. The more Mary thought about it the clearer it became. Still, she couldn't hate her mother for it, because she realized that she had done the very same thing, avoided her grandmother to get back at her father. How pathetic they all were.

Mary shook her head. "Boy," she thought, "I know what I should be, a psychologist."

She glanced over at her father, still concentrating on the road as if it was a perplexing maze he alone could solve. At least he had pictures of Sara in his house. There was one on his dresser that Mary loved; a framed photograph of Sara and Mike, her grandparents. They looked young and fit in bathing suits with their tan skin gleaming in the sun as if they had just gotten out of the water. Mike had his arm around Sara and the look on his face always made Mary take a second glance. He had the deepest green eyes that made you feel warm and safe just by looking into them.

Mary leaned back in her seat and closed her eyes, concentrating on the picture. They were sitting on the bottom step; the porch at the top and the green screen door were framed by the brown shingles of the house. She focused in on the door, and the picture blew up in her mind.

Suddenly she was there; she remembered the sun on her back and sand between her toes, running up those smooth wooden steps, opening the screen door, looking for Sara. The cool air inside enveloped her with its salty cotton smell. She loved that smell; summer. She tiptoed through the hallway and into the bright kitchen where Sara sat at the table reading. She looked up at Mary and a smile crossed her face and into her hazel eyes. Nana.

She saw her so clearly now she almost cried out to her. The ache in her heart took her by surprise. She could smell her perfume, touch her soft wrinkled skin, feel the soothing motion of rocking on her lap in that old wooden rocker out on the porch, listening to the sea gull's cry and the breaking waves.

Mary opened her eyes and sat up. "When was that picture taken, Dad," she asked. "The one on your dresser of Sara and Mike?"

He looked over at her sharply. "Since when do you refer to your grandparents as Sara and Mike?"

Mary couldn't believe it. She glared at him then turned back to the window. So much for conversation. So typical. Ask an innocent question. One you think he might even enjoy answering and he bites your freaking head off. So much for psychology.

When Mary asked him the question about the picture John was a million miles away. He was in the office, worrying about the Brady case, his mortgage, Mary's mother's mortgage, Mary herself and why the hell she couldn't stick it out and finish school like a normal twenty year old. Then she asks him about that picture, of all the topics in the world she had to pick that one and send it like an arrow straight into in his already troubled heart.

He always loved that picture of his parents. Did he know when it was taken? How could he ever forget? He took it himself and it was one of the happiest moments in his life. Because he had made his father proud.

Labor Day. John was ten, David was seven. Every year they had a big beach party with friends and neighbors to celebrate the end of summer. They had spent the morning helping their parents get ready and took a break for a swim before lunch.

John remembered his mother running, diving in, waving to the boys to follow. The four of them played around in the surf, drifting in and out as the wash filled their pants with sand. The boys rode some waves and Sara and Mike took a raft and paddled out past the breakers, yelling to John to keep an eye on David.

John caught a nice ride and took it all the way up the beach. He lay on the sand for a minute like a beached whale, but when he jumped up and turned to run back in something caught his eye. The crests of three enormous swells loomed about fifty yards out. His mom and dad spotted them too and turned toward shore with panicked looks at David who was flopping around in the danger zone, way too far in for them to help.

The danger zone; where the wave breaks, the point of no return. You can't make it under safely and you can't make it to shore no matter how fast you run. It's OK to fool around there if the waves are small but if it's a cruncher you're dead. People who don't know the ocean love that spot. They mistakenly think it's the safest place to be; not too far in, not too far out. John and his buddies always enjoyed watching them get smashed and tumbled and spit out on shore, especially girls who lost their bikini tops in the process.

But seeing his little brother there with those waves approaching wasn't funny. For a split second John contemplated doing nothing, keeping himself safe and getting ready to catch David when he washed up, but the next thing he knew he was running right into the danger zone. David didn't know what was going on but he knew enough to take a deep breath and hold it as John grabbed him tight around the waist and they went under the first wave just before it broke.

It broke over them, and John kicked as hard as he could and swam up, reaching for the surface, hoping they'd have time for another breath because he knew there were at least two more. They made it under the second wave and just as John thought they'd never make it to the surface he felt his father's strong arms take David out of his grip.

His mother was there when he broke the surface as the third and largest wave loomed ahead of them. He looked at her and she yelled, "Dive deep and grab the sand John. You can do it."

They dove under together. John went as deep as he could but he could still feel the powerful wave breaking, feel the pressure of the water pounding down on him, and when he tried to swim up his legs wouldn't kick. They felt like rubber and he was floating, swirling in the turbulent currents. His mother grabbed his hand and pulled him up with her, letting go when they broke the surface.

They swam to shore and sat for a long time catching their breath. His father looked at John and smiled. "I'm proud of you, son. You really saved the day."

During the party that afternoon his father told the story over and over again; the size of the waves, how brave John had been, what a good swimmer he was.

All the things a ten year old craves to hear. Later that day John took the picture and even as a grown man looking at it he could see the pride his father had felt in him that day.

He knew his father would not look at him with pride anymore. Far from it. He would look at him with disgust for treating his mother the way he had. It was all such a disaster. The past ten years, and even the five before that. The first five years of his marriage had been great, and so had his relationship with his mother. Then everything fell apart and he had never been able to figure out how to put it back together. So he'd given up trying. And now, he couldn't imagine how or why he had been so ignorant, and so blind.

He looked over at his daughter. She was so beautiful, even with that ridiculous black hair. It made her look more like her mother, though every time John looked at her he saw his mother's eyes, the tilt of her head when she spoke, her smile. He missed that smile...on both of their faces.

She seemed so dark lately, and it wasn't just the hair. She used to be so happy, so sunny, and he supposed he was to blame for that as well as everything else. She had asked him a simple question, and he had snapped at her and then ignored her. He was good at that. Ignoring the people he loved the most.

"You know, Mary. I never meant for any of this to happen."

There was no response. She stared out the window. She had learned too well from him.

He spoke softly. "I loved your Nana too, you know."

She turned to him quickly then, hate burning in her eyes.

Her words were filled with deliberate contempt. "You loved her? Is she dead and buried Dad? Or do you just hope she is so you don't have to worry about her anymore?" Mary shook her head in disbelief. "You loved her. Yeah, just like you loved Mom. Is that what you'll say about me someday? To your new family with what's-her-name? I really loved my daughter Mary you know, but things just didn't work out. I never meant for any of it to happen though."

More arrows to the heart. She had learned that from her mother. He reacted first with anger, shouted at her, "I knew I shouldn't have brought..." Then his eyes stung and his emotions shifted. He looked at Mary's face and saw his mother, and he couldn't bear to see it like that, full of hate. His eyes stung and to his horror he began to sob. He couldn't control himself. He pulled the car to the side of the road and wept like a little boy.

Mary moved to comfort her father as much out of shock as fear.

"It's OK Dad. I'm sorry. I didn't mean what I said. And anyway I'm sure she's alright. You heard the radio, they're still getting people out. And you know, her buddy, Charley. He wouldn't leave her alone, I'm sure she's fine."

John straightened up and took Mary's hand. "You're right," he said. "Of course she's fine. Thanks honey. I'm OK now." He blew his nose and wiped his eyes. He chuckled nervously. "She's probably sitting in Charley's store right now swapping storm stories over a cup of brandy with the old timers, watching the tourists in their four wheel drives taking pictures and getting stuck in the sand."

He pulled the car back on the road. "I don't know what I was thinking. I'll bet it wasn't any worse that the last 'storm of the century'! Wasn't Sara always saying how the media blew these things way out of proportion?"

John was on a roll now. They both relaxed. His voice still cracked but he went on, "She'll be surprised to see us that's for sure. We'll stick around for a week or two, I have some vacation time coming, we can help her clean the place up, it's such a great old house, you remember it don't you? Of course you do, you used to love your summer visits to Eastwind."

Mary wasn't so sure of anything at that point but she laughed nervously and said, "Yeah Dad, we'll all have a good laugh about you and me coming all this way to sweep a little sand off the porch, huh?"

John didn't answer right away. They were five miles from the Sandy Point Exit and traffic in front of them came to a stop. He turned on the radio. "Maybe we can get a local station, find out what's going on down there." Mary was relieved to see her dad back in control.

Their confidence was short-lived however as the radio produced only static and they saw outside their windows evidence of a more widespread devastation than they had expected. They inched along the highway, past office buildings with roofs missing and gaping holes where windows had been, uprooted trees lying in fields where a demented wind had left them, cars stranded by the side of the road.

As they approached the two mile exit sign they discovered more alarming clues to the impact of the storm. Boats of all sizes, some as big as 40 foot, had seemingly been lifted from their docks and sailed wildly over roads and driveways and now sat tilted hopelessly on their sides, masts and hulls mangled beyond repair. And amidst the rubble of the boats was household debris, a stove, toilets, a refrigerator.

The westbound side of the highway had been empty for miles. They hadn't passed a single car.

"Why is there so much traffic going this way. Where are they all going?"

John answered, "They could be coming to check on homes, or relatives, like we are. Or they might be curiosity seekers. A storm is a big attraction around here. People always come to look, before and after."

"Why are we stopped for so long? Can you see what's going on up there?"

"Traffic is always like this around here. In the summer city people sit in this mess all the time just to spend a day at the beach."

"That's pretty dumb." Mary said.

"What's so dumb?" John asked. He hated that word.

"People driving in a jam like this just to get to the beach."

John thought of his mother forever telling him how lucky he was to grow up at the beach, how as a child she loved to come for the summer and dreaded leaving every September. He grew tired of the stories, she was right, he didn't appreciate it. "I never understood it either Mary, but I know your grandmother would be unhappy to hear you say that. She loved the beach, and she loved how you used to come and share the summers with her because that's what she did when she was a little girl. She used to come down here every summer with her family and she lived for it. She could never understand people who didn't love the beach, or worse, people who did live there and never even noticed it..."

Mary interrupted him, "Look Dad, over there..."

An ambulance sped west on the road, so siren, no lights, there was no need.

Mary said, "Why aren't there any cars over there anyway?"

John didn't want to answer that question, but at least she didn't ask him about the ambulance, which was most likely carrying another victim of this goddamm storm. He knew why there were no westbound cars. Because anyone who wanted to leave had left a long time ago.

The only people who left now would be on a stretcher or in a body bag. And he suddenly remembered the story of Joshua Duncan. He could hear his mother clearly, telling him years before that when another storm threatened the island, she wouldn't leave, that she'd be as stubborn as Joshua and what would be, would be. And he knew then beyond the shadow of a doubt, that his mother had never left her home.

The Eastwind bridge was open, restricted. John saw two cars stop and speak to the officer at the foot of the bridge and then cross over, but all the others were waved away. They were stopped in the center of town, surrounded by the signs of a disaster that had become more frightening the farther east they traveled. The side streets were blocked off; cars sat where they had been left, some with water still over the tires. Trees branches drifted slowly by with assorted boots, a doghouse, two lampshades and various lawn chairs trailing behind them.

Main Street was still flooded, barricades tossed hastily aside. Most stores were closed, some still shuttered, some being freshly boarded until damage could be assessed and repaired. People wandered about in a daze. Duncan's General Store had both front windows blown out and emptied of everything but one lone survivor; a decoy sat nonchalantly high on a shelf, blissfully unconcerned with his surroundings as if nothing startling had passed his way in a few hundred years.

There was no sign of Charley around, and John wasn't sure if that was a bad sign or a good one. He craned his neck to get a look at the officer on the bridge. It would help if he knew him but the only one he knew was Fred Allen and it wasn't him. John got out his license, hoping the guy would recognize the name and let him pass. Mary asked him what he was doing and when he explained that they might not be allowed to cross she rolled her eyes at him, opened her door and said, "I'm walking. I'll meet you at the house." And off she went.

Mary walked toward the bridge hoping she would remember the way to Sara's house. There was a group of young guys standing at the top, surfer dudes. She knew the type well and wasn't impressed by them. As she got closer she listened, expecting the usual jargon about 'babes' and 'narly swells'.

But they were silently staring north over the island and one guy was shaking his head, saying "It's really weird, man. Just the other day she was standing right here describing exactly that scene to me and now, there it is, just like she said."

Mary stopped and looked out with them. It was certainly different from how she remembered it, though she couldn't quite say what was missing.

The surfer guy started talking again, "I'll bet old Mr. Blackmore is crying in his scotch this morning, huh? His whole deal blown away in one night; condos, townhouses, clubhouse, all gone in one clean sweep like it was never there. And it's gorgeous, man. It's so wild, isn't it? It's just like she said, look at those waves at the inlet; they're incredible. As soon as the cops back off we gotta blow out there and grab some of those curls. Let's go."

Mary stood for a long time after they left and stared out at the huge drifts of sand, the rocks piled out on the jetty and the gulls silently circling over head. Memories slowly began to take shape in her mind and she welcomed them. Enormous waves towered in the stiff west wind, then crested and broke gracefully, plunging onto shore. The torment of the storm was over, the sea was back in control and showing its strength in a methodical parade of powerful, even swells.

John approached the officer and was told no cars could pass unless they could show proof of residence. He was just about to argue his case when Fred Allen pulled up in his squad car. He didn't recognize John at first but when he did his face fell. The past twenty four hours had not been easy for Fred Allen. He had been in on a nerve wracking surf rescue, then evacuated his grandparents and the rest of his family, rescued a few more friends and neighbors, and then stood by helplessly as many of their homes and businesses were destroyed.

When dawn broke, and the wind shifted from sea to land and pushed Iris out in a mass of retreating storm clouds over the relieved blue ocean, Fred went up to the beachfront. He found that they had lost something more valuable than wood and plaster, sheetrock and glass.

He discovered that a precious life had passed, and was full of misgiving that he hadn't been able to save her. In his reasoning mind he knew that was simply because she hadn't wanted to be saved, but in his heart he felt such deep remorse that he doubted he would ever look at life the same way again.

And now he faced her son, who in all honesty might have been the only one who could have saved her, but this was neither the time nor the place to dwell on that. So he looked John Hankins in the eye and held out his hand.

They shook, but Fred didn't let go, and he delivered the sad news, and the more he looked into John Hankin's eyes the more he saw that nobody could pile any more guilt or blame on him than he had already buried himself under.

Mary walked along South Bay Ave, amazed at the extent of the destruction. Some lots were empty, a crumbling foundation and a pile of shattered lumber the only clues that a house had stood there yesterday. Sand lined the street, shells and huge chunks of driftwood, amid old buoys, water logged furniture and broken windows. People milled about in groups, some visibly shaken at the sight of their homes, others numbed into silent shock.

A beat up old station wagon slowly approached, and the driver, an old man, stared long and hard at Mary as he drove by. Ten yards past her he stopped the car and backed up and she recognized Charley Duncan. He looked exactly the same as he had ten years ago.

He got out of the car and walked up to Mary, took her hand and gazed at her. "You have to excuse me," he said. "I thought I was seeing a ghost. Same walk, same build, but the dark hair threw me. It is you, Mary, isn't it?"

She smiled at him but he didn't return it. He seemed so odd, not the cheery fellow she recalled. "Yes, Charley? It's me, Mary."

Mary was afraid to ask the question and Charley was terrified that she would and so they stood there looking at each other without saying a word. But it wasn't awkward. Mary was lost in his deep blue eyes, and Charley was lost in a Sara he remembered from a long time ago.

Finally she asked it, "Charley, where's Sara?"

He didn't look away. He held the girl's arms and answered the question. "Your grandmother is dead, Mary."

Then he waited for her to break down, to cry, to look away, but she didn't. She kept staring in his eyes. She smiled. "That can't be, Charely. You must be joking. Where is she? Is she at home?"

"No Mary. Sara is dead. She died last night in her sleep."

Mary didn't believe him, she couldn't believe him. It just wasn't possible. She stared at him blankly then took off in a sprint for Sara's house.

Charley got in his car and followed her. When she reached the house she collapsed on the back steps. He sat next to her and held her until she stopped crying. Then she asked fifteen questions all at once, "How can this be…what about the storm…was she sick…was she hurt…why did she stay here all alone…were you with her…why didn't somebody come and get her…?"

Charley patiently answered the ones he could and left hanging the ones that nobody ever would.

John pulled in, Mary ran to him and they sobbed together. Charley stood back and surveyed the house as he had done to countless other homes all morning, and to this one too, earlier, when Fred had called and told him about Sara.

He wasn't angry at her, though he had been at first, for leaving him all alone. He understood her too well to hate her for it, in fact he admired her courage, and cursed his own weakness. No, if it had to be, it was best this way, just not best for him. And maybe not for these kids either. She wanted so much to make a new start with them. That's when he remembered the letters and went inside to get them.

The house was a mess; water had been everywhere, moved every item from the shelves, pushed every piece of furniture against the back wall and then pushed the whole wall out. The winds had blown off every single shutter and then every pane of glass. The weather vane was gone, along with most of the roof. There was no trace of the garden shed, and he'd seen the purple martin house floating in the bay.

The massive rolltop desk was in the kitchen, and Charley wrestled with the swollen drawer to get the key out. The letters were there, tucked away in the highest cubby, untouched. There was one for John, David, and Mary, and with hers was a small box tied with ribbon. And there was a larger envelope for each of them too, and knowing his silly story was in them and all it meant to him and to Sara, finally made Charley Duncan, man of few words and fewer tears, drop to his knees on the soggy floor and cry for his loss.

Charley composed himself and went back outside. John and Mary sat on the steps like two forlorn children. Charley told them about Sara's last days, what she shared about them and the way things were, and most importantly about the way things would be.

Then he gave them their letters, and said, "You know, she was a great old girl. And someday, when we tell this story about how she stuck to her guns and fooled us all, we'll laugh about it…" His voice faltered and he had to stop. "But not yet. No, not today." He took one more look at the house, got in his car and drove slowly down the driveway.

John and Mary sat on the steps fingering their letters, trapped in their own private and bewildering worlds of grief, guilt and sorrow. They discussed calling Uncle Dave, and Mary's mother, where they might stay, and for how long; the practicalities were easier to deal with than the emotions.

After a few moments of silence they looked down at the envelopes in their hands and slowly, in unison, opened them and began reading the last words Sara would ever say to them. John read his letter carefully, and then read it again before breaking down in soft sobs of relief and gratitude that were necessary, yet so painful.

Mary's letter was much longer and she took her time reading it. She didn't shed a single tear, her heart was so muddled with sorrow and joy that she felt a new and unfamiliar sentiment that she wasn't sure how to react to.

John couldn't sit still any longer. He asked Mary if she was alright. She nodded and so he left her and walked into the house. Mary picked up the package and untied the ribbon. Inside was a necklace strung with tiny white clamshells. She held it up to the sky and the sea glass in the center weighted it down to form a perfect 'v', as she knew it would. She knew where it came from and where it had been, and as the sun sparkled on the blue glass she pictured the day Sara had first come upon it.

She took out the letter and read the ending again:

So, Mary, was my life much different than yours? Maybe on the outside but not on the inside. I am certain you are facing decisions, worrying and weighing your actions and thoughts, just as I did.

Circumstances change but the heart does not, and I suspect you and I are more alike than not. At twenty I wasn't much different than I am now at eighty. The farther along I travel, the farther back I seem to go.

I wish now that I had written you letters like this for the past ten years, not the ones I did write, but real ones where I told you how I was really feeling. Because then we would not have grown so far apart. And I take full blame for it, I am supposed to be the wise one; I should have known better. I am not foolish enough to hope it's not too late because of course I know it is. That is, we cannot recapture those years, one never can, but we can begin from here.

I want you to know that I love you, and that it is never too late to tell someone you love them. Have you told your father that lately? I, more than anyone can understand how hard it is to say, harder yet to show, but you must find a way. You have been through some trying times but I trust you haven't forgotten that one important thing; love.

I want you to know too that from what went on before I take only the good; the happiness we shared and the laughter and the smiles, for we did have that once and I am certain that we can enjoy it again. I guess, Mary, that I am trying with this letter to find a way to reach you, though in my heart I know I never lost you, you were always with me and you always will be, as I will be with you.

Love,
Nana

Mary folded the letter and placed it in the box with the necklace. She walked into the yard and conjured images from the past, welcoming them for the first time in a very long time; a picnic table covered with a red and white checkered tablecloth, a smoking grill, a swinging hammock. She encouraged memories she had kept hidden inside to flow as she passed the garden, now a bed of mud, and recalled the scent of roses, the feel of daisy chains, the blazing color of a bed in full bloom. She walked to the far end of the yard, where the green picket fence was splintered in a thousand pieces under a mountain of sand and grass. She could hear the sound of tiny creatures returning to survey the damage to their homes.

She tripped over a broom handle, dug it out and took it around to the front porch. The sand was piled like drifts of snow, a mountain here, a mere hill there. The steps were gone, either swept away or just buried under the sand, with just a slope of sand leading from the porch floor down onto the beach and beyond to the glittering sea.

The front door was gone, you could see straight through to the back door in the kitchen. More pleasant memories called to her from inside as her father rummaged about. She heard the laughter of the innocent child she once was, the patient, gentle voice of her grandmother, sounds of a simple time that didn't make her feel sad, but strengthened. She took the broom and began sweeping the porch, lifting the tiny specks of sand up and out, into the breeze that carried them back where they belonged. She was operating on a new dimension, removed from everything around her, yet intimately connected at the same time. She felt like she had found something dear that she hadn't even known was lost.

Underneath the front windows she uncovered two rocking chairs, and a lump rose in her throat. Silent salty tears streamed down her face as she sat in Sara's chair and began to rock, tentatively at first and then in gentle rhythm with the breaking waves before her. After awhile she stopped crying. Her father came out and sat in the rocker beside her. She reached for his hand and told him she loved him, something she hadn't said in a very long time.

They sat there together, calmed by the haunting symphony Sara played for them. As they listened it healed them until they too were at peace with the past, found forgiveness in their hearts, and heard hope for the future in the sounds of the sea.

ABOUT THE AUTHOR

Anne Sogorka Cook was born in Passaic, New Jersey, and spent her childhood summers in a shore cottage in Point Pleasant Beach. She now resides year round in Point Pleasant with her husband and three children. Ms. Cook is the author of various short stories and poems. *Sounds of the Sea*, her first novel, draws on her affinity for the ocean, nature, and family relationships.

A percentage of sales from *Sounds of the Sea* will be donated to The Surfrider Foundation, a nonprofit organization "dedicated to the protection and enjoyment of the world's waves, oceans and beaches for all people, through conservation, activism, research and education."